THE
LAST
BITE

Anna Higham

"Anna writes about fruit in the way it deserves, with such grace and respect. The recipes are unique and interesting, and Anna gives you so many options and ideas that this is more than just a standard recipe book but a lesson in pastry and fruit. This book will undoubtedly become a staple in any chef's collection – a true classic in the making."
Ravneet Gill

"A remarkable book, both poetic and grounded. Anna Higham has an inspiring love of fruit and is full of knowledge. If you're a fruit lover, you'll cook out of this book for the rest of your life."
Diana Henry

"Sweet delights abound on page after page of this lovely book that embraces the beauty of each season, superb produce and the sheer joy of making puddings."
Jeremy Lee

"I'm a huge admirer of Anna's considered approach to seasonal fruits and the treats that can be made with them (top tip: always order one of every dessert wherever she's cooking). Which means I'm delighted to find so much of her and her mind in this cookbook. There are, of course, wonderful, memorable recipes to be replicated. But beyond them are building blocks and principles that are going to help home and professional cooks alike make glorious sweet things forever."
Ed Smith

CONTENTS

From first to last bite   7
How I became a pastry chef   10
Using this book   15

SUMMER   16

Strawberries   18
Gooseberries   24
Tayberries, loganberries
   & raspberries   28
Mulberries   36
Blackcurrants   40
Cherries   48
Apricots, nectarines & peaches   57
Plums   64
Summer pudding   71

AUTUMN   74

Figs   76
Sweetcorn   84
Damsons   88
Apples   94
Pears   102
Grapes   108
Pumpkins   114

WINTER 120

Quinces	122
Dried fruits	128
Clementines	136
Lemons & citrons	140
Blood oranges	151
Forced rhubarb	156

SPRING 162

Sugars	165
Fats	172
Chocolate	186
Grains	192
Nuts	204
Outdoor rhubarb	214
Flowers, leaves & herbs	218

Index	230
Further reading	235
Useful tools & ingredients	236
Acknowledgements	239
Disclaimer	240

"Best of all is the fruit,
Sweetest and prettiest:
The strawberries and cherries,
The gooseberries and currants,
Raspberries and blackberries
(The best are wild), grapes, pears,
Apples early and late–
These gleamings in the sun
That gleam upon the tongue
And gleam put up in jars
And gleam within the mind."

The Farm, Wendell Berry

FROM FIRST TO LAST BITE

I've written this book to give you the confidence to feel just as at ease when it comes to dessert as you do for savoury food, to really cook. So often, sweet recipes are given as a fixed creed to be followed exactly. I want to create the space to show you the principles that underscore my recipes and where those principles can be pushed or manipulated and where substitutions can be made. I often hear people say that dessert is something they just can't do or that they don't understand. It is just cooking. Cooking in the same way that making a bowl of pasta is, or roasting a chicken or putting together a salad. Those things feel more straightforward because you practise them more. You probably cook a meal most days (I'll let "cooking" be a broad term here) so you get to see, smell and touch savoury ingredients over and over. You get to know them by repeated exposure. I've spent the past 10 years getting to know sugar, cream, flour and, most importantly, fruit. The goal of this book is to pass on that knowledge and familiarity to you.

I am privileged to have worked with many passionate people who have taught me not only how to search out the best ingredients but also how to make those ingredients taste the most of themselves. I want to communicate that passion, knowledge and skill to you. Working alongside savoury chefs has taught me to think beyond a recipe. Taught me to cook with my senses, with my instincts – and to trust my palate. After a decade as a pastry chef, I've learnt that there are many different approaches to dessert just as there are in the rest of the professional kitchen. These are the key points that define how I think about dessert; my pastry chef's manifesto if you will.

Make it delicious

Your first thought when you eat a dessert should always be "that's delicious". Your second can be "that's interesting" but never the other way around. You can engage the eater, you can challenge them, but the first mouthful should always inspire an "mmmmmm". I think chefs sometimes find this notion hard to grasp as it can seem too easy to make someone say "yum" when sugar and fat are involved. The challenge lies in not abusing those benefits. How to harness the power of sugar to intensify the flavour of fresh strawberries or to balance the bitterness of a lemon without overwhelming either? How to use cream and eggs to capture the floral scent of a blackcurrant leaf? How to use butter to make rich, crispy puff pastry while keeping a dessert light enough to enjoy every last bite?

Source well

Spend your time searching for the best-tasting fruit, chocolate, dairy produce, grains or sugar and your job becomes really quite simple. I will never be a pastry chef who sculpts sugar and chocolate; I have neither the patience nor the inclination. I can, however, spend hours in whatever weather picking sun-warmed strawberries, having my arms scratched while searching for ripe gooseberries or driving to meet a dairy farmer. I think seeing the produce grow, knowing the farm your cream comes from, meeting the miller responsible for your flour, is more inspiring than reading a hundred recipe books. Connecting to a producer transforms the way you think about – and treat – ingredients. If you want to reduce food waste, then grow or pick your own fruit and vegetables. People instantly respect food more when they have helped to harvest it. I am of the belief that once you taste a perfectly ripe berry, you no longer think that you can improve it through manipulation. Instead, the goal becomes to create a dessert that showcases that berry. The skill is in making it taste the most of itself it possibly can.

Cook like a savoury chef

Making a dessert is still cooking as much as, say, cooking a piece of fish. It took me a long time to really learn this. Cooking requires you to engage your senses no matter what you're making. You learn to understand the colour you like your caramels the more you make them; you feel the subtle difference between an undermixed and a perfectly silky dough, the correct bounce of a sponge and the wobble of a custard tart. Intuition and feel have as strong a place in the sweet kitchen as they do in the savoury, sitting alongside skill and technique in the same way. The more you cook, the more you learn to trust your instincts. Maybe the recipe says to bake for 20 minutes but after 15 you think it looks good and the other markers are telling you it's ready, so trust yourself. Maybe you'll get it wrong sometimes: a dish may be overbaked or underbaked but either way, you will have learned and you'll take that learning with you to the next bake.

Season

Sugar provides structure but, just as importantly, seasoning. Think of sugar in the same way you do of salt in savoury food. It should amplify flavours and should only be tasted when you want it to be a flavour. Use sugar to make fruit taste more intense, to balance the bitterness of coffee, as the base of caramel. Different sugars transform ice creams, doughs and meringues, lending their distinct structural properties. I don't mean to discount these properties but to shift your thinking from "the recipe says this much sugar" to "how much sugar does this need?". It is a small but transformational change.

The use of salt and acid as seasonings is also incredibly important but often ignored in the pastry kitchen. I love using flavoured vinegars in fruit dishes, often using the leaves of the same fruit to make a vinegar that reinforces and adds complexity to the dish. A splash of blackcurrant leaf vinegar added to poached blackcurrants helps balance the jamminess and sweetness by bringing some herbaceous, floral acidity. I don't think I need to say more than "salted caramel" to explain the importance of salt in desserts. A couple of flakes of Maldon (kosher salt) on your ice cream is revelatory the first time you try it. Salt also helps the structure of ice cream in the same way that sugar does by lowering the freezing point to give you a softer serve.

Sugar, salt, acids: all of these are at your disposal to balance and season your desserts but the only way to understand their effects is to taste. I know I have been guilty of just following a recipe without tasting along the way. Knowing how to make perfect rice pudding means learning what it tastes like a little undercooked and a little overcooked. To understand the sweet spot, you have to know the bitterness of either side. Fruit will change through the season, however brief it may be, and will require more sugar one day and less another. The only way you'll know is by tasting.

Eat the whole thing

It's really important. The only way you know if a dessert is balanced is by eating it all. Does it need a little more fruit? A bigger scoop of ice cream? More acid? More sugar? Do you feel satisfied at the end or a little sick? Is there enough texture? It will help you understand if the visual ideas are making the eating experience better or if they are detrimental. I really struggle with desserts that are spread out across the plate meaning you never get a cohesive bite. Not every bite has to be the same but you should be directing the way someone will eat your dessert by the way that you plate it. It all comes back to the first point: it has to be delicious from the first to the last bite. One of my absolute favourite things as a chef is watching desserts go to tables, watching people's faces burst into a smile as they eat, then seeing empty bowls returned to the kitchen. At that point, I know I have done my job well.

Find kitchens and people that get you excited about food

I'm talking to the pros here. This advice will take you further than any expensive culinary school. The kitchens that have defined me are places where everyone wants to talk about what they are cooking at home and where they have been eating. Where my colleagues are excited about ingredients, where the conversations are about wonderful things that someone has eaten or read about. I've mostly worked in a team of savoury cooks so have had to look to books for guidance on how to become the pastry chef I am now. Sentiments that have left a lasting impression include what Lindsey Remolif Shere wrote in *Chez Panisse Desserts*, "what will make you a really good dessert cook is your alertness to flavor, scent, and appearance, and especially your sensitivity to the dessert as a complementary part of a whole meal." Brookes Headley goes further in *Fancy Desserts* to say, "Remember, sweet stuff is still food. It needs to be seasoned and cared for; its traits must be championed." And of course, Claudia Fleming has a final say in *The Last Course* that rings true for me, always, "The only time a dessert doesn't make sense is if it doesn't taste delicious."

HOW I BECAME A PASTRY CHEF

I wish I could give you a romantic story of how my mum was an incredible baker or pastry chef and that's how I ended up in this career but I can't. My mother didn't bake. There is no long line of female bakers in my family. They all love to cook, though, and Mum was the best (sorry aunts!). She didn't know a thing when she got married at 21 but read and cooked her way through Elizabeth David, Jane Grigson and Leiths to become the food authority in our family. She had a rotation of three puddings: lemon tart, French apple tart and banoffee pie. They were all made in the same tart rings with the same pastry. She did, however, absolutely love fruit. Our family holidays were mostly spent in France. Her favourite days were those spent in the market. I have an incredibly clear memory of a paper bag filled with coral-blushed apricots which we ate sitting in the sunshine in a small market town. Besotted by the colours, she took a second bag home with us to paint. Another time we drove to Andalusia and stayed in a house with a fig tree. I've spent the past five years enraptured by the flavour of fig leaves but, at the age of 10, I cared more about the pool. She, on the other hand, spent the whole holiday painting and drawing the figs and their leaves. We seemed to eat figs with everything. She was delighted. She got excited by perfectly ripe fruit, by the flavour, by the colours, by the sunshine that hopefully accompanied them.

I hadn't thought much about her love of fruit until recently. All those sketchbooks filled with drawings and paintings of fruit, among other things, sit on a shelf in my childhood home in Scotland. The past seven years of my career have been spent working in restaurants and pastry sections that put fruit at the heart of what they create. Working with chefs who spend their time searching for the best examples of ingredients they can find. Speaking to fellow cooks, bakers and chefs who get just as excited when it's time for the forced rhubarb from Yorkshire; for that first hot week in June when the Malwina strawberries in Kent are at their sweetest; for the blood oranges from Sicily to finally arrive. My mum passed away six years ago but would have been so happy to see her love of fruit come to the fore in my work.

I am the youngest of four children whose parents enjoyed food, who cooked, who expected their kids to help to make meals and clean up afterwards. I wouldn't say we are competitive siblings but we were all keen to establish our own identities. Oli taught himself to make pasta; I remember Lydia baking bread and learning to make curries from Madhur Jaffrey, and Ellie later discovering her love of all things sour, spicy and south-east Asian. Well it seemed to me that the only thing left within the family dynamic was dessert. I made apple pie, gingerbread and anything and everything from Nigella Lawson's *How To Be A Domestic Goddess*; her Guinness cake became my go-to pudding.

When I left school, I had no intention of cooking professionally. I was going to study architecture at The Glasgow School of Art. I had the incredibly privileged understanding that there wasn't any other option than to go to university and get a degree. At school, I had been good at art and maths so architecture seemed like the most logical course to apply for. I think I pretty quickly understood that the people who were excelling in my class really loved it and that, though I enjoyed it, I most definitely did not love it. While studying, I worked part-time in a cheesemongers and then a delicatessen/bakery. I loved those jobs. I loved the people (cheesemongers really are the best of people), loved that they all wanted to talk about food and what they were cooking all the time. We would make hugely elaborate meals together, always with a great cheese course, where I learnt not just about food but also about generosity and hospitality. As my culinary education developed in those part-time roles, I came to realize that architecture was not where my passion lay. I remember really clearly looking around my classmates' third-year degree show, going from display to display thinking, "I understand this but it's not what excites me. Food excites me." It was a true epiphany.

After that wonderful realization, I had to work up the courage to tell my parents. I spoke to my mum first and then, a few weeks later, my dad. He listened and then asked lots of questions; I had answers for them all. The trickiest was a financial one. After some quick maths he said: "that's £600,000 you won't earn in your lifetime, what are you going to do?" I gave the only answer that made sense to me and that could have settled him: "I'll be happy." I knew that, at best, I would have made a mediocre architect but I felt I could be a really good pastry chef. He's very much warmed to my decision now he gets to come to all the nice restaurants.

Getting a foot in the door of a restaurant with no experience is never easy. I went to the local college to study pastry for a year and then set about applying for a lot of jobs but didn't hear back from any. I eventually got lucky and was offered a trial shift at a well-known restaurant opening in London. Chef trials are less intimidating to me now but they are always a disconcerting experience. You turn up to a restaurant's back door which is never clearly marked or easy to find and hope that you bump into another chef going in who will offer a lifeline. You don't know where anything is or who anyone is. The small act of finding a bowl to mix in can take you 10 minutes longer than it ever would on a normal day. I knew my first trial was going to be daunting. I just kept telling myself that as long as I worked quickly and cleanly it would be OK. I was given the job of piping baked Alaskas by the pastry chef. I made a giant mess of it: I was neither fast nor clean and was panicking. That pastry chef was pretty rude and very unhelpful – he later applied for a job with me and needless to say, I was not inclined to even give him a trial. Kitchens are a small world so never be rude or unhelpful to anyone; chances are your paths will cross further down the line). Another chef saw me struggling and came over to help. I was so thankful. I somehow got the job – I think because I spoke so passionately to the head chef. Over the next few years, I worked in restaurants including Bread Street Kitchen and Pétrus. It wasn't a perfect culinary education but it sure taught me how to move and get stuff done. Those kitchens pushed me further than I thought possible, taught me that I wouldn't break even on my fifth consecutive day on four hours' sleep. I credit those kitchens with giving me my unflappable demeanour. When you are pushed that far, you realize that you can get it done when you have to. So when you are in a calmer kitchen and you need to make something happen on the fly, you absolutely know that it is within you to do it.

They also taught me exactly the kind of chef I did not want to be. Towards the end of my time with one restaurant, I saw a junior chef being screamed at. I knew then that I never ever wanted to work somewhere that would make me feel like it was necessary to scream at someone like that. Somewhere that would put me under so much pressure and strain that I was capable of that level of anger. No part of the process should make you want to bring a colleague to tears. Our role is simply to cook nice things for people to eat. It is just food, not war, not surgery – just food.

I next went to Gramercy Tavern in New York and it could not have been more different. Everyone was so nice (I found this a bit disconcerting at first) and so excited about food. It opened my eyes to a whole different perspective on desserts. The pastry team at Gramercy was made up of about 14 cooks and chefs. It ran as an independent department meaning you got to move around sections within the kitchen and weren't expected to do everything at once as I had learnt to. I spent days making chocolates, other days making ice creams and others making doughs. I loved it. I was working with beautiful ingredients in an environment where I got to learn and develop my skills. I was also working with the most lovely, funny, skilled team of cooks. The group of pastry friends I made in New York has been invaluable to me, not just on a personal level but as professional advisers and inspirations ever since.

While I was in New York, I read about a new restaurant that had opened in Shoreditch called Lyle's. Their menu read very simply but was getting a lot of people very excited. I think there were only two desserts on the lunch menu and one on the set dinner menu back then. With such a short menu, I couldn't see that they needed, or would want, a pastry chef but I was curious about the restaurant so I emailed co-founder James Lowe when I returned to London and was offered a trial. It was immediately clear that this was the kind of food I wanted to be making. There was real respect for – and a great deal of knowledge about – all the ingredients being used. The food was delicious and simply beautiful. The team was warm and welcoming and the place had all the markers of a happy environment. I did a few other trials that week: one basement kitchen where the chefs looked positively grey from lack of sunlight and nutritious food; another with a head chef who spent the whole shift trying to tell me how nice he was to the staff and then proceeded to call his sous-chef a c**t for some minor infraction. Lyle's was the absolute best choice even without being reminded just how awful London fine dining kitchens could be.

I was very lucky to start working at Lyle's when I did. It had just won a Michelin star but was a fairly young restaurant, still figuring itself out and I got to grow with it. After the first two weeks, I remember James asking me for a new dish for the next day's dinner service. I had never worked somewhere where you just came up with dishes by sitting down at the end of the evening after service. I was pretty flummoxed and terrified. As far as I had experienced, desserts needed to be tested and worked out and tasted and tweaked. You couldn't just talk about and come up with a great dish then and there. It was a steep learning curve because that is exactly how dishes were conceived at Lyle's. We talked about delicious things, what was in season and what we had in the kitchen and then we made something the next day... easy! Steep is maybe an understatement. As time went on and I learned what James liked (ice cream), what ingredients excited him (pears! blackcurrants!), where the lines were (no fruit with other fruit, a maxim I still stand by), I figured out how to make desserts that matched up to the incredible food coming from the rest of the kitchen. As I learned and found my feet, so did the kitchen and the restaurant as a whole. We moved into the World's 50 Best Restaurants list and we climbed. The dessert menu increased to four dishes at lunch. People would come in the evenings after their meals elsewhere to eat dessert with us.

After five wonderful years at Lyle's and sister restaurant Flor, I made the difficult decision to leave. I no longer felt as creatively excited as I once had. It was hard to figure out where to go next as is often the case when you have moved up the kitchen ranks. There were very few restaurants that aligned with my love of ingredients and that I wanted to work in. Top of that list was The River Café. London dining owes so much to Ruthie Rogers and Rose Gray for starting, and managing to maintain, such an inspiring place. After the first lockdown in 2020, I joined the restaurant and have helped grow the *dolci* team. I am the same age as The River Café and feel the weight of its history and legacy, but also the total privilege of becoming part of that history as their first Executive Pastry Chef.

USING THIS BOOK

The desserts in this book are largely from my time at Lyle's and then from the wine bar and bakery, Flor, which we opened in 2019. They are highly seasonal and dependent on having excellent raw ingredients. I encourage you to create desserts and dishes in the same way we would at Lyle's: think about what ingredients you have to hand or what's excellent right now, what makes you say "yum" just writing it down. Make that dish, tasting everything constantly as you go and it will most likely be pretty delectable.

As you move through each section, the principles of how to prepare that fruit or ingredient – how to season it and how to construct a dessert centred around it – will build to give you an in-depth understanding. If you're cooking at home, it will be ambitious to regularly create desserts as if you were in a restaurant. My hope is that home cooks will learn to understand and make seasonal desserts, to create great rice pudding, ice cream and meringues to pair with fruit at the peak of its season. And that pastry chefs will find inspiration for their own menus as well as techniques to apply to the ingredients they discover.

Use this book to build desserts of your own. I don't expect you to replicate every dish but rather look to see how elements can be put together. What I really want to communicate is that you don't have to reinvent the wheel with each dessert you make. Draw on your knowledge and skill each time. You found one recipe you love? How can that be adapted to the changing season? Could you apply that technique to a different but similar fruit? Could you swap the nuts or the flour or sugar in a recipe to pair better with plums or raspberries or apples? The more you make and taste, the more you understand your own palate and sensibilities.

One of the most well-thumbed books in my collection is *Jane Grigson's Fruit Book*. It is top of the pile when I'm a bit stuck for inspiration or when I need to know more about a particular fruit. If you want to learn more about different varieties, this is a great place to start. I can't recommend highly enough finding a local fruit farm and going to pick your own. I usually spend one shift a week from May to September picking fruit for the restaurant. It means I get to speak to the farmer every week; to find out what is going to be at its best next; which variety is particularly special; where the trees that produce the best plums are. If you can't get to a farm then visit a farmers' market and speak to the growers. I've listed individual fruit varieties where I

have a personal preference, though they can be swapped for a variety local to you. Just remember to taste as you go since different varieties and climates will give varying levels of acidity and sweetness. Have fun and play with new fruits, find ones that are most similar to those I've named here and apply the same principles to see what happens.

The longer sections in the Spring chapter provide recipes for many of the elements I will use as a base for a dish. Ricotta ice cream accompanies magnolia in spring, and blackcurrant leaf oil in summer. Milk bread is used to build summer puddings at the end of August, and then fried in brown butter to go with apples in autumn. Olive oil ice cream is paired with peach sorbet and then later with Nebbiolo grape sorbet. Use the Fats, Nuts, Grains and Sugars sections as your foundations. The rest of the sections move through the year starting with strawberries in June, the first of the summer fruits that I would gather at the pick-your-own farm and the first to appear after the hungry gap of spring. They feel completely joyful and celebratory after months of waiting for the weather to warm – a fittingly ebullient beginning. The fruity year ends for me with rhubarb, both forced and then outdoor. I get just as excited for forced rhubarb in the new year as I do for those first strawberries. With each cycle I learn more: another technique, another way to look at the ingredient.

I move through the fruits as they come into season. Each year is slightly different and the timings may differ where you are. Fruit will ripen when it wants to and sometimes not at all. You'll find that some years will be exceptional for gooseberries but poor for strawberries, or you may be overrun with cherries for a few weeks but barely catch the good figs. The important thing is to revel in each fruit as it comes, to make the most of it. Where I can, I have offered different varieties that I know will behave in a similar way. My real hope is that you will use these recipes as a jumping-off point. That they will inspire you to search out the unusual varieties to be found near you. Look to see how I've used a particular fruit then apply that thinking to the ingredients you have. Don't be scared if something doesn't work out quite how you imagined. You will take that understanding and insight with you into the next dish. The more you make, the deeper your knowledge will become and the fewer disappointments you'll have. I still have disappointments even after a decade of making desserts but each one teaches me something and helps me to get better.

summer

STRAWBERRIES

Nothing says British summer time quite like strawberries and cream. Summer begins with strawberries. I'll have been driving out to Maynards Fruit Farm in East Sussex every few weeks since the end of April to pick cherry blossom and young blackcurrant leaves, excitedly checking the strawberry fields on every visit. Just waiting for that first gloriously sunny day in June when I can fill crate after crate with ripe, sun-warmed strawberries. It is one of my favourite days of the year.

Strawberries feel like a career-defining fruit to me, a distinct marker in my education where I learnt the kind of pastry chef I wanted to be. One of my early kitchen jobs was in a one Michelin star restaurant in west London. It was an abrasive, intense environment that I stuck at for two years because I felt like I was really learning how to work quickly and under pressure (I did but at the cost of only sleeping for four hours a night and working 95 hours per week at the height of it). One summer, we had a strawberry dish on the menu (strawberry gel, hazelnut sablé and basil, among other things). The sous-chef spent a long time aggressively telling me how the success of this dish depended on the strawberries we used. I needed to taste them each morning and send them back if they weren't good enough. I tasted the strawberries the next day; they were watery and lacklustre so I spoke to the sous-chef. He told me to go across the street to the supermarket and buy some from there instead. They were never good enough for us to make sorbet with so we just used bought-in purée. A dish that I had been told "lived or died by the strawberries" was kept on the menu despite the fact that we did not have

decent strawberries in a country that grows excellent fruit! This was in stark contrast to my next job at Gramercy Tavern in New York. As summer approached, all of the cooks and chefs began expectantly talking about when the Tristar strawberries would arrive in the greenmarket. They were so excited for the first appearance of this particular variety. I can't remember the dish they were used in but I do remember the anticipation and the knockout deliciousness of that fruit. I loved being in an environment where cooks got that animated about ingredients and recognized that exceptional produce made exceptional food. Ever since then, I have made sure to work in kitchens where people get excited about the coming seasons, where the passion is for wonderful produce, where the dishes still "live or die" by the ingredients but also where real effort is put into sourcing them so that they always "live".

You can get British strawberries earlier each year but I would always rather wait for that day in June when I can pick them myself. As the month progresses, so do the strawberry varieties. Vivaldi are the first to come through; a modern variety, they're large and juicy. Next come the Florence and Malwina varieties, my two absolute favourites. They tend to produce smaller fruit but each berry is more intense in flavour as a result. Please don't make sorbet from bought-in strawberry purée. It tastes sickly sweet and a bit flat; you can always tell when it's been used. Yes, it will be consistent, but consistency is pointless if it tastes consistently mediocre. Take the time to find someone growing or selling beautiful fruit and everything you make will be dependably sublime.

Strawberry juice and chewy dried strawberries

To bump up the flavour in any strawberry dish, the juice is my secret ingredient. I macerate strawberries in sugar and cook them at a low temperature to draw out their incredible juices. The elixir that is created is remarkable. I use it in the granita and ice cream recipes that follow and also in my summer pudding. It can even be served as a strawberry consommé or fruit soup.

You don't want them to be completely dry and crispy but they shouldn't feel damp or wet to the touch. Flip them over after a couple of hours to make sure they dry on both sides. Store in an airtight container between layers of baking parchment.

strawberries

caster (superfine) sugar

Hull the strawberries by removing the green top. Use a small knife to cut around the leaves and pull out the hull. Please don't just slice off the top of the fruit. Cut the hulled strawberries in half. Weigh the fruit and add 4–5 per cent of their weight in caster sugar, so 40–50g of sugar per kilogram of strawberries (or about 1½ tablespoons of sugar for every pound of strawberries). If your strawberries already taste very sweet, go for 4 per cent, but if they're a bit sharper or more balanced, go for 5 per cent. Toss the fruit to coat it evenly in the sugar.

You can cook this in one of two ways. Put the strawberries into a large bowl, cover it tightly with cling film and set over a saucepan of barely simmering water (bain-marie) for 30–40 minutes. The key is to cook them at a low temperature so that they keep their freshness.

PRO TIP
Alternatively, vacuum seal bags of the macerating strawberries and steam (or cook in a water bath) at 65°C (150°F) for 25–30 minutes.

The strawberries are ready when they have released lots of deep scarlet liquid. Drain them through a colander to capture as much of the liquor as possible. Refrigerate the strawberry juice. I like to keep a stash of this in the freezer to use all summer long.

The cooked strawberries won't look or taste great by now. They can be restored by drying them so they gain a chewy, gummy quality. Lay them cut face up in a single layer on racks and dehydrate at 50–60°C (122–140°F) for 5–6 hours. A dehydrator *(p236)* is ideal but a very low oven works as well.

Strawberry ice cream

If you get your hands on some extraordinary strawberries, make this ice cream. Intensely strawberry in flavour with a silky, creamy texture, I humbly say this will be some of the best ice cream you have ever had.

makes 870g (about 2lb)

300g (10oz) strawberries, hulled

90g (⅓ cup plus 1½ tbsp) caster (superfine) sugar

100g (scant ½ cup) strawberry juice *(p19)*

90g (⅓ cup plus 1 tbsp) condensed milk

250ml (1 cup) double (heavy) cream

pinch of salt

Put the strawberries and sugar in a blender and process until you have a smooth purée. Whisk in the strawberry juice, condensed milk, cream and salt. Pour the ice cream base into a container and chill for at least 4 hours. Churn in an ice-cream machine then transfer to a container and leave to set in the freezer before serving.

Dairy-free strawberry ice cream

As a pastry chef, it's always a good idea to have a few dairy-free or vegan recipes up your sleeve. I love all things dairy but I understand some don't and I want to serve them something just as mouthwatering. This ice cream is a lighter affair than its dairy equivalent but the oat milk provides a certain fatty creaminess that is equally luscious. Oat milk is great in dairy-free ice creams. Barista oat milks work best as they are formulated to be slightly fattier and to be able to trap and hold air, two qualities that are ideal for ice-cream making. The oat flavour doesn't come through in this recipe but I made a plum version using the same base where it was more pronounced. Plums and oats are a delicious combination so it worked well but just bear in mind you may taste the oat milk if you try this recipe with other fruits (which you absolutely should).

makes 750g (1lb 10oz)

400g (14oz) strawberries, hulled

60g (¼ cup plus 2 tsp) caster (superfine) sugar

250ml (1 cup) oat milk

50g (3 tbsp) liquid glucose

10g (2 tsp) tapioca flour

pinch of salt

Halve 100g (4oz) of the strawberries and combine with 10g (2 tsp) of the caster sugar. Cook following the method for strawberry juice *(p19)*. Once the fruit has released its juices, leave to cool.

Meanwhile, combine the remaining sugar with the oat milk, glucose and tapioca flour in a small saucepan and whisk well. Cook over a medium heat until the sugars have dissolved and the tapioca flour has thickened slightly. If using a thermometer *(p236)*, you're aiming for a temperature of 75°C (167°F). Take off the heat and leave to cool.

Put the cooked strawberries with their juices, the thickened oat milk and the remaining strawberries into a blender and process until you have a smooth purée. Stir in the salt, pour into a container and chill for at least 4 hours. Churn in an ice-cream machine then serve straight away.

Strawberry sorbet

makes 870g (about 2lb)

500g (1 generous lb) ripe strawberries, hulled

250g (1 cup) strawberry juice *(p19)*

120g (⅔ cup) caster (superfine) sugar, plus extra to taste

pinch of salt, to taste (optional)

lemon juice, to taste (optional)

citric acid, to taste (optional)

Put the strawberries and juice in a blender and process until you have a completely smooth purée. Add half of the sugar and mix well. Keep adding the remaining sugar a little at a time, tasting between additions. If you have a refractometer *(p236)*, you are aiming for a sugar level of 25°Bx. Taste the sorbet base and season with a small pinch of salt, lemon juice or citric acid. Go very lightly here; you are seasoning to brighten the sorbet base, not to impact the flavour profile.

Pour into a container and chill in the fridge. Churn in an ice-cream machine until frozen. Transfer to a lidded plastic container and store in the freezer. Put the container in the fridge about 30 minutes before serving.

Strawberry granita

This granita brings back memories of running around sunny parks as a kid eating one of my favourite lollies, a strawberry split: vanilla ice cream coated in an icy layer of strawberry. It's the easiest of recipes once you've made the strawberry juice.

strawberry juice *(p19)*

caster (superfine) sugar, to taste

Taste the juice to see if you are happy with the balance, adding a touch of sugar if it does not taste sweet enough. Pour it into a shallow container and freeze. Every couple of hours, scrape a fork through the freezing liquor so that you end up with large ice crystals rather than a fine snow. Once it is completely frozen, scrape a fork through to break it up further.

After many summers of making this granita, the sugar levels always come out perfectly if you follow the strawberry juice method on this page. If you have a refractometer *(p236)* and want to check, you are aiming for a sugar level of 12–15°Bx.

Strawberries and cream

I'm not usually one for dressing a plate with multiple "textures" of a fruit but when the strawberries taste their best, it seems foolish not to celebrate them in exuberant fashion. This dessert uses strawberries as ice cream, granita, dried and in their natural state. Be sure to serve the fresh strawberries at room temperature, never straight from the fridge. The difference in flavour between a cold strawberry and one at room temp – or even better, one that's just been picked and still warm from the sun – is astounding. Taste them side by side and you'll never serve a cold strawberry again. The rich double cream here should be spoonably thick (the one from Ivy House Farm is perfect). If it isn't, then whip it very lightly; the goal is a densely rich hit of cream rather than airiness.

serves 1

2–3 strawberries, hulled

2–3 chewy dried strawberries (p19)

1 large scoop strawberry ice cream (p20)

1 tsp rich double (heavy) cream

1 generous tbsp strawberry granita (p21)

Put a shallow bowl or lipped plate in the freezer to chill at least 30 minutes before serving. Cut the strawberries into halves or quarters depending on their size. You want each mouthful to have a piece of strawberry as well as all the other delicious things on the plate, so judge accordingly. Cut the chewy dried strawberries in half and toss them with the fresh strawberries.

Scoop a large quenelle of the ice cream onto the chilled plate, slightly left of centre. Make a deep indent in the ice cream with a clean, hot spoon. Fill the indent with the double cream and top with a generous spoon of the strawberry mix so that it tumbles over the ice cream into the centre of the plate. Sprinkle over a large spoonful of granita to cover most of the ice cream with glimpses of all the different treasures underneath.

GOOSEBERRIES

This wonderfully tart fruit will always inspire thoughts of old-fashioned British desserts: of fools and crumbles and syllabubs. Gooseberries grow well across our fair isle with the north of Scotland producing exemplary berries to rival those of sunny Kent. They have a reputation for aggressive acidity but I ask you to find a bush laden with fully ripe fruit and eat a bursting berry from it. They are sweet with a balanced zing, with the jellyish texture of grapes and are, of course, completely delicious. The acidity of underripe gooseberries can be harnessed and subdued without overpowering it with sweetness. That same acidity has the ability to thicken milk and set cream as it does to superb effect in the recipes for sherbet and a classic fool.

Gooseberries are often expensive by the punnet and commonly harvested before they realize their full sweetness. If you're able to pick them yourself, they'll be much better value, meaning you can pile them generously into a dessert or happily blend them to extract that glorious juice. Red gooseberries are the most beautiful deep burgundy at full ripeness and are my favourite, but the luminous chartreuse of green gooseberries is not to be snubbed. There is something so joyfully summery about the green varieties as the season starts, particularly when they're paired with elderflower.

Gooseberry compôte

The goal here is to cook the compôte hot and fast, then chill it down quickly. This helps to preserve brightness and avoids it tasting stewed. Two-thirds of the gooseberries are cooked down until completely soft then slightly thickened with cornflour before the remaining gooseberries are added off the heat, allowing them to retain their texture. The results taste vibrantly gooseberry-ish.

makes 850g (1lb 14oz)

750g (1½lb) gooseberries

100g (½ cup) caster (superfine) sugar

15g (1 tbsp plus 1 tsp) cornflour (cornstarch)

Top and tail the gooseberries and cut into quarters. In a small pan with a tight-fitting lid, combine 500g (1lb 2oz) of the quartered gooseberries with the sugar and cook over a medium-high heat for 5–10 minutes. The berries should have broken down and released their liquid; use a whisk to break them up further if necessary.

Mix the cornflour with enough water to make a slurry and pour into the cooked gooseberries. Bring back to the boil to cook out the cornflour then remove from the heat. Add the remaining gooseberries to the cooked fruit and stir well. Pour into a shallow container and set in an ice bath to cool then transfer to the fridge until ready to serve.

Gooseberry fool

Fools are a ridiculously easy dessert. In their simplest form, they are a tart fruit purée folded through whipped cream. The acid in the fruit helps to thicken and set the cream. Gooseberry fool is the classic but rhubarb, blackcurrant or raspberry all work brilliantly, too. I like to use yogurt as well as cream in a fool. The yogurt adds a little extra acidity, lightens the texture and takes away the cloying mouthfeel of cream. I tend to use a thick Greek-style yogurt but you could also use one made from sheep's or goat's milk, even if they are slightly thinner.

serves 4–6

200g (1 scant cup) gooseberry compôte *(left)*

350g (1⅓ cups) thick Greek-style yogurt

40g (3 tbsp) caster (superfine) sugar

300ml (1¼ cups) double (heavy) cream

Combine the compôte, yogurt and sugar together in a food processor. Pulse until you have a well-blended but still slightly coarse mixture.

Whisk the cream until it forms soft peaks. Gently fold the whipped cream through the yogurt mixture. You can set the mixture in individual portions or, if you are planning on creating the full dessert at the end of the chapter, decant into a container and store in the fridge for up to 3 days.

Red gooseberry sherbet

Sherbets are somewhere between a sorbet and an ice cream: a base of fruit and milk but without any cream or eggs. The acid of the gooseberry juice thickens the milk just as it would in a posset. Red gooseberries will yield a perfect millennial pink sherbet but this recipe works just as well with green gooseberries. Sherbets have a velvety mouthfeel that contrasts sublimely with the tart flavour of the gooseberries.

makes 1.5kg (3lb 3oz)

500g (1 generous lb) gooseberries

725ml (3 cups) whole milk

150g (¾ cup) caster (superfine) sugar

100ml (scant ½ cup) double (heavy) cream

Either pass the gooseberries through a juicer or blend them to a pulp in a food processor and strain through a sieve lined with muslin to release the clear juice. Leave the pulp to hang for a couple of hours to allow as much liquid as possible to drain out. Squeeze the pulp through the muslin to extract the last drops of juice and discard the solids. You should end up with about 275g (1⅛ cups) of juice.

Combine the milk and sugar in a saucepan. Bring to a simmer over a medium heat to dissolve the sugar. Take off the heat, leave to cool then chill in the fridge until completely cold. If the milk is at all warm, the gooseberry juice will split it rather than thicken it.

Whisk the cream into the chilled, sweetened milk followed by the gooseberry juice. The mixture will gently thicken. Pour this sherbet base into a container and place in the fridge to chill for at least 4 hours. Churn in an ice-cream machine then transfer to a container and leave to set in the freezer before serving.

Gooseberry sherbet with fool and oat biscuit

Oats and gooseberries are a very happy partnership. The combination brings to mind idyllic British countryside: farms and hay and unkempt hedgerows. I love this dish in the early summer before we get carried away with the heady delights of stone fruits. It is subtle in flavour and appearance but more unsuspectingly scrumptious for it.

serves 1

3–4 ripe gooseberries

2 generous tbsp gooseberry fool (p25)

1 generous tbsp gooseberry compôte (p25)

1 small scoop gooseberry sherbet (left)

1 thin sheet oat biscuit (p194)

Place a shallow bowl in the freezer to chill 30 minutes before serving. Cut the gooseberries into halves or quarters depending on their size. In a small bowl, very gently combine the fool and the compôte to create a ripple effect. Crumble a little of the oat biscuit into the bottom of the chilled bowl. Spoon the rippled fool on top followed by the cut gooseberries. Crumble a little more of the oat biscuit to the right of the fool and place an elegant quenelle of gooseberry sherbet on top. Try to keep the fool and the sherbet quite tight in the centre of the bowl. Top with a shard of oat biscuit, covering the fool but allowing the sherbet to peek out from underneath.

TAYBERRIES, LOGANBERRIES & RASPBERRIES

In my dream future, I have a large garden absolutely bursting with all kinds of fruit trees and bushes. I would have a big section dedicated to different berries: tayberries, loganberries, boysenberries, raspberries – anything I could get my hands on. The tricky thing with berries is that they taste best when at their ripest but they only achieve this perfect state when they are on the plant. If you pick them at their peak, bursting with aromatic juices (my mouth is watering just writing that) then you have a fruit that is now very fragile and not easily transportable. More often than not, berries are picked a little underripe to make sure they can be delivered from farms to their destination intact. If I had that garden, I would be able to harvest berries at their absolute peak without worry.

The next best thing is to find a pick-your-own farm. Not only do they tend to grow more interesting varieties but you can individually select each berry. They may cost you more in terms of scratched arms, aching thighs and sunburn but you will have gathered a superior product for half the price you'll pay for a punnet of slightly underripe fruit from your normal supplier. Plus, you get to sample as you go, learning exactly what colour indicates the most delectable berries.

Raspberries and blackberries have been crossed in every manner possible all over the world resulting in a wonderfully diverse range of berries. The most common to be found on fruit farms in the UK are tayberries and loganberries. Tayberries, named after the river Tay in Scotland, are large with a purplish magenta colour. They have a distinctly wild, almost tutti frutti flavour. Loganberries, named for their breeder, James Logan, are a brighter red and have a more pronounced acidity. They have both been further crossed to create other varieties such as boysenberries and marionberries, which are more commonly seen in the USA.

Perfectly ripe berries want little more than a pool of rich cream or custard. We shouldn't be fool enough to think we can improve upon nature. For all of those berries that slightly miss the mark, either underripe and in need of a little boost, or having slumped into juicy overripeness, I suggest you use them in a fool, ice cream or semifreddo. Dairy really is the best accompaniment to berries, so be joyous and generous in your use of cream. The season is brief so revel in it while you can.

Tayberry fool

This is the perfect home for berries that are a bit too soft, bruised or just not in perfect condition. There are several schools of thought on the origin of the name "fool" but the most apt one in this situation comes from *The Oxford Companion to Sugar and Sweets*: "A likely explanation is that fools, like trifles and whim-whams, are light and frivolous, mere trifles." This fool couldn't be simpler, a mere trifle indeed. The ratios here differ slightly from the gooseberry fool *(p25)*. You want to really show off the delicious affinity that berries and cream have so there are larger amounts of both, with the yogurt providing structural support and a gentle underlying acidity.

serves 4–6

150g (5oz) tayberries

80g (¼ cup plus 1½ tbsp) caster (superfine) sugar

400ml (1¾ cups) double (heavy) cream

200g (¾ cup plus 2 tbsp) thick Greek-style yogurt

Remove any stems or leaves from the berries and combine them with the sugar in a small saucepan. Warm gently over a low heat for about 5 minutes so that the sugar dissolves and the fruit starts to break down. You don't want to end up with a smooth purée; a little texture is welcome. Remove from the heat and leave to cool completely.

Whisk the cream to soft peaks. Mix the cooled berries and yogurt together. Fold in the whipped cream and then chill the mixture. I like to serve this with a few more tayberries and a shard of oat biscuit *(p194)* for dipping.

Loganberry ice cream

Loganberries come into their own with the application of a little heat. They make exceptional jam if you ever find yourself with a surplus. The berries are first roasted gently with sugar, which will release all of those delicious juices and bring out the wilder blackberry flavours. The tapioca flour will help keep the ice cream silky once churned.

makes 850g (1lb 14oz)

400g (14oz) loganberries

75g (⅓ cup) caster (superfine) sugar

250ml (1 cup) double (heavy) cream

250ml (1 cup) whole milk

75g (¼ cup) condensed milk

10g (1 tbsp) tapioca flour

Preheat the oven to 150°C (300°F). Combine the berries and sugar in a roasting dish, mix well and leave to macerate for 30 minutes. Cover tightly with foil and roast for 20 minutes.

Meanwhile, combine the cream, milk and condensed milk in a heavy-based saucepan. Heat gently to bring the mix up to 70°C (160°F). Mix the tapioca flour with 2 tablespoons of cold water to create a slurry. Pour into the hot milk and cream, stir well and leave to cool.

Once the milk and cream have cooled completely, combine with the roasted loganberries and blend to a smooth purée. Pour into a container and leave to rest in the fridge for 4 hours or overnight. Churn in an ice-cream machine then transfer to a container and leave to set in the freezer before serving.

Semifreddo

This may seem like a lot of steps but the outcome is more than worth it. A semifreddo is, in essence, a frozen mousse. It's lighter in texture and feel than ice cream. All the effort you put into aerating the egg whites, yolks and cream separately results in an ethereally light frozen dessert of which you can eat an alarming amount before feeling full. I love setting the semifreddo in a terrine and serving it in slices. You can also set different flavours on top of each other to create a layered effect. Try setting lemon verbena semifreddo *(p225)* on top of this recipe to achieve a two-tone effect.

This is a perfect use for any picked berries that have gone a bit soft or been damaged. You want super-ripe, soft fruit here.

---

serves 6

300g (10oz) tayberries, loganberries or raspberries

---

flavourless oil, for greasing

40g (2½ tbsp) egg whites, from 1–2 eggs

160g (½ cup plus 3 tbsp) caster (superfine) sugar

40g (2½ tbsp) egg yolks, from 2–3 eggs

250ml (1 cup) double (heavy) cream

Remove any stems or the bigger cores of the tayberries (if using) and blend the berries to a purée. If you are using raspberries, sieve the purée to remove the seeds. Set to one side. Lightly oil a loaf tin or terrine and line smoothly with a double layer of cling film.

Pour the egg whites into the bowl of a mixer with a whisk attachment. Put 80g (¼ cup plus 1½ tbsp) of the sugar into a small saucepan along with 50ml (¼ cup) of water. Place over a high heat. When the syrup reaches 110°C (230°F), turn the mixer to medium speed to start whisking the egg whites. When the syrup reaches 120°C (248°F), turn off the heat and turn up the mixer. Carefully pour the hot syrup onto the egg whites in a steady stream. Once all the syrup has been added, reduce to a medium speed and carry on whisking until the meringue base has cooled completely.

Meanwhile, combine the egg yolks and remaining sugar in a metal bowl set over a saucepan of simmering water (bain-marie) to make a sabayon. Whisk the yolks and sugar over a gentle heat until they are light and pale; when you lift the whisk out, it should leave a ribbon trail that holds on the surface of the mixture before melting back in. Remove from the heat and leave to cool slightly. Whisk the cream until it just holds soft peaks. Add the reserved berry purée and sabayon to the cream and gently fold through until just combined. Add the whisked meringue in two stages. Fold gently but firmly to ensure you maintain all of the volume you have worked hard to create but also to make sure you don't have any pockets of meringue or cream. Pour the semifreddo into the prepared tin, give it a gentle tap to make sure there are no air pockets, then freeze overnight.

To serve, invert the terrine to release the semifreddo. Cut 2cm (¾in) slices, then remove the thin strip of cling film surrounding it and serve on chilled plates. You can slice the semifreddo in advance and keep the slices between layers of baking parchment in an airtight container in the freezer.

Raspberry ice-cream sandwich

I was lucky enough to spend the summer of 2020 (which should have been an awful summer by all accounts) making ice-cream sandwiches and having the best time with Terri Mercieca at Happy Endings London. Our styles are very different but our approaches are firmly aligned. Terri puts extraordinary care into thinking about how her ice-cream sandwiches will be eaten, how each bite will taste and feel. They will be the perfect texture all the way through, even eaten straight from the deep freeze. This ice-cream sandwich is an ode to her.

When you're building an ice-cream sandwich, think about what the biscuit or cookie you use will be like to bite through when it's frozen. A chewy cookie is delicious served slightly warm but when it's frozen it can be like taffy. You want something that you can chomp straight through that is also sturdy enough not to crumble halfway through eating it.

for the raspberry jam

makes 850g (1lb 14oz)

500g (1 generous lb) raspberries

300g (1⅓ cups) caster (superfine) sugar

50ml (¼ cup) lemon juice

Combine the ingredients in a large heavy-based saucepan and mix well. Leave to macerate for about 30 minutes. The sugar will start to dissolve, shortening the cooking time and giving you a fresher-tasting jam. Place the pan over a high heat and bring to the boil, then stir occasionally as it cooks. I find raspberry jam is particularly prone to spitting everywhere so be careful when you stir it.

Cook the jam to 108°C (226°F). You can also test the setting point by using the wrinkle test. Place a small plate in the freezer when you start to cook the jam. To test, drop a small amount of jam onto the frozen plate. It should immediately thicken and set and the surface should wrinkle when pushed with your finger. If it is still quite liquid, cook the jam for another 3–5 minutes before testing again. Pour into a container and store in the fridge.

to serve

makes 1 sandwich

2 vanilla and hazelnut cookies (p208)

1 x 8cm (3in) disc raspberry semifreddo (p31)

2 tsp raspberry jam

Make the raspberry semifreddo according to the recipe (p31). Pour the mixture into a shallow tray, rather than a loaf tin, to a depth of around 4cm (1¾in). Bake the cookies and leave them to cool.

Once the semifreddo is completely frozen, use an 8cm (3in) round cutter to quickly stamp out discs. Dip the cutter into warm water between each use to get a clean, neat finish. Return the discs of semifreddo to the freezer to firm up. Any leftovers can be packed into a tub and stored in the freezer to enjoy another time.

Match your cookies into evenly-sized pairs then spread the underside of each one with a thin layer of raspberry jam. Once the semifreddo is firm again, sandwich a disc between each pair of cookies and gently press together to make sure it is well sealed.

The semifreddo and cookie dough will last well in the freezer for up to 2 weeks but it is best to construct the sandwiches shortly before you eat them.

Hay custard and tayberry tart

Supremely elegant, custard tarts are the perfect interplay between crisp pastry and just-set silken custard. This is based on the Marcus Wareing recipe that pretty much every London chef uses. In this version, the custard is infused with toasted hay and topped with tayberries, capturing the taste of an afternoon spent fruit picking in the summer sun. Pet shops are a good source of high-quality hay, or make friends with a local farmer.

makes 6 individual tarts

for the sweet pastry

350g (2¾ cups) plain (all-purpose) flour

100g (⅓ cup plus 1 tbsp) icing (confectioners') sugar

225g (2 sticks) cold unsalted butter, diced

pinch of salt

3 eggs: 3 yolks, 1 white

Combine the flour, icing sugar, butter and salt in a food processor and blitz to fine breadcrumbs. Add the egg yolks and mix until the dough is starting to come together. Turn out onto a work surface and knead firmly, just enough to bring the dough together. Wrap in cling film and chill until firm.

Roll out the dough on a floured surface to a thickness of 2–3mm (⅛in) then cut out 15cm (6in) circles. Press into 6 x 10cm (4in) tart cases, pushing the pastry into the edges. Chill the lined tart cases for 30 minutes in the fridge or freezer.

Preheat the oven to 180°C (350°F). Trim the excess pastry to give a neat finish. Line each tart with scrunched-up baking parchment, fill with baking beans and bake for 12–15 minutes until the top edge is starting to colour. Remove the baking beans and return the tarts to the oven for a further 5 minutes or until golden brown. Brush the insides with beaten egg white and leave to cool, still in their cases.

for the hay-infused cream

30g (1oz) hay

600ml (2½ cups) double (heavy) cream

Preheat the oven to 180°C (350°F). Place the hay on a baking tray and top with a cooling rack to help weigh it down. Toast in the oven for about 20 minutes until it smells very fragrant. Meanwhile, heat the cream in a saucepan over a low heat until it is starting to steam. Add the toasted hay and cover tightly. Leave to infuse in the fridge for 3–4 hours or overnight. Warm the cream gently then strain through a sieve, making sure to really squeeze out the hay to capture as much flavour as possible.

for the custard

140g (½ cup plus 1½ tbsp) egg yolks, from about 7 eggs

50g (¼ cup) caster (superfine) sugar

450g (1¾ cups plus 2 tbsp) hay-infused cream

Preheat the oven to 115°C (240°F) with as low a fan as possible. Whisk together the egg yolks and sugar. Slowly whisk in the warm hay-infused cream to combine. Pass through a fine sieve. Pour into a saucepan and heat gently until the custard reaches 40°C (104°F).

Place the tart cases on a baking tray and pour in the warmed custard. I like to put the tray in the oven before doing this so that I can fill the tarts as high as possible without spilling the custard on my way to the oven. Bake for 20–25 minutes until the tarts have that gentle wobble. Leave to cool before removing from the tart cases.

to serve

200g (7oz) tayberries, plus 100g (3½oz) per tart

100g (⅓ cup plus 1 tbsp) icing (confectioners') sugar

Blend 200g (7oz) of tayberries with the icing sugar and pass through a fine sieve. Use this purée to dress the remaining tayberries and to cover the surface of the tarts just before serving.

MULBERRIES

Deemed too delicate to machine harvest, mulberries are one of those fruits that have escaped mechanization or selective breeding and are still best picked by hand. That means that you won't find them in a shop to buy (or very rarely). Search out pick-your-own farms with mulberry trees. At Maynards in East Sussex, there's one tree near the entrance that only those in the know pay attention to. Otherwise old stately homes, parks and orchards are your best bets. Luckily for me, London is covered in mulberry trees (the upper west side of Manhattan and most of Queens is covered in mulberry trees, too). When people find one in their area, they often keep them a closely guarded secret; if others get to know of the one on your doorstep, you might miss out. Luckily, there is an online map of London mulberry trees, Morus Londinium, to help you find one nearby.

Wherever you find mulberries, don't wear a white t-shirt to pick them. Ripe mulberries will burst unexpectedly in your fingers, their deep magenta juices flowing down your arms and staining any and all clothing. The dense canopy of leaves can often hide the ripening crop below. If you can, get underneath the leaves so you are almost hiding inside the tree like a little child again. You'll then start to see all of the deep purple berries concealed beneath the shade. It is a truly joyful, nostalgic experience: searching and looking for the best berries; stretching as high as you can for those perfect fruits; revelling in the mess you're making as the juices splatter when you squeeze just a little too hard. Another reason mulberries aren't a commercial crop is that the trees ripen at startlingly different rates, which makes them more difficult to harvest. A trick for picking the ripe berries, though, is to lay a blanket or tarpaulin underneath the canopy and gently shake the branches. The fruit will fall off easily, without disturbing the unripe berries. In my experience, they land softly enough that no damage is done after their free fall.

The flavour and colour of mulberries speak of a certain wildness quite unlike any other berry. Perhaps their scarcity and the fact that they make you work so hard for such meagre amounts means they taste that bit more special. You can capture a little more of that enchanting flavour by using a handful of mulberry leaves infused into a sugar syrup or a neutral spirit, such as grappa or vodka. If you manage to come home from picking with any perfect whole fruits then simply pour some cream over them and enjoy. Otherwise, process them immediately into granita or ice cream to trap the brief magic of these jewel-bright berries. They will start to break down very quickly if kept in the fridge. If you aren't quite sure which route to take then freeze the berries as they are to delay the decision.

Mulberry ice cream

It was a good year when we had picked enough mulberries to make this ice cream at Lyle's. It didn't happen every year so when we could make a batch, it felt particularly precious. Serve this on its own, it needs no adornment.

makes 830g (1lb 13oz)

250g (9oz) mulberries

140g (⅔ cup plus 1 tsp) caster (superfine) sugar

250ml (1 cup) double (heavy) cream

100ml (scant ½ cup) whole milk

90g (6 tbsp) condensed milk

pinch of salt

Combine the mulberries and 50g (¼ cup) of the sugar in a saucepan, mix well and place over a very low heat. Cover the pan tightly and cook for about 5 minutes. You want the sugar to dissolve and the fruit to be releasing all of those delicious juices. Remove from the heat and leave to cool.

Once the mulberries have cooled completely, combine with the remaining ingredients and blend to a smooth purée. Pass the ice-cream base through a fine sieve then leave to rest in the fridge for at least 4 hours or overnight. Churn in an ice-cream machine then transfer to a container and leave to set in the freezer before serving.

Mulberry granita

makes 400g (14oz)

300g (10oz) mulberries

30g (2 tbsp) caster (superfine) sugar

malic acid or lemon juice, to taste

mulberry eau de vie, to taste (optional)

Combine the mulberries, sugar and 100ml (scant ½ cup) of water in a bowl set over a saucepan of barely simmering water. Cover the bowl and leave the mulberries to steep for 30 minutes or until they're starting to burst and release their incredible juices. Set the bowl in an ice bath to chill the cooked mulberries quickly.

Once they are cool, blend the fruit along with the juices. Pass through a fine sieve and taste. If it needs a little boost, season with a pinch of malic acid or a scant squeeze of lemon juice. If you are ever lucky enough to come across mulberry *eau de vie*, a splash here would be perfect. Pour into a shallow container and freeze.

Every couple of hours scrape a fork through the freezing liquor so that you end up with large ice crystals rather than a fine snow. Once it is completely frozen, scrape a fork through again to break it up further.

Mulberry leaf infusion

Often you get to your much sought-after mulberry tree only to find the birds or another enthusiast have got there first. There is still a harvest to reap. The leaves won't have the upfront jammy flavour of the fruit but they do carry that dusky quality that makes mulberries so special. This recipe will work whether you're infusing the mulberry leaves into a sugar syrup, cider vinegar or alcohol. Pick young, vivid green leaves. If they're left in the liquid for long enough, they will soften so they can be eaten like a vine leaf afterwards, stuffed and filled with something delectable, whether sweet or savoury. If you are using a sugar syrup, I would make it equal weights caster (superfine) sugar to water (or 1 cup of water to 1¼ cups sugar) as this will give the most versatility for future uses.

Try using the syrup to sweeten a fool, sorbet or summer pudding or to dress different berries for that elusive mulberry flavour. Add the vinegar infusion to a jam to give balance and help the set; it will season with that petrichor scent of mulberry leaves. The alcoholic version works wonders in a cocktail.

makes 1 litre (2 pints)

100g (3½oz) mulberry leaves, washed

1 litre (1 quart or 33.8 fl oz bottle) liquid (sugar syrup, cider vinegar, alcohol)

Warm your chosen liquid to 60°C (140°F). You don't want it to be too hot, just warm enough to aid the extraction of the flavour. Add the leaves and leave them to steep briefly. Transfer the infusion along with the leaves to a sterilized wide-necked bottle or jar while still warm and seal. If you have a spare handful of mulberries, add them for extra flavour. The infusion will be ready to use after 1 week.

Baked cream, mulberry granita and thyme

This feels like the archetypal Lyle's dish. Beautiful ingredients, thoughtfully paired and prepared with minimal manipulation. Use the richest, tastiest cream you can find. The honey should be deep and brightly floral: a wildflower or heather variety will work best. And the mulberries, well they can be nothing but completely themselves.

serves 1

1 generous tbsp baked cream (p179)

3–4 mulberries

3–4 dessert spoons mulberry granita (p37)

2 sprigs of lemon thyme, leaves picked

Prepare the baked cream as per the recipe (p179) but substitute the sugar for an equal quantity of honey. Once the cream has chilled, scoop a spoonful into the centre of a shallow bowl. Scatter over the mulberries then top with the granita, allowing it to mount over one side so that the baked cream is just visible underneath. Top with the lemon thyme leaves.

BLACKCURRANTS

The smell of a car full of blackcurrant leaves marks the ascent into summer for me. They are one of the first things we would pick in the spring just as I was itching to get back out into the countryside. Blackcurrants are the main crop for Maynards Fruit Farm where I spent one day a week picking for the restaurant. I had been somewhat nervously anticipating blackcurrant season the first summer I spent working at Lyle's. I knew they were going to be an important part of the summer menu so I hadn't mentioned my previous negative encounters.

I spent the first four years of my pastry career under the mistaken notion that I hated blackcurrants. At all the restaurants I worked in during that time I made cassis fluid gels, boiling the same bought-in purée with agar agar for exactly four minutes while it spat aggressively out of the pan, staining my whites and the walls; then fighting with the Vitamix as it cut out time and time again during blending. I think a lot of my hatred was situational (so much time spent cleaning and messing around with blenders) but it was also very much the flavour of those bought-in purées. They tended to be aggressive, sour and oddly one dimensional. Uninspiring, to say the least.

The first time I ate a ripe blackcurrant, picked from the sun-warmed stem, I realized how wrong I had been. A ripe blackcurrant tastes, yes, of that intense jamminess we all know, but of a jam balanced out with an amazingly floral and herbaceous quality. They are bright, pure and complex. A world away from the flat blackcurrant flavour I had known. The next revelation was the flavour of blackcurrant leaves *(below)*. I think this is one of the best smells in the whole world. Just crushing one gently in your hand releases so much aroma. Eating anything infused with blackcurrant leaf transports you to a summery field full of the promise of delicious fruit just hidden under a canopy of green leaves.

Two of my favourite desserts are based on blackcurrants and blackcurrant leaves. As they are so aromatic, the leaves infuse incredibly well into creams, custards and vinegars. They permeate whatever vehicle you choose with the heady, sweet, fresh flavour of blackcurrants, leaving you to use the actual fruit as the richer, more intense base for your dessert.

Blackcurrant cordial

A treat in and of itself but also brilliant for poaching blackcurrants. The leaves are not essential here but add a further herbaceous top note to the cordial. The overriding principle is to poach your fruit in a 20 per cent syrup, so a syrup that is 1 part sugar to 5 parts water; here 200g of sugar to 1 litre of water (1 cup sugar to 1 quart of water). A syrup based on these ratios gives a lovely sweetness level for cordials of most flavours. They aren't high enough in sugar to last without refrigeration but, if kept in the fridge, the cordial should last about 6 weeks.

makes about 1.5 litres (about 3 pints)

500g (1 generous lb) blackcurrants

200g (1⅓ cups) caster (superfine) sugar, plus extra to taste

a handful of blackcurrant leaves (optional)

1 tsp citric acid or lemon juice, to taste

Remove any small pieces of stem from the blackcurrants. Put them in a large saucepan with the sugar and blackcurrant leaves (if using) and 1 litre (1 quart) of water. Bring to a simmer over a gentle heat and cook for 15 minutes. Use a whisk or hand-held blender to break up the cooked blackcurrants, not to a purée but roughly so they can release more of their juices. Remove from the heat and leave to infuse overnight and then strain. Add the citric acid to the blackcurrant juice and taste, adding more sugar if required. Return to the boil and either pour into sterilized bottles or use straight away to poach blackcurrants. Store in the fridge.

Blackcurrant powder
Keep back the strained blackcurrant pulp from making cordial to create a dramatically deep purple powder. Discard any blackcurrant leaves left in the pulp and spread it in a thin layer on baking parchment. Dry in a low oven or dehydrator until completely crisp then blend to a fine powder in a spice grinder or mortar and pestle. You can also use frozen blackcurrants; just lay them on a tray and dry in the same way. They will take longer to crisp up as they have a higher moisture content.

Poached blackcurrants

Cooking fruits in a liquor made of their own juices adds an incredible intensity. I would tend to do large batches of these poached blackcurrants and then freeze them in 20-portion bags as we would pick such a large amount of very ripe fruit just once a week. We always kept a few bags in the freezer to use in summer pudding recipes, too.

makes 1kg (2¼lb)

1 litre (1 quart) blackcurrant cordial *(left)*

200g (1 cup) caster (superfine) sugar

a large handful of blackcurrant leaves

1kg (2¼lb) blackcurrants

blackcurrant leaf vinegar, to season *(p42)*

Combine the cordial, sugar and leaves in a wide pan, bring to the boil then turn down to a simmer. Add the blackcurrants and cook gently for around 5 minutes. The sugar will take the sweetness of the poaching liquor up to 40 per cent. Since the blackcurrants will absorb the liquor for such a short amount of time, a higher concentration of sugar is required. Keep tasting them throughout the cooking time. The blackcurrants will become sweeter and fruitier and will taste very lightly cooked; you don't want them to start bursting and lose their form. Once they are cooked, remove the poached blackcurrants from the liquor and set aside.

Bring the liquor back to the boil and reduce until it has thickened enough to coat a spoon but not be syrupy. Pour over the poached blackcurrants, leave to cool and then chill. Season with a little blackcurrant leaf vinegar to brighten.

Blackcurrant leaf vinegar meringue

Blackcurrant leaf vinegar is great to use as a seasoning for anything blackcurrant flavoured. I like an intensely infused vinegar so use 150g (5oz) or about two handfuls of leaves for 1 litre (1 quart) of Riesling vinegar or a light red wine vinegar. You can either warm the vinegar to just above body temperature and pour it onto the leaves in a Kilner jar, leaving for a minimum of a week to infuse; or vacuum pack the two ingredients together and again leave for at least a week before using.

makes 20 meringues

5g (1–2) blackcurrant leaves

200g (1 cup) caster (superfine) sugar

100g (scant ½ cup) egg whites, from 3–4 eggs

12ml (2½ tsp) blackcurrant leaf vinegar

3g (½ tsp) salt

First, make the leaf sugar: grind the blackcurrant leaves with 30g (2⅓ tbsp) of the sugar until fine and set aside.

Preheat the oven to 110°C (250°F) with minimal fan setting. Combine the egg whites, vinegar and salt in a mixer and whisk at low speed until soft peaks form. Add the remaining sugar one third at a time and continue whisking slowly until it is well incorporated. Once you have a stiff, glossy meringue, fold in the leaf sugar.

Line a baking sheet with baking parchment or a silicone mat and pipe the meringue into 5cm (2in) rounds. Bake for about 1½ hours until the meringues have a slightly mallowy centre and crisp exterior.

Blackcurrant leaf ice cream

This ice cream is based on an infused crème anglaise. The hot custard is poured over the blackcurrant leaves as it cools before being strained. I know I say this a lot but it is so completely delicious. I implore you to make it if you have access to some blackcurrant leaves.

makes 1.5 litres (2¾ pints)

45g (1½oz) blackcurrant leaves (about 1 handful), stems removed

800ml (3⅓ cups) whole milk

400ml (1¾ cups) double (heavy) cream

170g (⅔ cup) egg yolks, from about 9 eggs

100g (½ cup) caster (superfine) sugar

Put the blackcurrant leaves in a bowl set in an ice bath and place a sieve on top. Combine the milk and cream in a large heavy-based saucepan and bring to a rolling boil. Whisk together the egg yolks and sugar. Once the milk and cream have come to the boil, reduce the heat and pour about a third into the yolks and sugar, mixing well and quickly. Pour the now tempered yolks back into the pan with the remaining hot milk and cream and mix well. By bringing the milk and cream to a rolling boil first, there should be enough latent heat left in the pan to cook the egg to 82–83°C (180°F) without having to return it to the heat. Check the temperature and if it is below 82°C (180°F), continue to cook the custard over a gentle heat, stirring constantly until it reaches the required temperature. It will resemble a fairly thin custard that will coat the back of a spoon. This should be very quick if your milk and cream have just come off the boil.

Strain the custard through the sieve onto the blackcurrant leaves. Leave to infuse for around 20 minutes, taste and leave for another 10 minutes if the flavour is not yet strong enough. Leaves picked at the start of the season will be more fragrant; they taste milder as the summer progresses.

Strain out the leaves, pour into a container and chill overnight. Churn in an ice-cream machine then transfer to a container and leave to set in the freezer before serving.

Blackcurrant leaf sugar

Even a tiny taste of this will transport you to a blackcurrant field in the height of summer. I love a sprinkle over any blackcurrant or summer dessert: trifles, fools, Eton messes – it will improve them all.

140g (1 scant cup) caster (superfine) sugar

10g (2 tsp) Maldon salt

15g (½oz) blackcurrant leaves (4–5 leaves), main stem removed

Blend all the ingredients together in a spice grinder or blender until you have a vivid green sugar. It will feel quite wet. Store in the freezer until ready to use.

Blackcurrant leaf oil

This is really best made with leaves early in the season. They are more tender and more fragrant at that time. It freezes incredibly well so at Lyle's we would make larger batches at the start of summer.

blackcurrant leaves

grapeseed oil

Remove the stalks from the blackcurrant leaves then weigh them. Multiply the weight of leaves by 1.5 to work out how much oil you need, you are working to a ratio of 2:3 unblanched leaves to grapeseed oil (3 tbsp of oil for 1oz of leaves). Blanch the leaves in boiling water for 2 minutes until tender, strain and immediately put into either ice water or refresh under cold running water to stop them cooking.

Once they are cool, strain and squeeze out as much water as possible. Roughly chop the leaves then put in a blender along with the grapeseed oil. Blend at high speed until the oil gets hot and you see it split from a leaf green purée into a deep emerald green oil.

PRO TIP
If using a Thermomix, 10 minutes at 70°C (158°F) works perfectly.

Strain through a double layer of muslin or a clean tea towel set over a sieve. Don't push or squeeze it through but allow it to hang so that you get a clear oil.

You can freeze the oil in a plastic container to help clarify it further. Any remaining water and sediment will freeze as a block on the bottom while the oil will stay liquid enough for you to pour it off into a new container.

Blackcurrant leaf ice cream, meringue and poached blackcurrants

A celebration of all things blackcurrant. If you bake a larger, pavlova-style meringue instead of individual servings, this makes a most dramatic dessert to share. Every mouthful sings blackcurrant which could be overwhelming. The success of this dish is the respite that the ice cream provides from the poached fruit while reinforcing the herbaceous flavour of blackcurrants.

serves 1

1–2 tbsp poached blackcurrants *(p41)*

1 blackcurrant leaf vinegar meringue *(p42)*

2 large scoops blackcurrant leaf ice cream *(p42)*

2 tsp blackcurrant leaf sugar *(p43)*

Put a bowl in the freezer to chill 30 minutes before serving. Place a 10cm (4in) ring in the centre of the bowl and spoon in enough poached blackcurrants to form a single, tightly packed layer dressed generously in their syrup. Break a meringue into 3–4 pieces and place on top of the fruit. Spoon the ice cream on top and flatten off level with the top of the ring.

Remove the ring and sprinkle generously with the blackcurrant leaf sugar. Again, the deep purple currants, vivid green sugar and pale ice cream provide visual drama as you break through the layers.

Ricotta ice cream, blackcurrant leaf oil

I like to serve this dish in the spring when the blackcurrant leaves are just ready to harvest. The summer fruit avalanche still seems a way off but this dish always gets me excited for what's to come. Visually, this dish is dramatic and a pure joy to eat. I love the play between the green of the oil and the purple of the blackcurrant powder. The inky green oil looks almost black when pooled inside the ice cream but once you burst its banks, the most verdant green spills forth. The colours mingle as you eat, creating new swirls and shades with each mouthful. A feast for both eyes and palate.

serves 1

1 large scoop ricotta ice cream *(p179)*

1 tbsp blackcurrant leaf oil *(p43)*

1 tsp blackcurrant powder *(p41)*

small pinch of Maldon salt

Place a bowl in the freezer to chill 30 minutes before serving. Scoop a large quenelle of ricotta ice cream into the centre of the bowl. Using a warm spoon, create a deep well in the centre of the ice cream making sure not to breach the edges of your scoop. Fill the well with blackcurrant leaf oil.

Dust generously with blackcurrant powder and sprinkle a few flakes of Maldon salt into the centre of the oil. The simplicity of the dark oil spilling out and mixing with the deep purple of the powder is utterly beautiful.

CHERRIES

When sweet cherries are at their peakest peak, please just enjoy a bowl of them as is. They are one of the few fruits I think should be served chilled; on ice, they can't be beaten.

This would be a very short chapter if that was all I had to say but that's probably the most important thing to know. Sour cherries, on the other hand, really come into their own with a little heat and sugar. They can be a touch harder to find in the UK but are well worth tracking down; farmers' markets, pick-your-own farms and Eastern European grocers are all good sources. I am very jealous of people who live in countries where they are more widely available. If you want that classic cherry flavour in your desserts, include some morello cherries. I particularly love them in a pickle mixed with sweet cherries. The pickling liquor, along with any preserved cherry blossom, will bump any cherry-based dish up a notch. Use it to season compôtes, granitas, jams, ice creams or just drizzle it over cut fruit. To reinforce the cherry flavour and add further complexity to each mouthful, try a combination of the fruit, its flowers and leaves in your seasonings, whether through pickling, in syrups or infused into alcohol.

Cherries can go in so many different directions flavour-wise. They shine with dairy, particularly paired with goat's and sheep's milk. A bowl of cherries alongside sheep's ricotta or young fresh goat's cheese is one of life's great pleasures. Cherries also have a natural affinity with nuts that comes from the almond flavour of their stones. Almonds are the obvious choice but I love them with hazelnuts and walnuts, too. A cherry bakewell is hard to beat but try a frangipane made with hazelnuts instead for a slightly different take. Then there are the spices that combine with cherries to create something extraordinary. They love all members of the anise family: star anise, aniseed, fennel seeds and fennel pollen. The smoky, anise flavour of Mexican or Tahitian vanilla is a combination that will make each ingredient taste more intensely of itself and even more delicious. Lillie O'Brien of London Borough of Jam combines morello cherries with black pepper in her preserves with delectable results.

Pickled cherries

Make these just for the delicious smell coming from your kitchen and the gloriously jewel-coloured jars you end up with. They were used constantly at Lyle's, served with terrines, game and pork. I've definitely carried those ideas into my home cooking and often use a couple of spoonfuls to season braised duck legs or use the pickled fruit in a salad to serve alongside pork chops with some of the liquor in the dressing. Even if you don't like the idea of pickled cherries in your desserts, make them for a multitude of savoury applications. Used with a light hand, they are handy in the sweet kitchen, too. The surprising burst of acidity can break through the undercurrent of sweetness, providing balance and vitality to a dessert. Keep the stones in when you pickle the cherries; the longer they sit in their pickle, the more of the stone flavour will work its way into the liquor.

makes 2 x 500ml (1 pint) jars

500ml (2 cups) red wine vinegar

100g (½ cup) dark brown sugar

500g (1 generous lb) sweet or sour cherries

Combine the vinegar and sugar in a nonreactive pan and bring to the boil to dissolve the sugar. Turn the heat down very low and add the cherries. Leave to steep for 5–10 minutes depending on their size. You don't want the cherries to cook so much their skins burst but you do want the heat to penetrate all the way through to the stone. Immediately pour into sterilized jars and seal. These will keep for months somewhere cool and dark if properly sealed; refrigerate once opened.

Cherry granita

This granita works on a similar principle to the strawberry version. You cook the cherries with very little sugar at a low temperature to extract a small but intense yield of delicious juice. The amount of sugar will depend on the cherries you use – both sweet and sour cherries will be delicious, or even a combination of the two.

makes 500ml (1 pint)

500g (1 generous lb) sweet or sour cherries, pitted

25g (2 tbsp) light soft brown sugar

10ml (2 tsp) preserved cherry blossom vinegar (optional) *(p219)*

caster (superfine) sugar, to taste

Combine the cherries, brown sugar and vinegar (if using) in a large bowl. Toss the fruit to coat it evenly in the sugar. You can then cook this in one of two ways. Either cover the bowl tightly with cling film and set it over a saucepan of barely simmering water (bain-marie) and cook over a gentle heat for 30–40 minutes. Alternatively, vacuum seal bags of the macerating cherries and steam (or cook in a water bath) at 65°C (150°F) for 25–30 minutes. The key is to cook them gently at a low temperature so that they keep their freshness. The cherries are ready when they have released lots of deep cerise liquid. Leave the fruit and all the delicious juices to cool.

Blend the fruit and its liquor until it is completely smooth and pass through a fine sieve. Taste the purée and add caster sugar as required.

PRO TIP
If you have a refractometer, you are aiming to be in the range of 12–15°Bx.

Pour into a shallow container and freeze. Every couple of hours, scrape a fork through the freezing liquor so that you end up with large ice crystals rather than a fine snow. Once it is completely frozen, scrape a fork through again to break it up further.

Cherry and goat's milk sherbet

This works on the same principle as the gooseberry sherbet or Meyer lemon sherbet. The acidic fruit will react with the milk to thicken it. In order to help that process, I include a little cherry blossom vinegar, but pickled cherry liquor will also work. You really do need sour cherries for this recipe. Sweet cherries won't give the intense cherry flavour that you need to be able to carry through the flavour of the milk.

makes 1.3 litres (2¾ pints)

750g (1lb 10oz) sour cherries, fresh or frozen

70g (⅓ cup) caster (superfine) sugar

450ml (1¾ cups) goat's milk

20ml (scant 1½ tbsp) liquor from preserved cherry blossom (p219) or pickled cherries (p49)

25g (1¾ tbsp) ice-cream stabilizer (p237)

Pit the cherries. This seems like a long process but it is quicker to remove them at the start. Wrap the cherry stones in a square of muslin. This will help impart more of that delicious almond flavour into the sherbet. Combine the pitted cherries, sugar, bundle of cherry stones and 75ml (⅓ cup) of water in a shallow pan with a tight-fitting lid. Give them a stir to make sure the water and sugar are mingling with all the fruit. Bring the cherries to a simmer then put the lid on and turn the heat down low. Cook for 20–30 minutes until the cherries are very soft and starting to break down.

Remove the bundle of stones. Blend the fruit with the cooking liquor in a food processor until you have a fine purée. Leave to cool then combine it with the goat's milk, liquor and stabilizer and mix well. Transfer the sherbet to the fridge and chill for 4 hours. Churn in an ice-cream machine then transfer to a container and leave to set in the freezer before serving.

Cherry pits contain amygdalin, which is converted into hydrogen cyanide in the body and is harmful if ingested in large quantities. Caution should be observed and you should consult your physician if you have any concerns.

Cherry and buckwheat clafoutis

One of the very first cookbooks I received was Michel Roux's *Pastry*. It taught me to make perfect *pâte sablée* and saw me through my first attempts at choux pastry. The most used recipe in that book, though, was the one for cherry clafoutis. I have a love of desserts that have names that are as delicious to say as the dessert is to eat (syllabub... such a glorious word), and clafoutis is high up on that list. It is a traditional dessert from the Limousin region of France, which is famous for its cherries. A just-set batter with cherries (importantly with the stones left in to release their almond flavour) baked to a perfect wobble. Michel Roux bakes his clafoutis in a pastry case but I prefer it in a buttered and sugared dish. I use buckwheat flour along with the plain flour as I love the earthiness it brings to the cherries. You can bake these as individual portions but they lose a little of their magical texture so I would use larger shallow ramekins so they can be shared between two.

serves 4

500g (1 generous lb) dark cherries

25g (2 tbsp) caster (superfine) sugar

unsalted butter, softened, for greasing

demerara sugar, for dusting

2 eggs

270ml (1 cup plus 2 tbsp) whole milk

20g (1 tbsp plus 1 tsp) unsalted butter, melted

15ml (1 tbsp) cherry brandy

30g (2 tbsp plus 1 tsp) light brown soft sugar or panela sugar

pinch of salt

pinch of mahlab *(p237)*

35g (¼ cup) plain (all-purpose) flour

15g (2½ tbsp) buckwheat flour

Lightly crush the cherries, sprinkle on the caster sugar and leave to macerate for about 30 minutes.

Preheat the oven to 200°C (400°F). Brush two 15cm (6in) shallow ramekins generously with butter and then coat with demerara sugar to create a crust. Divide the cherries and their juices evenly between the ramekins.

Combine the eggs, milk, melted butter and cherry brandy together in a bowl and mix well. In a separate bowl, combine the brown sugar, salt, mahlab and both flours then make a well in the centre. Pour the liquid ingredients into the well and mix to create a thick batter. Pour the batter over the cherries in each ramekin.

Bake for 15–20 minutes, until the top is golden brown and the clafoutis has a gentle wobble. Serve warm with a generous scoop of vanilla ice cream.

Cherry blossom steamed sponge with sweet and pickled cherries

This dish was on the opening menu at Flor in July 2019. It celebrated both the preserved cherry blossom from spring and the peak sweetness of the English cherry season. The sponge is flavoured with cherry blossom vinegar and, in a nod to *sakura mochi,* is wrapped in a salted and pickled cherry leaf. The floral, almondy quality of cherry blossom is reinforced with almond milk and a pinch of mahlab *(p237)*. The sponges can be cooked ahead and then flashed in an oven to rewarm them. The cherries are best dressed an hour ahead and left to marinate. Use the sweetest, firmest cherries you can find to contrast with the softer, pickled cherries.

for the steamed sponge

makes 12

175g (1⅓ cups) plain (all-purpose) flour

1 tsp baking powder

pinch of mahlab

200g (1 stick plus 6 tbsp) unsalted butter, softened

220g (1 cup plus 2 tbsp) light brown or panela sugar

3 eggs

135ml (½ cup plus 1 tbsp) almond milk

15ml (1 tbsp) cherry blossom vinegar *(p219)*

110g (¾ cup) ground almonds

pinch of salt

flavourless oil, for greasing

preserved cherry leaves *(p219),* to serve (optional)

Sift the flour, baking powder and mahlab into a bowl. Beat the butter, sugar and salt together in a separate bowl until you have a pale, aerated mixture. Add the eggs one at a time, beating well between each addition. Add the almond milk and cherry blossom vinegar and mix gently to combine. The mix may curdle slightly at this point but don't worry, adding the dry ingredients will bring it all back together. Add the sifted flour, ground almonds and salt and mix to just combine. Be careful not to overmix once you've added the flour as this will make the cake tough. The cake batter will last in the fridge for 3 days at this point.

Set up a stovetop steamer or use the steam setting on your oven. You want the steamer to be nice and hot before you cook the cakes. Grease a 12-hole mini muffin tray with oil (a silicone muffin mould is ideal here but if you have only a small steamer, egg cups work really well) and carefully lay one preserved cherry leaf in the bottom of each mould (if using). Fill the moulds two thirds full with cake batter. Steam for 16–20 minutes; the sponges should have risen and will spring back when you press the top. Leave to cool for 2–3 minutes before turning out of the moulds.

for the cherry dressing

200g (7oz) sweet cherries, pitted

50ml (¼ cup) cherry blossom vinegar or liquor from pickled morellos

mahlab, to taste

salt, to taste

dark brown soft sugar or panela sugar, to taste

Put the cherries, vinegar and 30ml (2 tbsp) of water in a blender and process until you have a smooth liquid. Taste the dressing and use the mahlab, salt and brown sugar to season. You're aiming for a kind of sweet-sour agrodolce-style dressing. It should taste intensely fruity but with the background bitter almond flavour of the cherry pits and blossom (this also makes a delicious salad dressing if you add some peppery olive oil).

to serve

serves 1

4–6 sweet cherries, pitted

2–3 pickled morello cherries

2–3 tbsp cherry dressing

1 cherry blossom steamed sponge

Cut the sweet cherries into 2–6 small wedges, depending on their size. Cut the pickled morello cherries into quarters. Combine the cut cherries with the dressing and leave to marinate for an hour in the fridge. Warm the sponge gently in the oven or microwave. Place in the middle of a warm bowl and surround it with the chilled, dressed cherries.

Goat's cheese and cherry tart

The timely confluence of the seasonal peak for both young goat's cheeses and cherries means that they are delicious together, as is so often the case. Young goat's cheeses are at their best in summer when the goats are in kid. Cheeses that have short maturation times are able to showcase the milk produced as the animals graze on sweet summer pastures. The goat's cheese here needs to be grassy and lactic-tasting. You want citrus high notes, rather than too much goaty funk, and a firm, moussey texture. I like cheeses such as Dorstone or St Tola, but it's worth a conversation with your cheesemonger to find out what is best at the time.

This tart is all about the alternating layers and textures of cherries and goat's cheese. The flaky pastry case gets a layer of sweet, sticky cherry compôte followed by the cherry and goat's milk sherbet. It's then topped with plenty of raw cherries and a showering of shaved goat's cheese. You need the sherbet to be quite soft and pliable in order to spread it inside the tart so leave it to soften slightly if it needs to.

for the cherry compôte

serves 6

150g (5oz) sweet cherries

150g (5oz) sour or morello cherries

150g (¾ cup) caster (superfine) sugar

juice of 1 lemon

Pit and halve both types of cherry. If you can't get morello cherries, you can use all sweet cherries but add a tablespoon of cherry blossom vinegar or pickling liquor for balance. Combine the cherries with the sugar and lemon juice in a small nonreactive pan. Cook over a medium heat for around 15–20 minutes, stirring occasionally, until the cherries are soft and the compôte has reduced down to a sticky, jammy consistency. Leave to cool.

serves 1

1 x 8cm (3in) circle rough puff pastry (p135)

2 tbsp cherry compôte

2 scoops cherry and goat's milk sherbet (p50)

4–5 sweet cherries, pitted and halved

1 small young goat's cheese

Make the pastry according to the recipe (p135). Roll it out to a thickness of 2–3mm (⅛in) and use it to line an 8cm (3in) tart tin. Chill the lined tin in the fridge or freezer for at least 1 hour.

Preheat the oven to 180°C (350°F). Bake the tart blind for 10–15 minutes, remove the baking beans then bake for a further 5 minutes or until the pastry is cooked through and deeply golden. Leave to cool.

Spoon a small amount of the cherry compôte onto the centre of a plate and place the baked tart shell on top. Spread a dessert spoon of cherry compôte inside the tart case. Scoop a large ball of cherry sherbet on top of the compôte and spread out. Cover the surface of the sherbet with halved cherries.

Finally, use a coarse Microplane grater to shave the goat's cheese over the top of the cherries, allowing it to fall onto the plate.

APRICOTS, NECTARINES & PEACHES

Apricots will always make me think of my mother. Wandering joyfully around a French market with a brown paper bag full of perfect, blushing examples on our summer holidays, then snacking on a punnet of ever disappointing fruit back in Scotland while she waited to pick us up from school. Those apricots bought in Scotland were a chilly shadow of a reminder of the sun captured in those Provençal paper bags. Good stone fruit was very tricky to find in Scotland in the early 2000s; it can still be a bit tricky to find in London 20 years later.

The problem is that stone fruits do not store starch so will not get sweeter once they are picked. Their sweetness is fed by the tree itself. They will soften and increase in aroma once they are picked but that transcendent sweetness won't develop. Picking the sweetest fruit means picking the most delicate and least transportable. In order to get peaches and nectarines and apricots from their sunny orchards to our chillier isle, growers tend to pick the slightly underwhelming, more robust fruit. Thankfully, we have importers who are taking the risk and bringing in more delicate but superior examples but it's always a gamble. When you are in a country or area that grows peaches, apricots or nectarines, eat as many as you can. Enjoy those juices dripping down your chin and hands with absolute abandon.

Thankfully, these fruits respond well to heat and sugar when cooking so even that tray of peaches that smelled great but tasted bland can be saved. Apricots poached in a syrup flavoured with chamomile, thyme or vanilla will be softened and imbued with any sweetness they lacked. I have a nostalgic soft spot for tinned peaches but now prefer to poach my own in wine, enjoying the resulting liquor as much as the peaches themselves. Poaching will give you soft, yielding fruit that can still hold its form. Roasting or grilling at a higher heat will intensify the sugars in the fruit and evaporate off excess water. Adding sugar and a splash of spirit will give you deliciously caramelized edges and melting flesh.

When choosing stone fruits, don't be tempted by the very first trays that appear at the start of summer. Wait patiently for a couple of weeks for the season to really get going and the sweeter fruit to arrive. Apricots will come first in June, followed by peaches in July as the weather warms. Choose fruit that is firm but yields to a gentle squeeze with no major bruising or soft spots. And, most importantly, smell each fruit; it should be richly perfumed and make you want to bite into it right then and there. Try not to keep your fruit in the fridge, as this can deaden the flavour. If you can find *pêches de vigne*, buy as many as you can. These dusky-hued heirloom peaches are traditionally grown at the end of rows of vines in wine-producing regions in France and have the crimson flush of a blood orange. They make the most dramatic sorbet.

Poached stone fruit

The key to poaching stone fruits is to be gentle. Think about it as if you are almost candying them; you want to introduce more sugar into the fruit but maintain the structure of the cell walls. You create a flavoured, sweetened liquor and then cook the fruit at a very low temperature. It is the perfect technique for fruit that is a little underripe, in need of sugar or a flavour boost.

The flavourings are where you can play around. I will forever love apricots with chamomile (it should be flowering when apricots come into season), vanilla, lemon or thyme. Apricots have quite an intense flavour so benefit from something more subtle to back them up rather than anything too dominant which can clash. Peaches can take a little more punch. Rosemary and bay leaf both impart some of their wild woodiness into peaches, which is a lovely marriage. They will be further enhanced by poaching in a syrup made with wine. You can use red or white: a white with peachy characteristics or a red that has berry notes will both yield delectable results. Apricots and peaches are firm friends with honey and darker sugars, so play a little with what you have and see what brings out the best in the fruit. You don't want any of the flavours to dominate but to harmonize with it.

Apricots poached in chamomile

300g (1½ cups) caster (superfine) sugar

600ml (2½ cups) water

2–3 sprigs of fresh chamomile

2–3 strips of lemon peel

5 apricots

Peaches poached in white wine and bay

400g (2 cups) caster (superfine) sugar

350ml (1½ cups) white wine

350ml (1½ cups) water

3 fresh bay leaves

5 peaches

The method for both recipes is the same, the only difference will be how long the fruit takes to cook. The pan you use should fit the fruit snuggly in a single layer and be deep enough to allow it to be submerged in the poaching liquor. Combine the sugar, liquid(s) and aromatics in a saucepan and bring to the boil to dissolve the sugar. You can keep the fruit whole or cut it in half, or even smaller; just bear in mind that the smaller you cut the fruit, the shorter the time it needs to cook. I like to halve the fruit to allow the flavour as much chance to permeate as possible without sacrificing the structure.

Once the poaching liquor has come to the boil, turn it down to the lowest possible heat. Add the fruit and place a circle of baking parchment (a cartouche) directly on the surface. The fruit is ready when you can pierce it with a knife and feel no resistance. This will depend on the ripeness and size of your fruit. For a whole peach, start to check after 20 minutes, for a halved apricot check after 5 minutes. Leave the fruit to cool in the liquor to allow the exchange of flavours to continue.

Roasted peaches

Now is the time for aggressive heat. The key to roasting fruit is to use a high heat and just enough sugar to kick start the caramelization of the natural sugars. Roasting won't rescue hard, flavourless fruit (poach it instead) but it will intensify the flavour of fruit that is a little lacklustre or underwhelming. The heat of the oven will cook off some of the water content in the fruit, which will concentrate both flavour and sweetness. Think about roasting fruit like you would a piece of meat: you want it to develop colour while in the oven and then use the residual heat to finish cooking once you take it out. Utilizing the residual heat will mean that the fruit doesn't cook to the point of collapse. Roasting will yield an intensified version of the fruit so you don't necessarily want to add more flavourings but a healthy pour of a spirit like amaretto, grappa or brandy will always be welcome. You want something that boosts and supports the flavour rather than adding another dimension. If you ever get hold of fresh peach leaves then roast your peaches on them so they can impart their gentle almond flavour.

---

3 peaches, halved and stoned

20–30g (1½–2 tbsp) demerara sugar

30ml (2 tbsp) brandy

---

peach leaves (optional)

Preheat the oven to 220°C (430°F). Use a shallow roasting dish that snuggly holds the fruit. Cover the base of the dish with peach leaves if using. Lay the peaches on top, cut side facing up. Sprinkle the sugar over the face of each peach half and then pour the brandy over, allowing it to pool in the hollow where the stone was. Roast for 20–25 minutes. The surface should have bubbled and caramelized by this point so if they are still pale, give them a little longer. Remove from the oven and cover the roasting tray tightly with foil and leave for another 20 minutes. The fruit should now be tender all the way through and very juicy.

Nectarine ice cream

Kitty Travers of La Grotta Ices believes that nectarines make better ice cream than peaches and I agree. They have the richness needed when combining the fruit with a custard base, otherwise the flavour is easily lost. This is pretty much Kitty's recipe. Once it's churned, I fold in small chunks of frozen nectarine; they're like tiny ice cubes of concentrated fruit.

makes 1.2 litres (2½ pints)

600g (1lb 5oz) nectarines (about 4–5 fruits), plus 2 more to fold through

140g (⅔ cup) caster (superfine) sugar

lemon juice, to taste

200ml (¾ cup plus 2 tbsp) whole milk

200ml (¾ cup plus 2 tbsp) double (heavy) cream

60g (¼ cup) egg yolks, from about 3 eggs

50g (¼ cup) light brown soft sugar

pinch of salt

Cut the 600g (1lb 5oz) of nectarines into small chunks and mix with 90g (⅓ cup plus 1 tbsp) of caster sugar and a squeeze of lemon juice. Leave to macerate, covered, in the fridge for 2 hours.

Combine the milk and cream in a large saucepan over a medium heat. Meanwhile, whisk together the egg yolks, remaining sugars and salt. Set a sieve over a bowl and place in an ice bath (or a sink filled with very cold water). When the milk and cream are at a full rolling boil, turn off the heat and slowly pour into the egg yolk mix, whisking constantly. Return the mixture to the saucepan and check the temperature. If the custard hasn't reached 83°C (181°F), return the pan to a gentle heat and cook, stirring constantly, until it reachs the correct temperature. Strain into the waiting bowl in the ice bath. Chill completely and let the custard rest in the fridge for at least 4 hours.

Dice the remaining nectarines into 5–10mm (¼–½in) pieces, dress with a little lemon juice and place in the freezer. Pour the chilled custard into a blender along with the macerated nectarines and their juices and blend until smooth. Churn in an ice-cream machine then fold through the frozen chunks of nectarine. Transfer to a suitable container and leave to set in the freezer before serving.

Stone fruit sorbet

Stone fruit sorbets have to be some of my favourites. Their innate creaminess really comes out when they have been blended and churned. Use the ripest fruit you can get your hands on. The quality of the fruit will be front and centre. Removing the skin from the peaches, nectarines or apricots is very much down to personal preference. If you want to remove it then cut a small cross into the base of each fruit. Bring a large pan of water to the boil and add the fruit. Remove after 1–2 minutes and immediately plunge into a bowl of ice water to halt any cooking. The skin should peel off easily.

makes 1 litre (2 pints)

1kg (2¼lb) ripe stone fruit, peeled if preferred

lemon juice, to taste

about 150g (¾ cup) caster (superfine) sugar

Cut the fruit into rough chunks and remove the stones. Blend with a squeeze of lemon juice and half of the sugar until you have a smooth purée. Pass through a fine sieve. Whisk in the remaining sugar a little at a time, tasting between additions. If you have a refractometer *(p236)*, you are aiming for a sugar level of 25°Bx, so whisk in more sugar as required. Season with some more lemon juice if it tastes a little too sweet. Go very lightly here as you are just brightening the sorbet, not changing the flavour profile.

Chill the sorbet base in the fridge for at least 4 hours or overnight. Pour into an ice-cream machine and churn until frozen. Transfer to a lidded plastic container and keep in the freezer. Put the container in the fridge about 30 minutes before serving. Peach sorbet is pictured overleaf *(p62)*.

Roasted peach with peach sorbet, olive oil ice cream and rosemary

I'm not sure where I first heard of the combination of peaches and rosemary but the thought of it has stayed with me for many years. Nigella Lawson writes of rosemary for remembrance in her funeral chapter in *Feast*. I first made a version of this the summer my mum was dying. It was the height of peach season and I was re-reading Nigella in the hope of finding comfort in her words and recipes. I spent a lot of that summer sequestered in the kitchen trying to distract myself. I made rosemary ice cream with roast peaches that day. It was delicious and I think my mum managed to enjoy a mouthful or two. This version uses olive oil ice cream to allow the peach to shine a bit brighter, with the rosemary providing its peppery and camphorous character as small bursts in the tuile.

serves 1

4 shards rosemary tuile *(p167)*

1 large scoop olive oil ice cream *(p181)*

1 large scoop peach sorbet *(left)*

½ roasted peach *(p59)*

extra virgin olive oil, to serve

pinch of Maldon salt

For the rosemary tuile, follow the sugar tuile recipe *(p167),* sprinkling 1 tablespoon of chopped rosemary over the tuile mix just before it goes in the oven.

Place a shallow bowl or plate in the freezer to chill 30 minutes before serving. Place a 10cm (4in) metal ring on the plate slightly off centre. Crumble a little of the rosemary tuile into the centre of the ring. Fill half the ring with olive oil ice cream and the other half with peach sorbet and use the back of a spoon to press down to form a kind of ying-yang shape before removing the ring. Cut the roasted peach into three wedges and place two on top of the ice cream and the other slightly to the side. Drizzle with a little olive oil and a few flakes of Maldon salt, then cover with 2–3 shards of rosemary tuile.

PLUMS

The tricky thing with plums is that there are just so many varieties out there to choose from and they differ from one location to another. In supermarkets, the most common plum is the Victoria. It is probably the least exciting variety but it grows well with consistently good yields so is widely available. As is the case with so many of our foods, its success in the field, along with its profitability, have outweighed its somewhat lacklustre performance in the kitchen. My advice, as always, is to find out what grows near you. So often, waterways, train lines and parks are lined with wild plum trees just crying out to be picked. Greengrocers or smaller local shops often have a wider range of varieties grown in the surrounding area. Farmers markets and pick-your-own farms will always be a good bet for finding something delicious.

The first varieties that people get excited about here in the UK are the greengages – or Reine Claude in France – and mirabelles. The sweet and delicate mirabelle is a small yellow plum flushed with a little orange that is generally grown in France but can also be found here. I love them in frangipane tarts and jam, or just eaten raw straight from the punnet. Greengages became popular under François I and were named after the French king's wife, hence the name Reine Claude. Some trees were brought over to England and were cultivated on the land of Sir Thomas Gage, where they quickly adopted his name. There are different varieties within the greengage family but all share the same sublime translucent flesh and honeyed sweetness. I never really get round to cooking with greengages as the season is so short and I end up eating them all before they can make their way into a pan or oven. I would recommend you enjoy them in a similar fashion. Once the greengage and mirabelle season has passed, the darker plums arrive and last throughout September. If you find Germanic or eastern European varieties, such as the quetsch, then keep them to make jam, tarts and pies. Their deep purple colour comes out best under heat and their prominent acidity makes for a great cooked plum. I have a real soft spot for the Warwickshire Drooper. Such a great name isn't it? Droopers are a glorious golden yellow colour, flecked with orange, pink and purple, with the occasional russetted scar. They have a slightly thicker skin which gives a mellow bitterness to balance the candy sweetness of its flesh. I first tasted pluots, a cross between a plum and an apricot, in California. Their deep magenta flesh recalls the jammy sugariness of apricots.

Maynards Fruit Farm in East Sussex produces a wonderful range of plums. These summer fruits really are a passion for them so I always want to showcase each variety as it comes along. Back in the 1960s, the farm developed some new varieties as part of a testing programme. When the scheme was scrapped under Thatcher's government, the farm kept the test varieties and has grown them ever since. They started with the Excalibur and followed with Guinevere and Lancelot. Lancelots are my favourite to eat and cook. They are a purple-pink colour with a bluish dust over the skin. I take endless photographs of Lancelot plums as they ripen on the tree each year and occasionally try to paint them. I am certain I never fully capture their beauty but I'll keep trying.

Plums are closely related to cherries. When coming up with desserts many of the same flavours that complement cherries will work just as beautifully alongside plums. All things almond create a felicitous pairing, picking up on the bitter notes found inside the plum kernels, just as in cherry stones. I often use a pinch of mahlab to heighten that bitter almond flavour rather than crushing the kernels, which contain toxic compounds.

Poached plums

Different varieties of plum will poach very differently. Some will hold their shape perfectly as they cook, while others will disintegrate almost as soon as heat is applied. It is very much a case of trial and error. As a general rule, freestone varieties (where the flesh does not cling to the stone) hold their form well. At Lyle's, we would pick huge quantities of plums when the season rolled around and then race to process them each week before they went bad. We would macerate them with sugar, vacuum seal and then steam them at 75°C (165°F). The vacuum sealing helps to break down the cell walls and means they release a generous amount of precious plum liquor.

You can achieve a similar effect at home by putting the plums and sugar in microwave steam bags, squeezing out as much air as possible and then cooking in a stovetop steamer. Start with 3–4 minutes and keep checking as they steam; you want to remove them from the steamer when they are still holding their shape but are cooked through.

The key to poaching plums is to use minimal sugar and liquid to preserve the intense syrup they generate. Use just enough sugar to season them, making them taste like the most concentrated version of themselves. After a lot of trial and error, I've found that adding 12–14 per cent of the weight of the plums in sugar works best for most varieties (except greengages as they are so sweet naturally).

---

plums

caster (superfine) sugar

lemon juice

Cut the plums in half and remove the stones. Taste a small piece to see how sweet they are. Weigh the plums and calculate how much sugar you need by multiplying the weight by 0.12 or 0.14, so for 1kg of plums, you would need 120–140g of sugar (or ¼ cup sugar for every 1lb of plums) depending on the percentage required. Toss the plums with the sugar and a squeeze of lemon juice and leave to macerate for 15 minutes. Pour the plums and their juices into a saucepan that fits them snuggly. Turn the plums so they are cut side down and add 50–100ml (3–6 tbsp) of water, just enough to dissolve the sugar and generate a little steam. Place a circle of baking parchment directly on top of the plums and tuck it in so it is tightly fitting. Place the pan over a medium heat and bring to a simmer. Once the water starts bubbling, turn down the heat to the lowest possible setting. After 3–4 minutes, gently flip the plums and continue cooking until the flesh is tender but not so soft it is collapsing. You should be able to pierce it with a skewer or small knife with little resistance. The cooking time will depend on the size of the fruit but, for a Victoria plum, it will be a further 2–3 minutes; for a larger variety or pluot it could be a further 5–6 minutes once they've been flipped.

Remove the pan from the heat and leave the plums to cool, still covered, to room temperature. The colour in the fruit and the plum juices will intensify. Store them in a container with their cut faces down and keep them submerged in their juices, or place a piece of baking parchment directly on top, to prevent oxidation.

Dried

I am always keen to preserve as much of the season as I can. I also have a tendency to overdo it when I go fruit picking and inevitably end up with way more than I can get through. This is particularly true with plums which are so easy to pick, and then to pick just one more, oh and just that one more... and just... well, you get the picture. I would often poach far more plums than we needed, so would cut the excess into quarters or sixths and dry until fudgy. You can dry uncooked plums but they will be very sour and have a tough skin. Poached plums will still taste a little sour but in a much more palatable way.

---

poached plums

Cut the poached plum halves into 2 or 3 depending on their size and lay on a rack so that the flesh is facing up. Dry in a very low oven for 4–6 hours. Keep an eye on them as the sugar is likely to caramelize and the flesh will collapse if the temperature gets too high. Alternatively, dry in a dehydrator at 60–70°C (140–160°F) for 4–6 hours. Once the plums are dry, they can be stored in an airtight container somewhere cool and dark. I love to add them to any dried fruit-based recipe like Christmas pudding, or serve as we did at Lyle's alongside duck, goose or game.

Plum leather

Fruit leathers are sheets of sweetened fruit purée that have been dried so that they are solid but still malleable. They look beautiful laid over the top of a dessert. You can also cut them into strips or squares and store in an airtight container for a moreish snack. Plum leathers will oxidize as they dry so you are likely to end up a brownish colour. The most attractive leathers are made with the most pink/purple plums. I would steer clear of any yellow plums or Victorias but instead look for quetsch varieties or those specifically grown for cooking. Their acidity will be stronger and will balance better in the final product.

1kg (2¼lb) cooking plums

lemon juice, to taste

500g (2¾ cups) caster (superfine) sugar

Preheat the oven to 200°C (400°F). Wash and remove any stems from the plums. Lay the whole plums in a single layer on a baking tray and roast for 20–25 minutes. The skins should have split open and the juices will have started to caramelize. Leave to cool for 10–15 minutes until you can handle them comfortably. Remove the stones from the fruit and blend the pulp to a smooth purée.

Weigh the purée and multiply by 0.5 to calculate the weight of sugar required (or ¼ cup sugar for every 1 cup purée). Add the sugar to the fruit purée and mix to dissolve. If the purée has completely cooled, then gently warm it in a pan until the sugar is well dissolved. Season with a little lemon juice if the plums are not acidic enough.

You can either use a very low oven or a dehydrator set to 60°C (140°F) to dry the leather. Spread the sweetened purée evenly onto pieces of baking parchment or silicone mats to a thickness of 2–3mm (⅛in). Dry the leather for around 6 hours until it is no longer tacky and peels easily from the paper. Store layered between sheets of baking parchment in an airtight container.

Plum sorbet

For greengages, mirabelles or any yellow or green plums, gently poaching will help preserve the fruits' more delicate colour and flavour. For plums with red, pink or purple skins, a quick hard roast will set the deep colour and bring forward their jamminess. As a general rule, just think: pale, poach; red, roast.

---

makes 500ml (1 pint)

500g (1 generous lb) plums, halved, stones removed

70g (⅓ cup) caster (superfine) sugar

pinch of mahlab *(p237)*

juice of ½ lemon

1 tbsp plum brandy, kirsch or grappa (optional)

Red-skinned plums
Preheat the oven to 220°C (430°F). Put the plums in a roasting dish so that they're tightly packed in a single layer. Mix half of the sugar with the mahlab and sprinkle over the plums then squeeze over the lemon juice. Roast for 10–15 minutes, until the fruit is soft and starting to bubble at the edges and the cut face is slightly caramelized. Leave to cool slightly.

Pale-skinned plums
Combine the mahlab with half of the sugar in a large saucepan. Add the lemon juice and 300ml (1¼ cups) of water and heat gently to dissolve the sugar. Add the plums so they form a single layer. Place a piece of baking parchment directly on top to help them steam. Turn the heat up until you see the syrup bubbling around the plums then turn it down so that they cook gently without caramelizing. Cook for 15–20 minutes until the fruit is completely tender. Pour into a shallow tray and chill quickly over ice.

Pour the cooked fruit and juices into a blender and process until smooth. Gradually add the remaining sugar until it tastes slightly too sweet. If you have a refractometer, you're aiming for a sugar level of 25°Bx. Season with the lemon juice if it needs brightening up then add the alcohol (if using). Go lightly as too much will stop the sorbet from freezing. Chill completely. Pour into an ice-cream machine and churn until frozen. Transfer to a lidded container and store in the freezer. Put the sorbet in the fridge about 30 minutes before serving.

Baked cream with Brighton Belle plums

This dish would appear on the menu as soon as we started to feel the gentle ending of high summer when the mornings are not quite so bright and the evenings come a little quicker. The flavours are slowly moving from bright berry to something a little earthier. Use a dark-skinned plum here. My favourites are Brighton Belles but as I know only one farmer who grows them, and he has about six trees, I don't expect you to be able to get them. You want a plum that will impart a deeply plummy flavour to every element and that can hold its shape once poached; red-skinned varieties such as pluots or quetsch will work well.

I use mahlab to flavour the baked cream. Made from the dried and crushed seeds of the St Lucy's cherry, mahlab shares the warming bitter almond flavour of the plum kernel.

serves 1

1 generous dessert spoon baked cream *(p179)*

2 poached plum halves *(p66)*

½ dried plum *(p66)*

3–4 tbsp plum poaching juices *(p66)*

light brown soft sugar, to taste

lemon juice, to taste

plum brandy or amaretto, to taste (optional)

1 small scoop plum sorbet *(p67)*

1 small sheet plum leather *(p67)*

Make the baked cream according to the recipe *(p179),* adding 5g (1 tsp) of mahlab to the cream as you warm it before whisking it into the sugar and egg whites.

Put a wide shallow bowl in the freezer to chill 30 minutes before serving. Slice the poached plum halves into 3–5 thin wedges depending on their size. Chop the dried plum into small pieces, around 5mm (¼in) wide.

Add the plum poaching juices to a small saucepan and warm gently. Taste and add some brown sugar if it needs any extra sweetness, or a tiny squeeze of lemon juice if acidity is required. You could also add a splash of alcohol at this point such as plum brandy or amaretto. Once seasoned to your liking, set the pan aside.

Place the baked cream slightly to the left of centre in the bowl. Add the chopped, dried plums in a small mound just to the right of this. Top the baked cream with the wedges of poached plum, allowing them to tumble off of it into the bowl. Scoop an elegant quenelle of sorbet and place on top of the dried plums. Tear a small sheet of plum leather and artfully drape it over the baked cream and poached plums. It should be placed so you get little peeks of what lies underneath. Try to create texture and a little height with the folds of the leather.

Finally, warm the plum juices until steaming and pour a couple of spoons over the top of the leather so that they spill over the cream and plums.

Summer pudding

From a quick poll among some food-loving friends and colleagues, summer pudding can be divisive: people either love or loathe it with very little middle ground. This may be a bold statement but I think it is very much the case that the people who loathe it have just had bad summer pudding. It doesn't necessarily sound like a recipe for success: a pudding basin lined with slightly stale bread and a mixture of tart summer fruits. As with all stale bread dishes, this is much greater and more delicious than the sum of its parts. There are a few crucial points that you need to pay attention to for a successful pudding. The bread should be a good white sandwich loaf. Please don't use a "plastic" sliced white loaf, it will result in a slimy slop of a pudding. You want a slightly stale loaf with a close crumb and a little sweetness. I like to use milk bread as it lends a cakey feel to the finished pudding. The second crucial point is that the pudding should be well soaked and juicy. Nobody likes the bread if it is still dry and white in the middle; each slice should have soaked up so much liquid, it's barely holding itself together.

Start thinking about and preparing for summer pudding just as the berry season takes hold. Every time you pick a fruit at its peak, nab a little extra and store it in the freezer. All of those berries that tip just over the edge into overripe mush, pop them in the freezer. The extra yield of strawberry juice, elderflower cordial, poaching liquor from cherries, peaches or apricots – all into the freezer. Once the redcurrants arrive in mid- to late July, you can start to think about making summer puddings. At Lyle's I would squirrel away all of the excess summer fruit from picking just waiting for the day we would make our huge batches of summer pudding mix. The late-summer pudding follows exactly the same principle as summer pudding but utilizes all of the dark berries, currants and fruits instead of mostly red fruits. We would defrost everything we had, separating out syrups and juices from whole or cooked fruits. Then we'd create a master syrup using the juices, summer cordials and assorted syrups to which the fruit could be added. That master syrup can have a whole range of things in it depending on what you have. This year, I have added the last of the magnolia cordial to one batch and an experimental litre of mimosa syrup to another (the mimosa syrup tastes of pure summer so will definitely make it into future puddings). In previous years, I have used elderflower in the summer pudding and blackcurrant leaf in the late-summer version. At the River Café, they add a couple of bottles of Valpolicella, which have been reduced to burn off the alcohol to make up the bulk of their master syrup. I'm not going to offer you a prescriptive recipe here but rather a framework into which you can slot whatever fruit you have.

Summer pudding

Redcurrants should make up the largest proportion of any classic summer pudding. They are a defining flavour, adding acidity and texture. Other than that, you have free rein. I like to use some of the cooked strawberries left over from making strawberry juice, always a handful of gooseberries, a heady mix of tayberries, raspberries and blackberries, some pitted sweet cherries and recently a few apricots or overripe peach chunks.

makes 2 puddings

for the fruit

500g (1 generous lb) mixed currants (mostly redcurrants but feel free to add some blackcurrants)

400g (14oz) mixed berries (mostly red berries like raspberries or tayberries but a handful of blackberries or even mulberries will be welcome)

250g (8oz) strawberries, a mix of raw and cooked

50g (1½oz) gooseberries

for the master syrup

150g (⅔ cup) fruit juices (from strawberries, raspberries or poached cherries)

400ml (1¾ cups) summer cordial or 750ml (1 bottle) red or white wine reduced to 400ml (1¾ cups)

250g (1¼ cups) caster (superfine) sugar, plus extra to taste

1 loaf milk bread *(p201)*

flavourless oil, for greasing

Late-summer pudding

This should be full of all the darker fruits. Blackcurrants occupy top billing just as redcurrants do in summer pudding. Blackberries, poached plums, the first of the Fragola grapes, all meld together to create a slightly more autumnal take on the summer classic.

makes 2 puddings

for the fruit

500g (1 generous lb) mixed currants (mostly blackcurrants with a handful of redcurrants)

300g (10oz) poached plums *(p66)*, cut into bite-sized pieces

400g (14oz) mixed berries (mostly blackberries but raspberries or tayberries are welcome)

50g (1½oz) black cherries

for the master syrup

150g (⅔ cup) fruit juices (from plums, raspberries or poached cherries)

400ml (1¾ cups) summer cordial (a mix of blackcurrant and blackcurrant leaf works well) or 750ml (1 bottle) wine reduced to 400ml (1¾ cups)

250g (1¼ cups) caster (superfine) sugar, plus extra to taste

1 loaf milk bread *(p201)*

flavourless oil, for greasing

The method for both recipes is the same. Combine everything for the master syrup in a saucepan large enough to hold the syrup and the fruit. Bring the syrup to a simmer to dissolve the sugar. It should taste too sweet at this point as the mixture is hot and you are about to add a lot of acidic fruit. If it needs a little more sugar, whisk it into the hot liquid until it's dissolved. Once the syrup is tasting just right, turn down the heat as low as you can and add the fruit. Give the mix a good stir and leave for 10–15 minutes on a very low heat for the fruits to get to know each other. Taste the mix again to check the sweetness level and then leave it to cool to body temperature before starting to build your pudding. At this point you can chill and then freeze your summer pudding mix if you don't want to use it all at once. Be sure to divide the mixture evenly so that you have equal amounts of fruit and syrup for each portion.

To construct the puddings, lightly oil two 1-litre (2-pint) pudding basins or bowls. Slice the milk loaf into 5mm (¼in) slices and remove the crusts. I prefer a thinner shell of bread in my pudding to maximize the amount of fruit with each mouthful. Dip the slices of bread into the warm juices in the saucepan to soak and then build a single layer of sodden slices inside the bowl. Start with a slice at the bottom of the bowl and then build up the sides, leaving no gaps from which the filling could spill. You can tear the bread apart or smoosh it together as needed to create your patchwork. Fill the pudding with the fruit and juices, reserving a little to serve with the pudding the next day. It is very important to add more of the juices than you think is sensible as nobody wants a dry pudding. Once the pudding is full to the brim with fruit and juice, top with a final layer of soaked bread so that the fruit is sealed within. Place the filled pudding basins into a shallow dish to catch any excess juices. Top each one with a small plate or saucer weighted down with a couple of cans or jars. Place in the fridge and leave overnight to press and carry on soaking. Don't try to speed up this stage or you'll end up with an unpleasantly anaemic-looking pudding.

The next day, turn the pudding out onto a plate and marvel at how all the odds and ends of summer have resulted in something so glorious. Serve the pudding with an extra spoon of any leftover fruit and a huge scoop of vanilla ice cream or pour an extremely generous glug of double (heavy) cream over the top. The cold creaminess of either will be a perfect foil to the punchy fruitiness of the pudding.

autumn

FIGS

You may be asking why there is a section on figs in what is very much a British dessert book. Think of this more as an ode to the fig leaf. London is covered in fig trees; honestly, once you start spotting them you'll find them everywhere. The first year I started using them in the restaurant, I didn't know of any local trees from which I could unobtrusively pick a few leaves. It was a constant panic each time I wanted to make another batch of fig leaf ice cream. I even got my aunt in Sussex to post some from her garden at one point. But then the scales fell from my eyes and I started seeing fig trees all over town. Churchyards and parks will usually supply you with a well-established tree or two. Try to find a few that you can pick from in rotation so that you never overpick an individual tree.

Fig leaves can be toasted or used raw. Toasting will draw out the more coconutty flavours while raw leaves will deliver a brighter, green-fig flavour. Fig leaves contain a milky sap that is an irritant to human skin (be sure to wash your hands after picking them). This sap will also cause milk to curdle so you need to be careful when infusing any dairy product. To reduce the risk, always trim the thick stem right up to where the leaf starts. You can, however, turn that curdling to your advantage and use fig leaves to both flavour and curdle milk to make ricotta. You can also use them in a similar way to vine leaves: to wrap fish, chicken, cheeses like feta or halloumi, or whole fruits like figs or peaches before roasting or grilling. Their gentle perfume will permeate whatever they surround while helping it to gently steam.

We don't quite get enough heat in this country to ripen the most delicious figs so rely on those grown around the Mediterranean and Aegean seas. Figs, like peaches and nectarines, need to be ripened on the tree. You cannot ripen a picked fig. This means they are more difficult to transport and the juicy figs are more fragile and therefore susceptible to damage en route. Because of their delicacy, they often arrive individually wrapped in complementary coloured tissue paper to help protect each fruit, looking like a joyful box of sweets. I have never loved green figs but I suspect this is mostly because I haven't had a great one rather than because they are no good.

I prefer the black and deep purple varieties. I love the bright jamminess of black figs as opposed to the honeyed subtlety of the green varieties. Bourjasotte Noire and Violette de Bordeaux, both French varieties, appear in the UK around mid-August and last through until the end of September. They have a thin skin that you can bite straight into to reveal bright ruby insides. When they are at their peak, you will see small splits in the dark violet skin and beads of their nectarous insides squeezing out.

If your figs are a little lacklustre then a blast of heat will help them along tremendously. Placed atop a fig leaf and into a medium oven or under a grill, that slightly underwhelming fig will remember all of its sunny perfume and sweetness. You can also lower them into a poaching liquor made of sweetened or fortified wine (Marsala or Pedro Ximenez sherry work beautifully) and a split vanilla pod, then cook on the gentlest heat to introduce even more deliciousness.

Fig leather

When you have figs that are so overripe you can see them collapsing in real time, fig leather is the way to go. Fruit leathers are sheets of sweetened fruit purée that have been dried so that they are solid but still malleable. They look beautiful laid over the top of a dessert. You can also cut them into strips or squares and store in an airtight container for a moreish snack. The figs will have so much natural sugar there is no need to add any extra.

overripe figs

Trim any bruised or damaged parts from the figs. Put them in a blender or food processor and blend to a smooth purée. Preheat the oven to 60°C (140°F) or use a dehydrator set to 60°C (140°F). Spread the fig purée evenly onto pieces of baking parchment or silicone mats to a thickness of 2–3mm (⅛in).

Dry the leather for around 3–4 hours until it is no longer tacky and peels easily from the paper. Store layered between sheets of baking parchment in an airtight container.

Fig jam

I get overexcited when the fig season starts and will inevitably buy too many. I can never resist when a fruit supplier calls to say they have a couple of boxes of overripe figs and asks if I can take them off their hands. Why would you say no? These figs generally arrive in need of immediate attention and preparation. Jam is always a good idea in this situation. The fig leaves will add an extra top note of bright, figgy perfume to the intense jamminess but if you can't find them feel free to leave them out. I use fig jam to fill crostatas, in thumbprint cookies or to ripple through ice cream.

makes about 6 x 200g (7oz) jars

1kg (2¼lb) very ripe figs

650g (3¼ cups) caster (superfine) sugar

juice of 1 large lemon

1–2 fig leaves, stalks removed and finely sliced

Trim the stems from the top of the figs and tear each one into about 8 pieces. You can slice the figs with a knife but I enjoy the rougher texture of torn figs. Combine the torn figs with the sugar, lemon juice and fig leaves. Mix well and leave to macerate for at least 1 hour.

Add the juicy mix to a large, heavy-based saucepan and place over a low heat. Once the mixture has loosened and the sugar is well dissolved, turn the heat up high. Bring to a rolling boil and cook, stirring occasionally to prevent the fruit from sticking, until it reaches setting point, 105°C (221°F). If you don't have a thermometer, you can use the wrinkle test *(p32)* to check if the jam is ready.

Remove from the heat, pour into sterilized jars and seal immediately.

Fig leaf oil

This is really best made with young leaves picked in July or August as they're more tender and fragrant. It freezes incredibly well so you can make a large batch and store it in smaller portions. It's wonderful poured over ice cream (fig leaf, vanilla, ricotta or almond all work brilliantly) or used to dress a plate of roasted figs or peaches. I also love it in a savoury context as a dressing for tomatoes.

fig leaves

grapeseed oil

Remove the stalks from the fig leaves, then weigh them. Multiply the weight by 1.5 to work out how much oil you need – you are working to a ratio of 2:3 unblanched leaves to grapeseed oil. Blanch the leaves in boiling water for 2 minutes until tender, drain and immediately put into either ice water or under cold running water to refresh them and stop the cooking. Once they are cool, strain and squeeze out as much water as possible.

Roughly chop the leaves and put them in a blender along with the grapeseed oil. Blend at high speed until the oil gets hot and you see it split from a leaf green purée into a deep emerald green oil.

PRO TIP
If using a Thermomix, 10 minutes at 70°C (160°F) works perfectly.

Strain through a sieve lined with a layer of muslin *(p236)* or a clean tea towel; don't push it through but allow it to hang so that you get a clear oil.

Freezing the oil in a plastic container will help to clarify it further; any remaining water and sediment will freeze as a block on the bottom while the oil will stay liquid enough to pour into a new container.

Fig leaf ice cream

Probably the best ice-cream flavour out there. This became something of a signature at Lyle's. We would try to serve it with fresh figs but if we couldn't wait for the season to be in full swing, we'd top it with a generous pour of fig leaf oil as soon as there were enough leaves on the fig trees to pick. Back then, I would simply make a custard base and pour it hot over the washed fig leaves. Once the flavour was strong enough, I would strain it and then blend in the green, leafy pulp left over from making fig leaf oil to give it a bright green colour. This works well but requires you to have a stash of fig leaf pulp in the freezer. I've adapted the recipe here, first infusing the milk and cream with fig leaves for flavour before blending them in. The pale green fig leaf milk is then used to make a custard base.

makes 1.75 litres (3½ pints)

60g (2oz) fig leaves

1 litre (4 cups) whole milk

360ml (1½ cups) double (heavy) cream

240g (1 cup) egg yolks, from 13–14 eggs

150g (¾ cup) caster (superfine) sugar

pinch of salt

Remove any large stalks from the fig leaves then slice into thin ribbons. Combine the milk and cream in a heavy-based saucepan and bring to a gentle simmer over a medium-high heat. Once the milk and cream are starting to steam but not boil, remove the pan from the heat and add the sliced fig leaves. Leave the mixture to infuse in the fridge for at least 3 hours or overnight.

Pour into a high-powered blender and process until the liquid is bright green with an intensely figgy taste. Pass the infusion through a fine sieve to remove any small fibrous bits of fig leaf. Pour into a clean pan and place over a medium heat.

Meanwhile, whisk together the egg yolks, sugar and salt. Once the infusion reaches a rolling boil, remove from the heat and slowly pour half into the yolk mixture, whisking as you go to prevent curdling. Pour the now tempered custard back into the pan with the remaining infusion and stir well. There should be enough latent heat left in the pan to cook the egg yolks to 82–83°C (180°F) without having to return it to the heat. Check the temperature and if it is below 82°C (180°F), continue to cook the custard over a gentle heat, stirring constantly until it reaches the required temperature.

Immediately strain through a fine sieve and chill in the fridge for a minimum of 4 hours. Churn in an ice-cream machine then transfer to a container and allow to set in the freezer before serving.

Almond and fig cake

This is similar in many ways to the brown butter cakes *(p174)* but less fudgy and with a lighter crumb. The figs aren't fully submerged in the shallow batter so that their edges slightly caramelize as the cakes bake.

makes 6

125g (½ cup) brown butter, softened, plus extra for greasing *(p173)*

3–4 tbsp demerara sugar

125g (1 scant cup) whole almonds

pinch of salt

125g (⅔ cup) light brown or panela sugar

2 eggs

6 ripe figs

Preheat the oven to 180°C (350°F). Line the bases of six 10cm (4in) flan tins or solid base tart cases with a circle of baking parchment. Brush the parchment and the inner sides of the tins generously with brown butter. Sprinkle with a little demerara sugar and shake the tins so that you have a crust of sugar and brown butter over the whole surface.

Grind the almonds in a food processor with the salt until they resemble fine breadcrumbs. Cream together the brown butter and brown sugar in a mixer or by hand. You are not looking to aerate them, you just need to make sure the two ingredients are well incorporated. If you overbeat, you'll end up with a puffier final product. Add the eggs, one at a time, mixing well after each addition. Stir in the ground almonds.

Pour the batter into the prepared tins. Cut each fig into 8 wedges and arrange on top of each cake. Sprinkle with a little demerara sugar. Bake for 15–20 minutes until golden and the cakes spring back to the touch. Leave to cool for 5 minutes before removing from the tins. These can be baked ahead and then rewarmed before serving.

Fig leaf ice cream with fig leaf oil and warm almond cake

I have a real love of warm cake and cold ice cream eaten together – pure childhood pleasure. For this dessert, the ice cream is scooped into a small bowl with a pool of verdant oil; and plated alongside the warm almond and fig cake. I like to spoon the ice cream, still dripping with fig leaf oil, onto the cake for perfect bite after perfect bite.

serves 1

1 almond and fig cake *(left)*

1 large scoop fig leaf ice cream *(p81)*

1 tbsp fig leaf oil *(p80)*

pinch of Maldon salt

Place a small bowl in the freezer to chill 30 minutes before serving. The ice cream should be quite soft so take it out of the freezer around 10 minutes before serving. Warm the cake in a hot oven for about 5 minutes and place on a small plate. Put the fig leaf ice cream into the chilled bowl. Use a clean, hot spoon to press down into the ice cream to create a slight hollow. The flattened scoop should fill most of the bowl. Pour the fig leaf oil into the hollow and sprinkle on the Maldon salt.

SWEETCORN

Whether in a cake, ice cream or pudding, sweetcorn extols the energy of late-summer harvests, of golden sunshine and of plenty. It inspires images of bounty. Though rarely the first pick for desserts, it pours forth its generosity whenever it is used. Perhaps it is just the buttercup yellow colour but I have never seen a sweetcorn dessert that looks anything other than completely joyful.

A variety of maize, sweetcorn is actually the result of a natural mutation that prevents the sugars in the kernels from being converted to starch, giving it an identity all of its own. Each cob bursts with an intense sweetness that lends itself to all manner of interesting pairings. It is not an ingredient we produce in huge quantities in the UK. We don't have the warmth for it except in the very south. The season is short here, starting in August and lasting through to September.

Sweetcorn is a natural friend to blueberries, blackberries and bilberries – or blaeberries as we Scots call them – their colours and flavours symphonic together. It is useful to look to the savoury kitchen to see the flavours that pair well with sweetcorn, too. At Lyle's, we would serve grilled cobs (ears) doused in brown butter, honey and lemon thyme. That combination is crying out to be turned into a dessert somehow. It lends itself to American-style desserts like a thickened pudding (Jeremy Fox's *On Vegetables* has the best recipe you will ever find) or sundaes layered with different textures of sweetcorn and sauced with any purplish berries.

Sweetcorn ice cream

I originally made this ice cream with sweetcorn grilled over charcoal, which is particularly delicious but it's much easier to roast the corn in the oven. I urge you to try it.

makes 1 litre (2 pints)

4 corn cobs (ears), husks and silks removed

50g (3 tbsp plus 1 tsp) brown butter *(p173)*

750ml (3 cups) whole milk

100ml (scant ½ cup) double (heavy) cream

80g (⅓ cup) egg yolks, from 4–5 eggs

75g (¼ cup plus 2 tbsp) caster (superfine) sugar

pinch of salt

Preheat the oven to 220°C (430°F). Remove the kernels from the corn cobs with a sharp knife. Cut the cobs into thirds then place in a roasting tin, along with the kernels. Melt the brown butter and toss through the kernels and cobs to coat them. Roast in the oven for 15–20 minutes, stirring every 5 minutes until the kernels are caramelized and the cobs have started to colour. Pour the milk into a bowl and, when the corn is ready, add to the milk while still hot. Leave to cool to room temperature, cover, then infuse in the fridge overnight. The next day, strain the infused milk through a sieve. Squeeze the milk out of the cobs then discard, reserving the kernels for later.

Put the infused milk in a pan with the cream and bring to the boil. Meanwhile, whisk the egg yolks, sugar and salt together. Once the infusion reaches a rolling boil, remove from the heat and slowly pour about half into the yolks, whisking as you go to prevent curdling. Pour the tempered egg mix back into the pan with the remaining infusion and mix well. There should be enough latent heat left in the pan to cook the egg yolks to 82°–83°C (180°F). Check the temperature and if it is below 82°C (180°F), continue to cook the custard over a gentle heat, stirring constantly until it reaches the required temperature.

Pour into a blender along with the roasted kernels and blend until completely smooth. Strain through a fine sieve and discard the solids. Chill in the fridge for a minimum of 4 hours. Churn in an ice-cream machine then transfer to a container and leave to set in the freezer before serving.

Corn cake

Christina Tosi of US bakery Milk Bar will always be associated with freeze-dried sweetcorn. Her Milk Bar pie (also known as Crack Pie) made liberal use of it in powdered form, so it's impossible not to reference her whenever I use it in a recipe. It really does add an inexplicable intensity to all manner of desserts. This cake is all about texture: crispy edges from the sugar, gooey centre from all the butter, and the gravelly crunch of polenta. It will taste intensely "corny" in all the best ways.

170g (¾ cup) brown butter *(p173)*

160g (⅔ cup) egg whites, from 5–6 eggs

255g (1¼ cups) demerara sugar

85g (¾ cup) ground almonds

40g (⅓ cup) cornflour (cornstarch)

50g (⅓ cup plus 1 tbsp) polenta

20g (3 tbsp) freeze-dried sweetcorn, ground to a powder *(p237)*

6g (1 generous tsp) salt

butter or flavourless oil, for greasing

Melt the brown butter over a low heat so that it is liquid but not hot. Whisk the egg whites in a mixer at medium speed until they are stiff but not dry. Combine the dry ingredients in a large bowl and mix well with a whisk. Gently fold the egg whites into the dry ingredients. Add the brown butter, mixing it in one third at a time. Don't worry about knocking too much air from the whites as these are dense cakes by nature. Once all the butter is well incorporated, rest the batter in the fridge for at least 8 hours or preferably overnight. Don't be tempted to skip the resting; you'll end up with overly puffy, uneven cakes.

Preheat the oven to 180°C (350°F). Grease a mini muffin tray with butter or oil so that it's very well coated. Pipe the batter to fill three quarters of each mould then bake for 16 minutes. Allow to cool for 2 minutes before turning out. Serve warm.

Corn ice cream with caramelized corn cake and whey cajeta

This dish was conceived for one of the annual game dinners at Lyle's. A group of international chefs would descend on the restaurant to create two game-inspired menus over two evenings, after spending a week shooting and fishing in the Scottish Highlands. It was always total chaos, the most stressful week of the year for the team, but great fun. Game desserts were always a conundrum. One of the visiting chefs would generally want to prepare a pudding one evening but it was never the course they were fighting over to cook. It often fell to me and James to come up with something. My first year, we made a hare's blood ganache with chestnut ice cream; the next year, chocolate mousse with plums and a sauce made from braised venison and chocolates filled with mallard (wild duck) fat caramel. Sweetcorn is often served alongside grouse and other game birds so I knew I wanted to make sweetcorn ice cream at some point. For the event, we served this dish with candied black trumpet mushrooms and a candied meat floss made from duck. When the restaurant menu returned to normal the following week, we kept this dish but simplified it a little, taking away some of the more challenging elements. What was left was a real celebration of corn. The goat's milk whey cajeta (similar to dulce de leche) can be made with cow's milk whey which is much easier to get hold of.

The corn cake should be served warm and coated in a crumb made of caramelized corn kernels and freeze-dried corn. To make the caramelized corn, remove the kernels from one cob with a sharp knife. Combine with 1 tsp of brown butter and 1 tsp of honey in a shallow pan and cook over a medium heat until the kernels are cooked through and have deliciously caramelized edges. Season with a sprinkle of fine salt then dry out in a dehydrator or very low oven for several hours until crisp. Combine the dried caramelized corn with an equal amount of freeze-dried corn kernels in a spice grinder or mini food processor and grind to a coarse powder.

serves 1

1 corn cake *(p85)*

1 tbsp caramelized corn crumb *(see intro)*

1 large scoop sweetcorn ice cream *(p84)*

1 tsp bee pollen

pinch of Maldon salt

2 tbsp goat's whey cajeta *(p176)*

Place a high-sided bowl in the freezer to chill 30 minutes before serving. Warm the cake in an oven preheated to 160°C (325°F) for 3–5 minutes or until it has slightly crispy edges. Roll the warm cake in the caramelized corn crumb so it is completely coated. Use a flat spoon to take a wedge of ice cream, place it in the chilled bowl and sprinkle with the bee pollen and a few flakes of Maldon salt. You aren't after the formality of a round scoop or quenelle of ice cream here but rather an elegant chunk. Place the warm, coated cake next to it and pour the whey cajeta into the bowl. The three elements should be plated so they are tightly packed together.

DAMSONS

A distant relative of the sloe, these *plums of Damascus* (they're thought to originate from the city in modern-day Syria), can often be found in British hedgerows. The trees are hardy, low maintenance and bountiful so are a happy addition to any garden or orchard where they can act as a sturdy windbreak for less robust fruit trees. Damsons are particularly beautiful, their skins morphing from softest, velveteen green to deepest dusty indigo as they ripen, concealing chartreuse-coloured flesh within.

These small, ovoid plums have the advantage of being high in sugar and acid, making them ideal for preserving. Bite into a ripe fruit and you'll find it's super-sweet with a shadow of sloe-ish astringency. A perfectly ripe damson is a bit of a rarity so the fruits are often picked slightly underripe and then cooked, turning a deep, purplish magenta. The midnight skins will impart their colour into any liquid they are immersed in, whether that be a poaching syrup or a spirit such as gin, losing any memory of the yellow-green flesh they once had. I pretty much always follow the same rhythm each year when damsons are ripe: first cooking them in a little water to make damson jelly, then puréeing the softened fruit and freezing it in batches to make fruit leather and ice cream later. Each part of the process leads to the next, using the whole fruit, including the stones – a perfect flow from raw ingredient through preservation to myriad outcomes.

Damson jelly

In the context of preserves, jellies are made only from the juices of a fruit. Normally transparent, they have a jewel-like quality to them. They're a good option for fruits that would require intensive labour to remove the flesh from the seeds or stones, or where the fruit can handle longer cooking. Both are true for damsons. The stone at the centre is fairly large in relation to the fruit and clings to the flesh whether raw or cooked. Damsons are high in both acid and pectin, so achieving a perfect set is never tricky.

makes about 6 x 200g (7oz) jars

1kg (2¼lb) damsons

caster (superfine) sugar

50ml (3 tbsp) cider vinegar or homemade fruity vinegar

Put the damsons in a deep pan and add enough water to come up 1cm (½in) above the fruit. Bring to the boil then gently simmer for about 45 minutes with the lid on so the water won't evaporate. The fruit should be very soft and the water have taken on a deep magenta colour. Leave the fruit and cooking liquor to get to know each other better in the pan while it cools to room temperature. Strain the liquid through a jelly bag or a colander lined with a layer of muslin (or two layers of cheesecloth) set over a deep bowl. Allow the fruit to hang overnight so gravity draws the liquid out. You can squeeze the fruit but your resulting jelly won't be as clear.

The next day, weigh the drained liquid, keeping the damson pulp to process for purée. I like jellies set with 60 per cent sugar as it's enough to preserve while giving a balanced sweetness. Simply multiply the weight of the damson liquid you have by 0.6 to work this out (or, for every pound or 2 cups liquid, add 1 cup plus 2 tablespoons of sugar). Add the sugar and damson liquid to a large preserving pan. Bring to a gentle boil, stirring to dissolve the sugar. Turn up the heat to high and hard boil until it reaches 108°C (226°F) on a sugar thermometer or until the jelly passes the wrinkle test on a cold plate (p32). Pour into sterilized jars and seal.

Damson purée

Now to deal with the fruit pulp left over from jelly making. Damsons are the best reason I know to buy a moulin or food mill. It will still be a laborious process to remove the flesh from the stones but it will feel easier. If you don't have one then the next best thing is to push the cooked damsons through a coarse sieve or fine colander. Try to get as much fruit off the stones as possible. Set the stones aside and blend the fruit to a smooth purée. This can be frozen to use later in the following recipes.

Damson leather

These sheets of dried, sweetened fruit purée are solid but still malleable. They look beautiful laid over the top of a dessert. Damson leather will keep its deep magenta colour once dried so looks particularly striking. You can also cut it into strips or squares and store it in an airtight container for a handy snack. The tangy acidity of the damson balances well with the amount of sugar needed.

damson purée *(p89)*

caster (superfine) sugar

Preheat the oven to 60°C (140°F) or set a dehydrator to 60°C (140°F). Weigh the purée and multiply by 0.5 to calculate the 50 per cent sugar required. Gently warm the purée and sugar together in a pan until the sugar is well dissolved.

Spread the mixture evenly onto pieces of baking parchment or silicone mats to a thickness of 2–3mm (⅛in). Dry the leather for around 6 hours until it is no longer tacky and peels easily from the parchment or mat. Store layered between sheets of baking parchment in an airtight container.

Damson ice cream

If for no other reason, make this for the beautiful pinky, mauve colour. The balanced acidity of the damsons will cut through the rich custard base making this much more than a treat for the eyes. If you don't want to go through the jelly-making process first, simply roast the damsons in a hot oven until their skins burst and they smell heavenly, remove the stones and blend the fruit to a purée.

makes 1kg (2¼lb)

250ml (1 cup) whole milk

150ml (⅔ cup) double (heavy) cream

90g (⅓ cup) egg yolks, from about 5 eggs

140g (¾ cup) caster (superfine) sugar

pinch of salt

400g (1⅔ cups) damson purée

Combine the milk and cream in a large heavy-based saucepan and set over a medium-high heat until it reaches a rolling boil. Meanwhile, whisk together the egg yolks, sugar and salt. Set a sieve over a clean bowl and place it in an ice bath (or a sink filled with very cold water) so that you can quickly strain and cool the custard.

When the milk and cream are at a full rolling boil, turn off the heat and slowly pour the liquid into the egg yolk and sugar mix, whisking constantly. Return the custard to the pan and check the temperature. You want it to hit 83°C (181°F). If it doesn't, return the pan to a gentle heat and cook the custard, stirring constantly, until it reaches the correct temperature. Immediately strain into the waiting bowl in the ice bath. Add the damson purée and mix well.

Chill the ice-cream base in the fridge for a minimum of 4 hours or overnight. Churn in an ice-cream machine then transfer to a container and leave to set in the freezer before serving.

Damson stone vinegar fudge

And finally we get to the damson stones. It feels impossible to get all of the flesh from the stones, particularly when you start with kilos and kilos of damsons. There will always be a little left clinging on. I don't want to waste any part of the fruit I have spent so long picking. One day, after processing about 30 kilos of damsons, I thought I would try cracking the stones and tipping them into a jar with plenty of red wine vinegar. I put it on a shelf in the restaurant and forgot about it for a few weeks. When I came back to it, it had turned into the most deliciously almondy fruit vinegar. I added the vinegar to a batch of fudge I was making and felt very pleased with myself when I ate a piece of cooled fudge an hour or so later. We served this as a petit four but I've also made blocks to give as presents at Christmas.

yourself. You can add the damson stones to the vinegar without crushing them but bear in mind that the flavour will not be as strong.

makes 25 squares

flavourless oil, for greasing

275g (1⅓ cups) caster (superfine) sugar

100g (⅓ cup) golden syrup

230ml (1 scant cup) double (heavy) cream

5g (1 tsp) salt

60g (¼ cup) damson stone vinegar

for the damson stone vinegar

makes 500ml (1 pint)

125g (4½oz) damson stones

500ml (2 cups plus 1 tbsp) red wine vinegar

Spread the stones out on a heavy chopping board and cover with a tea towel. Bash the stones with a rolling pin to crack them open. Scoop the cracked stones into a jar and pour over the vinegar. Seal the jar and leave for at least a week. Give it a shake after a couple of days if you remember. Use this vinegar sparingly. It will have extracted a higher amount of amygdalin (the naturally occurring compound which converts to cyanide after eating) from cracking the stones so only use a couple of spoons and don't eat this whole batch of fudge

Line a rectangular or square plastic container with lightly oiled baking parchment. Put all the ingredients in a large saucepan and mix to combine; the fudge will bubble up as it boils so make sure the pan is generously sized. Place over a high heat and bring to the boil, stirring often, until the mixture reaches 118°C (244°F).

Transfer to a mixer with a paddle attachment. Beat the fudge on a slow speed to cool and start crystallizing it. The fudge will go from a glossy caramel to something matte and slightly grainy in texture. You can do this by hand, using a whisk to intermittently beat the mixture as it cools. Once the fudge is cool to the touch and has thickened, pour into the lined container and place in the fridge to set. Cut into bite-sized pieces to serve.

Damson stones contain amygdalin, which is converted into hydrogen cyanide in the body and is harmful if ingested in large quantities. Caution should be observed and you should consult your physician if you have any concerns.

Damson ice cream with warm oat sponge and whisky

Warm cake eaten with cold ice cream has to be one of life's great pleasures. Pour over a wee dram of whisky and I just don't know what more you could want. This dessert is totally comforting, and the plating not particularly formal; it's meant to be eaten quickly to enjoy the contrasts of temperature and texture.

Oats and whisky are true pals, both being perfectly suited to the Scottish climate. The quality will greatly impact the success of this dessert. Pinhead oats or steel-cut oatmeal have a very different texture from rolled oats. For rolled or porridge oats, the grain is flattened between rollers so they cook quicker and release more of their starch. Pinhead oats are produced by breaking or cutting the whole oat groat (the hulled kernel) into small pieces. They have a distinct crunch and bring a deeply nutty, cereally flavour when toasted. Now, which whisky to use? This will depend on your preferences but I do think it should be Scottish, though I may be biased. You are only using a small amount so use something a bit special: a whisky that has been matured for some of its life in bourbon barrels will give lovely, vanilla notes to the dessert. I would probably avoid anything too smoky or heavily sherry aged. My favourites with this dish are the single-harvest whiskies produced by Bruichladdich. They are designed to showcase the differences in each barley harvest and have a beautiful creamy, cereal quality to them.

Toast the pinhead oats in a dry frying pan over a medium heat until they are fragrant, nutty and deeply golden. Tip onto a plate and set aside. Sift both flours and the baking powder together. Beat the butter, sugar and salt together until you have a pale, aerated mixture. Add the eggs one at a time, beating well after each addition. Add the oat milk and stir gently to combine. The mix may curdle slightly at this point but don't worry, adding the dry ingredients will bring it back together. Add the dry ingredients except for the pinhead oats and mix to just combine. Avoid overmixing once you've added the flour as this will make the cake tough. The cake batter will last in the fridge for up to three days.

Set up a stovetop steamer or use the steam setting on your oven. You want the steamer to be nice and hot before you cook the cakes. Grease a mini muffin tray well (a silicone muffin mould is best here but if you have only a small steamer, egg cups work really well). Fill the mould two thirds full with cake batter. Steam the cakes for 16–20 minutes; they should have risen and will spring back when you press the top. Leave them to cool for 2–3 minutes before turning out of the moulds. Roll each cake in the toasted pinhead oats until well coated. The cake surface will be slightly tacky when warm so the oats should stick easily. The sponges store well for 1–2 days and can be rewarmed in the steamer or in a microwave.

Steamed oat sponge

makes 30 mini sponges

150g (1½ cups) pinhead oats (steel-cut oatmeal)

90g (¾ cup) plain (all-purpose) flour

90g (¾ cup) oat flour

5g (1 tsp) baking powder

200g (1 stick plus 6 tbsp) unsalted butter, softened

220g (1 cup plus 1½ tbsp) light brown or panela sugar

pinch of salt

3 eggs

135ml (½ cup plus 1 tbsp) oat milk

110g (1 cup) ground almonds

serves 1

1 tsp toasted pinhead oats (steel-cut oatmeal)

1 scoop damson ice cream (p90)

1 tsp damson jelly (p89)

1 steamed oat sponge

10ml (2 tsp) whisky

Put a small bowl in the freezer to chill 30 minutes before serving. Sprinkle a little of the toasted pinhead oats into the bottom of the bowl and place a large quenelle of damson ice cream on top. Use a ¼ tsp measuring spoon to make 3–4 scoops of damson jelly and dot them to the right of the ice cream so they are almost hidden underneath it. Warm the oat sponge in a steamer or in the microwave and break it into two. Place the pieces to the right of the ice cream to cover the jelly. Drizzle the whisky over the sponge and ice cream.

APPLES

I feel as though apples, like vanilla, have become all too ubiquitous in our pastry kitchens; a reliable staple that seems seasonless despite its strong association with autumn. Due to their ability to be stored long after picking, apples can be available all year round. They are not celebrated in the same way as the first flush of strawberries, or the first gleaming citrus fruits. They should be. There are about 7,000 varieties of apple across the world, 2,500 grown in the UK. Imagine all the different ways to coax out the flavour of those varieties: whether to roast, poach, dry, purée, juice, ferment, slice into thin crescents, enjoy in thick wedges, chomp into straight from the tree? Infinite possibilities and variations.

One of the three desserts my mum made when I was little was a "French apple tart" – a shortcrust pastry case filled with crème pâtissière and thin slices of apple that had been first browned in plenty of butter and dark muscovado sugar. I loved helping her cook the apples in the pan before laying them out in a perfect (or rather, childishly imperfect) spiral. I do think pretty much every apple dessert I've ever made references those buttery, beautifully caramelized slices of apple that I used to steal from the pan.

One of the great things about apples is how well they work with so many other flavours without losing their own identity. They pair beautifully with warming spices (black pepper, ginger, star anise, cardamom, cinnamon) but my favourites by far are allspice berries and nutmeg. Apples are equally happy luxuriating in all fats (butter, cream, nut oils, rapeseed oil) as they are kept bright and acidic. Woody herbs like thyme, rosemary and bay work brilliantly alongside them too. Whichever direction you go in, just make sure that the apple variety you choose is celebrated as the star of the dish.

Rehydrated apple crisps

This is a technique adopted from the savoury side of the kitchen. In the early days of Lyle's, there was often a main course garnish of celeriac that had been dried in thin sheets and then rehydrated in a butter emulsion. The result was intensely flavoured with the silky texture of perfect pasta. I loved snacking on that celeriac during service so wanted to see how I could apply this method to desserts.

The process of dehydrating a fruit removes the excess water and intensifies the flavours and sugars within. Once the apples are dehydrated, you can then rehydrate them with a liquid using the fruit's own juice as a base to further reinforce the flavour and make it taste even more of itself. I've given two different options for rehydrating the apple crisps here: one hot and one cold, both delicious. Always use a pressed apple juice, not one that's made from concentrate. I like the blend of Cox and Bramley apples from Chegworth Valley, which has a great balance of sweetness, acidity and tannins. Try playing around with single variety juices to see what works best for you.

for the crisps

apples, such as Braeburn, Cox or Pippin

Use a mandoline or electric meat slicer to cut the apples into slices around 2–3mm (⅛in) thick. You want them to be just thick enough to hold their shape once rehydrated but not so thick that they become unpleasantly chewy. You can dry these in an oven at the lowest temperature with the door slightly ajar to help the moisture escape. Keep an eye on them to ensure they don't colour. Alternatively, lay the slices on racks and dry in a dehydrator for 3–4 hours at 55°C (130°F). Once dry, the apple crisps will last for about a month.

You end up with quite a lot of trim when making the crisps: slightly wonky slices or ends too small to slice. Put these in a saucepan, cover with water and simmer for about an hour to create an apple stock. Strain, discarding the apple pieces, then return the liquid to the pan and reduce by about half. Keep tasting as it reduces until the stock is pleasantly appley. You can use it to replace up to half of the apple juice in the following recipes.

Rosemary butter emulsion

Inspired by that celeriac dish, I use this to rehydrate apple crisps: they become silken with a buttery apple flavour and a gentle whisper of rosemary.

300ml (1¼ cups) apple juice, or a mix of apple juice and apple stock *(left)*

200g (1 stick plus 6 tbsp) unsalted butter, cubed

1 sprig of rosemary

½ tsp xanthan gum

muscovado or demerara sugar, to taste

Pour the apple juice into a medium saucepan and bring to the boil then turn down the heat to a gentle simmer until it's reduced by a third. Add the butter one piece at a time, blending it in with a whisk or hand-held blender until the mixture has emulsified. Blend in the xanthan gum to help prevent it from splitting. Add the rosemary and return to a low heat to let it infuse for about 20 minutes. Keep tasting as it infuses; the rosemary shouldn't overpower the apple flavour so remove it once it tastes balanced. Remove from the heat and add a little muscovado or demerara sugar if it needs more sweetness.

Apple, honey and rapeseed dressing

Use a darker wildflower, heather or buckwheat honey, rather than the lighter acacia or meadow honeys. Cold-pressed rapeseed oil has a biscuity, almost oaty flavour, which is delicious with apples.

500ml (2 cups) apple juice or a mix of apple juice and apple stock *(left)*

25g (1¼ tbsp) honey

50ml (¼ cup) cold-pressed rapeseed oil

Pour the apple juice into a large saucepan and bring to the boil over a medium-high heat then turn down to a low simmer until it's reduced by half. Leave to cool to room temperature before whisking in the honey followed by the oil. This will now look like a vinaigrette. Pour the dressing over dried apple slices and leave for 30 minutes to soften slightly. Add cider vinegar to any remaining dressing and use it to dress a salad.

Brown butter-poached russet apples

Russet apples have a wonderfully dry texture and are more beautiful with their khaki papery skin than any shiny Red Delicious if you ask me. I've used Egremont Russets for this recipe. You want a reasonably sweet, dense apple and, importantly, one that will hold its shape when cooked.

serves 4

4 russet apples, cored

500g (4 sticks plus 2 tbsp) unsalted butter

6 allspice berries

Cut each apple into 6–8 wedges depending on the size of your apples. Lay them on racks and either dry them in an oven at the lowest temperature with the door slightly ajar to help the moisture escape or put them in a dehydrator at 60°C (140°F) for approximately 1½ hours. The aim is to ensure the cut flesh is no longer wet to the touch and is starting to pucker around the edge of the skin. The apples will keep in a sealed container for 3 days.

Melt the butter in a large saucepan over a medium heat until the milk solids have separated from the liquid and begun to caramelize. Whisk the butter to stop the solids from sticking to the bottom of the pan. Keep cooking until it is deep brown in colour with a nutty aroma. Strain through a fine sieve.

Preheat the oven to 100°C (210°F). Lightly toast the allspice berries in a dry frying pan over a medium-low heat until they start to smell fragrant. Crush gently in a mortar and pestle and add to the brown butter.

Place the apples in an ovenproof dish just big enough to hold them snugly then pour over the brown butter until they're completely submerged. Bake in the oven for about 8 hours. They should be slightly fudgy from absorbing the butter and very tender. Leave to cool still submerged in the butter. When you are ready to serve, simply warm them gently to melt the butter and remove the apple pieces as required. Use the leftover apple-infused butter in cakes or for frying pancakes.

Apple sorbet with Calvados or cider

I go in one of two directions with this sorbet depending on the apples available. When I have sweet, rosy-fleshed varieties such as Rosette or Pink Pearl, I pour over a glug of dry sparkling cider for balance. With sharply acidic green apples like Granny Smith, Mutsu or certain varieties of Pippin, a measure of Calvados or apple brandy brings a gentle boozy depth and a rounded sweetness. This Calvados-doused sorbet is often served during a multi-course meal. Known as *le trou normand* (the Norman hole), it's thought to reawaken the taste buds and create space in your belly for cheese and pudding. Be sure to chill the cooked apples down quickly.

serves 4–6

550g (1½lb) apples, cored (about 6 medium apples)

100g (½ cup) caster (superfine) sugar

100ml (scant ½ cup) dry (unsweetened) apple juice

juice of ½ lemon

malic acid, to season *(p237)*

35ml (2½ tbsp) sparkling cider or Calvados, to serve

Cut the apples into 6–8 pieces, keeping the peel on. Place in a saucepan with the sugar, apple juice, lemon juice and 100ml (scant ½ cup) of water so they fit snugly in a single layer. Cover with baking parchment, tucking it down the inside of the pan to keep in the moisture. Place over a medium heat for around 10 minutes until the apples are cooked through and tender but still hold their shape. Remove from the heat and transfer the apples with all of their juices to a shallow tray, cool slightly then chill in the fridge.

Once the apples are completely cold, place them in a blender and whizz until smooth, adding a little more sugar if the mix is too sharp. Pour into an ice-cream machine and churn until frozen. Transfer to a lidded plastic container and keep in the freezer until ready to serve. Transfer the container to the fridge about 30 minutes before serving.

Scoop a large ball of the sorbet into a bowl or glass and make a slight indent in the top. Pour over a generous measure of cider or Calvados so that it pools into the sorbet and around.

Apple crisps with rosemary butter, yeast ice cream, croutons and apple caramel

This perfectly autumnal dessert is definitely at the richer end of the spectrum. It celebrates butter and cream and their special affinity with apples. Choose a variety with a strong natural acidity, such as those from the Cox family, so it will still make its presence felt against the rosemary butter emulsion.

serves 1

2.5cm (1in) thick slice of milk bread *(p201)* or brioche

25g (3 tbsp) icing (confectioners') sugar

25g (1½ tbsp) brown butter *(p173)*

1 large scoop yeast ice cream *(p196)*

2 tsp apple caramel *(p166)*

500g (1lb 2oz) rosemary butter emulsion *(p95)*

6 apple crisps *(p95)*

1 sprig of lemon thyme, leaves picked

Place a shallow bowl in the freezer to chill 30 minutes before serving. Remove the crusts from the milk bread and cut into 2.5cm (1in) cubes. Toss in the icing sugar to get a heavy, even coating on all sides. Fry the cubes in the brown butter over a medium heat. Carefully colour each side before turning until you have caramelized, deeply golden croutons. Leave to cool on a rack.

Scoop a large quenelle of yeast ice cream into the centre of the chilled bowl. Make a well in the centre of the ice cream and fill with the apple caramel. Top with 3–4 caramelized croutons of milk bread.

Bring the rosemary emulsion up to a gentle boil. You need plenty of emulsion to cook the crisps in. Drop in the apple crisps and cook for 30–60 seconds, until they have gone soft. Remove with a slotted spoon and drain on kitchen paper. Arrange on top of the croutons to cover the entire scoop of ice cream. Garnish with the lemon thyme leaves.

Brown butter-poached russet apples with St Jude cheese ice cream and buckwheat shortbread

The fudgy poached apples are served warm and sit upon an incredibly short buckwheat biscuit in a nod to the classic Breton combination of buckwheat and apple. St Jude is a small, mould-ripened cow's milk cheese from Suffolk. Named after the patron saint for lost causes by its maker Julie Cheyney, it is a young creamy cheese whose buttery flavours come to the fore in winter when the cows are brought in from pasture. It provides a beautiful backdrop to the butter-poached apple along with a bit of lactic tang for balance. Make sure to use the cheese when it is young for this dish. A more mature, funky cheese will clash with the sweetness of the apples and overwhelm the earthiness of the buckwheat.

serves 1

6–8 pieces of brown butter-poached apple *(p96)*

1 scoop St Jude ice cream *(p180)*

1 buckwheat shortbread *(p194)*

whole nutmeg, to grate

Heat the apples in a saucepan over a low heat to about 50°C (120°F), until they are warm but not hot and the butter has melted. Drain the pieces of butter-poached apple on kitchen paper so that they are no longer greasy. Place the buckwheat shortbread off-centre on a plate and layer the apple pieces on top to build a stable nest for your ice cream. Place a quenelle of ice cream on top and then sprinkle generously with grated nutmeg.

PEARS

Pears can be divisive, a Marmite (love it or loathe it) kind of fruit. Partly because of their somewhat grainy texture, partly because it seems impossible to catch them when perfectly ripe so most people have either eaten underripe, flat-tasting pears or overripe, mushy/grainy pears. There can also be something a little sickly in their perfumed aroma. I used to very much be in the "loathe it" camp. We went on many long car journeys as a family (where I was always in the boot seat as the youngest) and there were two constants: I would get travel-sick; and my mum would buy pear drops as her car sweet of choice. Pear drops aren't a fair representation of pears, as few candies are; they are a hard boiled sweet that is sickly sweet and overly perfumed. Travel sickness and pear drops will unfortunately be forever linked together for me.

So, at a young age, I had decisively declared my dislike for pears. Then came my trial shift at Lyle's. I spent a day at the end of November making bread, chocolates and ice cream, enjoying the atmosphere in the kitchen and the food coming from it. The dessert on the set menu that night was warm pear with caramel ice cream covered in a ginger and chocolate crumb. The pears were simply cut into wedges and put in a lidded container on top of the oven just before service to get warm and extra juicy. I didn't much like the pudding if I'm honest but I loved the approach and appreciation for the ingredients. There was an excitement about – and understanding of – ingredients I hadn't seen in another British kitchen. I sat down at the end of the shift with head chef James to talk about the job and how the day had been. I explained about wanting to work somewhere I could make simple desserts that didn't require highly formal plating or 20 elements but focused on being delicious. James talked to me about pears... for a solid 20 minutes. How it was vital that, as a British restaurant, we serve pears; how chefs are scared to serve ripe pears and cop out by always serving them poached or cooked; how much he loves pears. I nodded and agreed (I really wanted to work in this kitchen and for this chef) and kept my mouth shut about my total aversion. I kept my mouth shut the entire time I worked there, so James, just so you know, I used to *really* hate pears. Five years of tasting them almost every day during the season has given me a real appreciation and respect for this particularly beautiful and special fruit. I'd still rather bite into an apple, though.

I don't offer any recipes on poaching or roasting pears here. There are many out there that will yield delicious results. I offer the thought instead that no poached pear is ever as delicious as a perfectly ripe just warmed pear so why bother? Let nature do what it does best and bring fruit to its peak, all we have to do is watch and wait for it. The easiest and most difficult recipe of all.

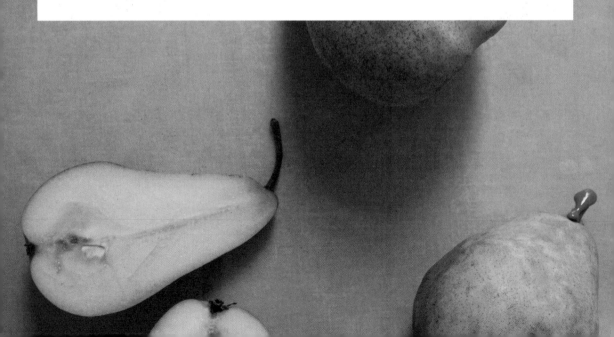

Pear sorbet

This should be made with nothing but the ripest pears. Ripe to the point of collapse and fit for no other use. I love Comice and Williams for sorbet but choose whichever variety is best at the time. This pear sorbet may not be a perfect pale cream colour – it's a sort of muddy pink and slightly oxidized – but it is the best tasting and I know which I'd rather have. You can use some ascorbic acid or lemon juice to help preserve the colour but go incredibly lightly as you don't want citrus acidity to overwhelm the subtle pear flavour.

makes 900g (2lb)

1kg (2¼lb) overripe pears

lemon juice or ascorbic acid, to taste (optional)

90g (½ cup) caster (superfine) sugar

malic acid, to season

Cut the pears into chunks (don't bother to peel or core them) and place in a blender along with any juice they might have released. Add a small squeeze of lemon juice or a pinch of ascorbic acid, if using. Blend on the highest speed until liquid and immediately pass through a chinois or fine sieve to catch any grainy peel, pips or core.

Gradually whisk in the caster sugar. As ever, go gently and keep tasting until it is just right. Season with malic acid. If you have a refractometer *(p236)*, you're aiming for a sugar level of 25°Bx. Pour into an ice-cream machine and churn until frozen. Transfer to a lidded plastic container and keep in the freezer. Put the container in the fridge about 30 minutes before serving.

Chewy pears

These grown-up sweets are wedges of pear that have been slowly dehydrated and tossed in a mix of sugar and malic acid. The results are fudgy and chewy, intensely pear flavoured and slightly tangy. They appear as a little extra on most of my pear dishes, or I've served them whole as petits fours. Conference, Comice and Bartlett varieties all work well here. Very ripe pears will collapse from the heat in the dehydrator so choose firm, slightly underripe fruit.

makes 36

6 firm medium-sized pears

500g (2¼ cups) caster (superfine) sugar

25g (3 tbsp) malic acid

Cut the pears through the centre into 6 wedges then remove the core, trimming as little fruit as possible. Lay the wedges on racks, flesh side up, and either dry them in an oven at the lowest temperature with the door slightly ajar to help the moisture escape or put them in a dehydrator at 55°C (130°F) for approximately 1½ hours. They should be just dry to the touch and no longer sticky or wet on the cut flesh.

Combine the sugar and malic acid, then gently toss and coat each wedge in the sugar mix, shaking off any excess. Return to the oven or dehydrator for 2 hours then toss again. The sugar mix can be reused for successive batches. Once the pears have had their two coats of sugar and malic acid, return them to the oven or dehydrator for 6–8 hours. The pears are ready when they are wrinkled and fudgy rather than wet and have shrunk by at least half. Be careful not to go too far as you will end up with crispy rather than chewy pears. Store in an airtight container in the fridge or at room temperature.

Pear, oats and goat's cheese

This became a Lyle's classic, returning each winter as pears came into season. The original credit for this dish goes to James Lowe. It was often described by guests as somewhere between a dessert and a cheeseboard. A base of our fragrant pear sorbet topped with slices of chewy pear and then a sweet oat biscuit covered in grated goat's cheese.

The balance here is vital to its success. We would plate and eat it in its entirety every day to see how the sorbet (brighter, more acidic, sweeter?) and the cheese (different batch, stronger, milder, nuttier?) played against each other, varying the ratios of cheese and sorbet as needed. We originally used Innes Burr, a small mature goat's cheese produced by Joe Bennett at Highfields Farm in Staffordshire. Neal's Yard Dairy would take Joe's excellent Innes log and mature it to become a denser, more savoury goat's cheese similar to a French crottin. Sadly, the Bennetts decided to sell their flock and give up cheesemaking during the pandemic. Their goats have gone to another excellent British cheesemaker so there is hope it will return. Whatever cheese you use here, it should be firm enough to be either shaved or grated and have a savoury, hazelnutty flavour.

serves 1

115g (4oz) aged goat's cheese

1 thin sheet oat biscuit *(p194)*

2 large scoops pear sorbet *(p103)*

2 pieces chewy pear *(p103)*

Place a shallow bowl in the freezer to chill 30 minutes before serving. Remove the rind from the cheese. Break off one or more pieces of oat biscuit to a width of 12cm (5in). Finely shave or grate the goat's cheese to cover the surface of the oat biscuit. Place a 10–12cm (4–5in) diameter cooking ring in the chilled bowl. Fill the ring with pear sorbet and flatten off to create a level disc. Scatter the surface of the sorbet with wedges of chewy pear and then carefully top with the cheese-covered oat biscuit.

Cocoa husk ice cream with warm Passe Crassane pear

This dish is a tribute to the classic dessert *Poires Belle Hélène* created by Auguste Escoffier, which consists of a poached pear served with vanilla ice cream, warm chocolate sauce and crystallized violets. I love to eat it in January and February when I still want the comfort of chocolate but my palate is yearning for bright flavours after the excesses of Christmas. In this version, the heavy chocolate is replaced by the lighter, cleaner flavour of cocoa husks *(p237)*, and the ripe pear is simply left somewhere warm to get as juicy as possible. Passe Crassane pears are a variety grown in France, which come to the fore in late winter when spring is just around the corner. They have firm flesh, even when very ripe, thin skin and beautiful natural acidity. If you can't get Passe Crassane then varieties like Bartlett or Decana share many of the same qualities. It's best to use a bright, fruity dark chocolate such as the Jamaica 75% from Pump Street Chocolate.

serves 1

1 ripe Passe Crassane pear

50g (1¾oz) chewy pears *(p103)*

30g (1oz) fruity dark chocolate *(see intro)*

1 generous scoop cocoa husk ice cream *(p188)*

30g (¼ cup) cocoa nibs

About an hour before you're ready to serve, find a warm spot to leave the ripe pears. In the kitchen I would often put them either in or just above the hot cupboard where plates are stored. A warming drawer or a dehydrator on a low heat will also work well. You're not looking to cook the pears, you just want them to be slightly above body temperature so they're as sweet and perfumed as possible.

Place a bowl in the freezer to chill around 30 minutes before serving. Chop the chewy pears into small pieces, about three times the size of a cocoa nib. Chop the chocolate so that some pieces are about the same size as the chewy pear and some are a fine dust. Combine the chewy pear, chopped chocolate and the cocoa nibs in a small bowl. Drop a large spoonful of ice cream into the bowl and move it around so it's completely covered in the crunchy, chewy, chocolatey pieces. The ice cream should be fairly firm so that it holds its form. Place into the chilled bowl and serve with a large wedge of warm pear.

GRAPES

Where would we be without grapes? One of the earliest fruits to be cultivated, grapes are arguably a defining crop for humanity. The generic seedless varieties grown as eating grapes are not much more than a fruity source of sugar, their year-round presence on our supermarket shelves tricking us into forgetting their distinct seasonality. The most interesting tasting grapes are pretty much always kept for wine. In the northern hemisphere, grape picking stretches between August and October, with the very first wines produced from that year's harvest appearing by November in the case of Beaujolais Nouveau.

Thankfully, we are starting to see a few more grape varieties make it out of the vineyard and into our kitchens. Chasselas is a white variety generally grown in the Loire region of France, as well as in Germany and Switzerland. Its pale yellow-green colour is beautifully subtle and as for its flavour, well 20th-century food writer Edward A. Bunyard puts it best: "sweet, short of sickliness, and the musky flavour not overdone". Muscat grapes, on the other hand, embrace that musky flavour and bright sweetness. I love them roasted and served alongside vanilla ice cream. Italy boasts of the Fragola – and rightly so – and in the US, it is the

Concord that earns the highest praise. If you are lucky enough to live near a grape-growing region, then use what you find on your doorstep. I am always jealous when I hear of the wide variety of grapes that Californian cooks have access to from the vineyards there.

It wasn't until I worked in New York that I saw grapes being used in desserts. I started at Gramercy Tavern at the height of Concord season and boy, were all the chefs excited about them. Their deep colour is somewhere between amaranthine and burgundy, and their flavour is distinctly wild and musky. They are the classic flavour of grape jelly used in peanut butter and jelly sandwiches, a flavour utterly familiar to Americans but very much novel to this British chef. The Concord is often paired with peanut or other nut butters in desserts to play on that childhood nostalgia. In Europe, the closest thing we have is the Fragola. It is similar in colour but with a gentler muskiness and a distinctly strawberry flavour; *fragola* means strawberry in Italian. It's generally grown in the north of Italy and comes into season around September. A handful scattered over focaccia just before it goes in the oven is a delightful marriage of sweet and savoury.

Nebbiolo sorbet

Nebbiolo grapes are grown in Piedmont in the north of Italy where they're used to produce the famous wines of the region, Barolo and Barbaresco. Since they're high in tannins, wines made from Nebbiolo are typically aged in oak to round out the flavours. The lemon in this recipe is boiled whole and then added to the grapes once they have been macerated. Whole citrus fruits are an incredibly useful tool in sorbet making. Their pith and peel add body to any sorbet that could be a little too thin to churn smoothly, while the added pectin gives a silky texture. They do dull the colour of the sorbet slightly and you need to be careful that their flavour harmonizes rather than dominates. I like to cook the lemon for this sorbet to mellow its flavour but keep the bitterness. Grapes can be flatly sweet so having a background bitterness gives balance.

The other trick to this sorbet is to allow the grapes to macerate overnight in their juices so that the skins provide their deep colour and the seeds release their tannins. This will give the sorbet structure and real bite. The addition of ascorbic acid helps to maintain the colour of the grapes and restrict oxidation. If you can't get hold of it, then substitute with the juice of a lemon.

makes 1 litre (2 pints)

1 small lemon

1kg (2lb 3oz) black grapes, such as Nebbiolo

125g (generous ½ cup) caster (superfine) sugar, plus extra to taste

½ tsp ascorbic acid

lemon juice, to taste

Put the lemon in a small saucepan and cover with water so it's completely submerged. Boil for around 45 minutes until the lemon is tender, topping up the water as necessary. Leave to cool.

Combine the grapes with the sugar and ascorbic acid. Tip into a food processor and blend to a purée. Leave in the fridge overnight to macerate. The next day, pass the grapes through a fine sieve, reserving the pulp and skins to make grape powder.

Combine the grape liquid with the whole cooked lemon and blend to a completely smooth purée in a food processor. Taste the sorbet base and adjust with a little extra sugar or lemon juice as required. Remember that freezing will dull the sweetness.

Pour into an ice-cream machine and churn until frozen. Transfer to a plastic container with a lid and keep in the freezer until ready to serve. Put the container in the fridge about 30 minutes before serving.

Grape powder
Due to the high sugar content of grape skins, this powder will get sticky and clump together if left for too long. Grind small amounts at a time and keep in an air-tight container with a sachet of food-grade silica gel if you can.

black grape pulp

Rinse the grape pulp in cold water to remove any surface sugars then spread out in a thin layer on a baking tray or dehydrator rack lined with a silicone mat. Dry in the oven or a dehydrator until crisp then blend in a spice grinder.

Roasted Fragola grapes

A very hot oven is your friend here. The grape halves will cook extremely quickly so you need a blast of heat to caramelize the edges before cooking the flesh through. They're particularly delicious when done in a wood-fired oven. The grapes release their heliotrope-coloured juices which mix with the oil to create the most fragrant sauce. It is important to add the vinegar as soon as the grapes come out of the oven so that any aggressive acidity evaporates. This technique will work well with any dark-skinned grape. For pale-skinned grapes, simply switch to golden caster sugar and white wine vinegar.

makes 350g (12oz)

300g (10½oz) red grapes, such as Fragola

10g (¾ tbsp) dark soft brown sugar

50ml (¼ cup) extra virgin olive oil

15ml (1 tbsp) red wine vinegar

Preheat the oven to 230°C (450°F). Cut the grapes in half and remove the seeds. This is a slow and fiddly process; I find a small paring knife is the best tool to flick out the seeds.

Place a heavy-based, ovenproof dish in the oven to preheat for 10 minutes. Combine the seeded, halved grapes with the sugar and olive oil. Toss the grapes in the mix so that they are evenly coated. Pour them into the hot ovenproof dish and roast for about 5 minutes. They should have started to caramelize and have released their delicious juices. Remove from the oven and immediately add the red wine vinegar and mix through the grapes. The harsh vinegar will evaporate and help to deglaze the pan. Leave to cool slightly and serve warm.

Chasselas grape granita

Wine grapes make delicious granitas. Their subtle aromas and flavours can sometimes get lost in a dairy ice cream or sorbet. Something about the delicate flakes of granita seems to match the subtlety of their flavour. The vermouth adds a little alcoholic structure that boosts rather than overwhelms the grapes. I love the idea of serving this on top of a sheep's milk ice cream or goat's cheese mousse.

makes 650ml (1¼ pints)

500g (1 generous lb) white grapes, such as Chasselas

100ml (scant ½ cup) dry vermouth

50g (¼ cup) caster (superfine) sugar

juice of ½ lemon

Add all the ingredients to a saucepan with a tightly fitting lid, along with 50ml (¼ cup) of water. Mix well to start dissolving the sugar, put the lid on and cook over a medium heat for 15–20 minutes. The grapes should burst and release their juices. You can help this along by gently crushing them with a fork or whisk once they have started to soften. Turn off the heat and allow the grapes to carry on cooking in the residual heat for a further 10–15 minutes.

Blend the grapes with all their liquid in a food processor then pass through a fine sieve. Taste the granita base and add a little more sugar or lemon juice if it tastes too sharp or too sweet. Pour into a shallow container and freeze. Every couple of hours, scrape a fork through the freezing liquor so that you end up with large ice crystals rather than a fine snow. Once it is completely frozen, scrape a fork through again to break it up further.

Nebbiolo sorbet, olive oil ice cream with roasted Fragola grapes

Grapes and olive oil are a natural pairing. Often sharing the same pockets of land in Italy, the olive trees are planted where vines will not grow. The flavours mirror and complement each other: both have an earthy, vegetal quality and an inherent piquancy which is balanced by savouriness in the case of the oil, or fruitiness in the grapes.

It is important that the ice cream and sorbet are well tempered and have a similar texture so that you can press them together into a smooth puck. The goal is to fill the centre of the ice cream and sorbet with the roasted grapes so that they're hidden inside. As you break into the ice cream, the grapes will spill out their fruity surprise, a bit like those kids' birthday cakes that spew out a rainbow of Skittles, but much more elegant.

serves 1

1 x 8cm (3in) olive oil and ricotta cake *(p181)*

1 scoop Nebbiolo sorbet *(p109)*

1 scoop olive oil ice cream *(p181)*

1 generous tbsp roasted Fragola grapes *(p110)*

1 tsp extra virgin olive oil

1 tsp grape powder *(p109)*

Make the olive oil cake batter according to the recipe *(p181)*. Preheat the oven to 180°C (350°F). Line a roasting tray with baking parchment and spread the cake batter to a thickness of around 5mm (¼in). Bake for 12–15 minutes until golden, remove from the oven and leave to cool completely. Use an 8cm (3in) cooking ring to cut out a perfect circle.

Put a shallow bowl in the freezer to chill 30 minutes before serving. Place a 10cm (4in) cooking ring in the centre of the bowl. Lay the circle of cake in the centre of the ring. Scoop a dessert spoon of each ice cream into the ring. Use a spoon to press the ice cream and sorbet into the base and up the sides of the ring. Take a generous spoonful of the roasted grapes with a little of their juices and place in the middle of the ring. Use equal amounts of the ice cream and sorbet to cover the grapes and fill the ring to the top. Press down again with a spoon then use a hot palette knife to flatten off the top and get rid of any excess. Remove the ring. You should be left with a smooth, sharp-edged puck of the ice cream and sorbet with the roasted grapes hidden within. Dot a little olive oil into the surface and then dust the plate with the grape powder.

PUMPKINS

Leave the first pumpkins of the season for savoury dishes. Pumpkins and squashes get sweeter as the season goes on, having had more time to ripen and cure after picking, so hold out for that deep sweetness to build within the fruit before making desserts. My time spent in New York definitely made me think more about pumpkins and squashes than I ever had before. I still can't quite get on board with pumpkin pie (it's a texture thing), or really understand the draw of a pumpkin spice latte, but I really appreciate all the ways that American cuisine celebrates the pumpkin season. I like to take inspiration from this, incorporating them as a purée into custards, creams and batters with joyful abandon.

They play well with other candy sweet flavours like brown sugar, maple syrup or candied chestnut as well as woody herbs like sage, rosemary and thyme. Pumpkin, sage and brown butter is one of those classic combinations that really can't be improved upon. The pumpkin ice cream and sage meringue dish riffs on that trio of flavours; it tastes familiar and comforting but not like a sweet plate of pasta. Don't be shy about using acid and salt to balance all of the extreme saccharine flavours in a dish centred around squash. Whey and sour dairy like crème fraîche are great foils, as are vinegar caramels. I generally avoid the well-trodden path of pairing pumpkin with warming spices like cinnamon, ginger and clove. If you do choose that route, then spice lightly so that pumpkin is the dominant flavour. The spices should enhance and edify the fruit, not overwhelm it. Nutmeg is a lesser used but excellent spice to use to achieve that balance.

Pumpkin ice cream

The important thing with this recipe is to use a pumpkin or squash that has a dense, sweet flesh. Don't be tempted to use a "Halloween" pumpkin; they are stringy, pumped full of water and not very tasty. My favourites are Delica or Violina pumpkins but Crown Prince, Kabocha or Red Kuri squashes will work well too. This ice cream takes a couple of days to make as you need to roast the pumpkin, purée it and then press that purée to remove any excess liquid, giving you the most intense, silky-textured ice cream possible.

makes 1.5 litres (3 pints)	
1.3kg (2lb 14oz) Delica (sugar or pie) pumpkin	
630ml (2⅔ cups) whole milk	
140ml (⅔ cup) double (heavy) cream	
100g (½ cup) egg yolks, from about 5 eggs	
170g (¾ cups plus 1 tbsp) light muscovado sugar	
5g (1 tsp) salt	

Preheat the oven to 160°C (325°F). Cut the pumpkin in half, scoop out the seeds, then peel it. This seems like the wrong way round but these pumpkins are easier to peel when you can hold them better. Cut each piece in half again and place in a roasting dish. Cover with a double layer of foil and seal tightly. Bake for 30–40 minutes until the pumpkin is completely tender. The tight foil will help it steam rather than colour.

Blend to a smooth purée in a food processor and then pour into a colander lined with a clean tea towel. Fold the tea towel over the purée and place the colander inside a bowl to catch the excess liquid. Place a plate on top of the purée and put a couple of heavy tins or another bowl full of water on the plate to use as a weight. Leave the purée in the fridge overnight until the excess water has been pressed out. Give the tea towel a squeeze to remove any liquid still in there. You should end up with approximately 350g (1½ cups) of pumpkin purée.

Combine the milk and cream in a large pan set over a medium-high heat until it reaches a rolling boil. Meanwhile, whisk together the egg yolks, sugar and salt. Set a sieve over a clean bowl and place in an ice bath (or a sink filled with very cold water) so you can immediately strain and cool the custard. When the milk and cream are at a full rolling boil, remove from the heat and slowly pour half into the yolk mixture, whisking as you go to prevent curdling. Pour the now tempered egg mixture back into the pan with the remaining milk and cream and stir well. There should be enough latent heat left in the pan to cook the egg yolks to 82–83°C (180°F) without having to return it to the heat. Check the temperature and if it is below 82°C (180°F), continue to cook the custard over a gentle heat, stirring constantly until it reaches the required temperature. Immediately strain into the waiting bowl in the ice bath. Add the pumpkin purée and mix well. Chill completely in the fridge for a minimum of 4 hours. Churn in an ice-cream machine and leave to set a little before serving.

Pumpkin ice cream with sage meringue and whey caramel

This is the very first dish I put on the menu at Lyle's. I still think it is utterly delicious and a great example of looking to the savoury kitchen for inspiration. The vegetable course on the set menu at that time was a dish of steamed and roasted pumpkin with kales, chestnuts and a whey sauce. I had never really cooked with whey before but loved the sourness it brought to that dish so when we decided to do a pumpkin dessert, it seemed a natural choice. And, of course, pumpkin and sage is such a classic combination. New York chef Brooks Headley has a recipe for sage gelato that he pairs with kabocha squash so I felt confident that it could work in a sweet setting. So, I began playing and testing with pumpkin ice cream, sage and whey. I went through several iterations (including an ill-conceived whey granita) before arriving at this dessert. There is a hidden spoon of very rich double cream in the centre, which acts as a palate break from the rest of the punchy flavours. I would use a very thick cream such as the one from Ivy House Dairy, which does not need to be whipped, but you can gently whip standard double cream instead.

Sage sugar

140g (¾ cup) caster (superfine) sugar

10g (2 tsp) salt

10g (about 10) sage leaves

Grind the ingredients together in a spice grinder or mortar and pestle until the sage is completely broken down by the sugar. You should have a bright green, wet mixture. Store in the freezer until ready to serve.

Sage meringue

9g (about 9) sage leaves

600g (3 cups) caster (superfine) sugar

300g (1¼ cups) egg whites, from about 10 eggs

9g (2 scant tsp) salt

Preheat the oven to 120°C (250°F), on the non-fan setting. Grind the sage with 200g (1 cup) of the sugar in a mortar and pestle or spice grinder until it has broken down then set aside. Whisk the egg whites with the salt using a mixer or electric hand whisk at medium speed until they are at the soft peak stage. This will give a stronger meringue so don't be tempted to turn up the speed on your mixer. Add half of the remaining caster sugar and continue whisking until it has been fully incorporated then add the other half. Once the sugar is fully mixed in, add the sage sugar and whisk until you have a shiny, stiff meringue.

Either pipe 5cm (2in) rounds onto baking trays lined with baking parchment or use two dessert spoons to make quenelles of meringue. Bake for 1½–2 hours. Leave to cool in the oven with the door slightly ajar then store in an airtight container until ready to serve.

serves 1

1 scoop pumpkin ice cream *(p115)*

2–3 tbsp whey caramel *(p167)*

1 tsp thick double (heavy) cream

1 sage meringue

1 tbsp sage sugar

Place a bowl in the freezer to chill 30 minutes before serving. Scoop a medium-sized quenelle of ice cream into the bowl, just to the right of centre. Use a warm spoon to flatten the top of the scoop. Spoon the whey caramel to the left of the ice cream to form a pool. Place the cream on top of the flattened ice cream and then break the meringue over it, putting the largest pieces on top of the ice cream. Sprinkle over the sage sugar to finish.

Maple-roasted pumpkin

As with the pumpkin ice cream, you want a dense-fleshed, sweet pumpkin or squash. A butternut squash actually works very well even though I would normally avoid its rather flat flavour in desserts. The salt and vinegar are important here so don't be shy with the amounts. The pumpkin and the syrup are both very sweet so the seasoning and acid will stop the dish from becoming sickly.

1 small pie pumpkin or squash, about 600g (1lb 5oz)

200g (¾ cup plus 2 tbsp) light brown butter *(p173)*

1 heaped tsp Maldon salt

100ml (scant ½ cup) maple syrup

20ml (4 tsp) apple cider vinegar

Preheat the oven to 200°C (400°F). Peel and deseed the pumpkin then cut into 4cm (1½in) cubes. These cubes look quite large but will shrink as the pumpkin cooks. Combine the remaining ingredients in a saucepan set over a medium heat and whisk together as the butter melts so they're loosely combined but haven't started to caramelize. Remove from the heat and pour over the cubed pumpkin. Toss well to make sure each surface is coated and then tip the whole lot into a roasting tray so that it fits quite snugly in a single layer.

Roast in the oven for 15 minutes then turn each cube to make sure it colours evenly and return to the oven for a further 15–20 minutes until deeply caramelized. The butter and maple mix will have reduced and formed a delicious caramel. Leave to cool before serving.

Maple-roasted pumpkin with caramelized cream panna cotta and walnuts

This is pure autumn in a bowl. You can plate it with a panna cotta that has been turned out but I like it served in the bowl it's set in with the pumpkin and walnut elements built on top.

serves 1

1 caramelized cream panna cotta *(p175)*

walnuts, to serve

4–5 cubes of maple-roasted pumpkin *(left)*

1 walnut shortbread *(p208)*

1 tsp green walnut liqueur *(p205)*, *nocino* or other walnut liqueur

Preheat the oven to 170°C (340°F). Spread the walnuts out on a baking tray and toast in the oven for 7–10 minutes until they're starting to brown and smell deliciously nutty. Use a coarse Microplane grater *(p236)* to shave the toasted walnuts over the surface of the panna cotta.

Warm the pumpkin gently in its maple glaze in a small saucepan. The pumpkin is really at its best served just warm. If it is too hot, it will melt the panna cotta. Once it's ready, place the caramel-coated cubes on top of the walnut-blanketed panna cotta. Break the walnut shortbread into small shards and scatter over the pumpkin, then drizzle the nocino on top.

winter

QUINCES

When I started cooking, baking and reading recipes, quinces sounded utterly magical to me. There seemed little to no hope of finding these glowing, fragrant fruits in rainy Glasgow but I read and reread Nigella Lawson's passages about this transcendental ingredient. Imagining having a beautiful kitchen full of them in my future life diminished the disappointment of not finding them in my home city. Nigella wrote about buying them just for their beauty and ability to perfume the whole house; about trapping their heady scent (a mix of apples, pears, honey and some wild floral quality) in brandy and the enchantment they bring to everything from apple crumbles and mincemeat to Middle Eastern stews. I moved to London and found the fabled quinces in a Portuguese shop in Brixton. I bought a huge bowlful for the kitchen table and received many mocking comments from my housemates who would find me standing alone, sniffing the quinces. Their signature golden yellow is my favourite colour and their smell one of the best in the world.

Quinces are part of the same family as apples and pears so work in many of the same dishes and alongside the same flavours. They do, however, need to be treated in a very different manner. Quinces are not generally eaten raw (although I worked with a Chilean chef who enjoyed them that way as a childhood treat) but need to be cooked low and slow to achieve that classic fiery blush and tender flesh. Raw quince is astringent with quite an unpleasant texture. If I want larger chunks as part of a dessert, I will cook the quinces first. If I'm adding it to a crumble or compôte then I keep the raw quince pieces small (grating it works well) so they cook quickly, imparting their flavour but not their colour. Once poached, they last for a long time submerged in their syrup in a sealed container, and can then be added to purées, crumbles, pies, tarts, cakes and breads as you wish. They add an ethereal touch to a dish whether as the star or a member of the chorus. Their transformation from glorious yellow to ruby red still feels like alchemy no matter how many times I cook them.

Poached quinces

While poaching will release perfume from any quince, it is always best to start with heavily aromatic, ripe fruit.

quinces
2 tsp citric or ascorbic acid, or juice of 2 lemons
caster (superfine) sugar

Wash any downy fluff from the quinces, then peel and cut into quarters. Have a deep container filled with cold water and either a generous spoon of citric or ascorbic acid or the juice of a couple of lemons to plunge the peeled quinces into to stop them oxidizing. Keep all the peel to add into the poaching liquor as it is highly aromatic. The neatest way to add them is to tie them up in a square of muslin as you would with spices. You don't need to core the quinces at this point. They are notoriously tough to cut through but once poached the core can easily be cut out of the now-yielding flesh.

Make a 1:1 syrup, ie one that is equal weights water and caster sugar (or 1 cup water to 1 cup plus 2½ tbsp sugar). You will need enough syrup to cover the quinces. Pour it into an ovenproof casserole or baking tray and bring to the boil then add the drained quinces and the peelings in their muslin pouch. Return to the boil then remove from the heat. Place a circle of baking parchment directly on top of the quinces and then cover the tray or casserole tightly with foil. Place into an oven at 90°C (195°F) and bake for 6–8 hours or overnight. The quinces are unlikely to overcook at such a low temperature. This low, gentle poaching should yield fruit that is tender but holds its form and is a deep garnet hue.

Remove and squeeze out the muslin bag of peelings then chill the quinces ensuring they remain submerged in the poaching liquor to keep them moist. You can use this syrup again with subsequent batches. The colour and flavour will deepen with each use. From here you can do pretty much anything with them: purée, sorbet, sliced over a panna cotta, chopped into sweet and savoury dishes alike. Whatever you decide, remember to cut out the tough core before you use them.

Pickled quinces

A short step along from the poached quinces is a lightly pickled version. A slice or two on the plate alongside poached quinces can really lift a dessert and be a lovely surprise. To make the pickle, combine equal quantities of poaching liquid and apple cider vinegar in a saucepan and bring to the boil. Core some poached quince quarters and slice into slim crescents and place in a container or jar. Pour over the hot pickling liquor then cover and chill. The liquor is excellent used as a seasoning to stop the poached quinces tasting sickly sweet. This will last happily for about a month in the fridge but will start to lose its texture after that.

Quince posset

A posset is one of those wonderfully British words and desserts (along with syllabub) that is as pleasing to say as it is to eat. In essence, cream and sugar is boiled for a few minutes then removed from the heat before an acidic fruit juice is whisked in. The acid immediately thickens the cooked cream and, once cooled, it sets to an unctuously rich texture. As with the recipe for poached quinces, slower and lower cooking is necessary to extract the magic of the fruit, so this posset has a very different technique to the classic version.

This recipe came about after seeing a guest chef we hosted at Lyle's during one of the annual game dinners cook rabbit in double cream. It was the most delicious dish and seemed like the most decadent way to prepare an ingredient. When I tested this initially, I was more interested in the fruit than the cream. I was hoping the quinces would be meltingly tender and rich. In fact, when you take them out of the cream after their long poaching, they look quite unattractive and anaemic; they need to be cooked a second time to caramelize into amber fruit. The cream the quinces are poached in, on the other hand, is transformed. While the fat captures the characteristic perfume, the acid and pectin in the quinces work their alchemy to thicken and set the cream as it cools in the same way lemon juice sets a traditional posset. A note on

this recipe: the cream must have a high percentage of fat (in the UK, double cream is 48 per cent which is perfect) and, just as with the poached quinces, the fruit must be ripe and perfumed.

serves 6–8

2 tsp citric acid or the juice of 2 lemons

800g (1¾lb) quinces

800ml (3⅓ cups) double (heavy) cream

150g (¾ cup) caster (superfine) sugar

Dissolve the citric acid in a large bowl of cold water or, if using lemon juice, mix it into the water. This prevents the quinces from oxidizing and also adds a little extra acid to help the posset set. Peel, core and quarter the quinces, keeping the peeled fruit submerged in the acidulated water. Put the peel and cores into a muslin square and tie loosely. These trimmings carry an incredible amount of the fruit's perfume and pectin, which we want to capture as much as possible.

Combine the cream, sugar, drained quinces and peel in a flameproof casserole with a lid, such as a Dutch oven. Bring to a rolling boil for 2 minutes. Lay a piece of baking parchment over the surface and put the lid on. Bake in the oven at 90°C (195°F) for 6 hours or overnight. At Lyle's, we would bring this up to the boil after we had cleaned the kitchen and then take it out first thing in the morning.

Once cooked, the quinces should be tender but won't feel as soft as a classically poached piece of quince. Strain the hot cream into a blender, really squeezing the muslin bag to extract maximum flavour. Reserve the quince pieces for roasting. Blend the cream briefly to help it re-emulsify. Pour into small pots or ramekins of 160g (⅔ cup) per serving, as the posset sets much better in small quantities. Leave to set in the fridge for at least 2 hours before serving.

Quince posset with chestnut meringue

One of my favourite dishes ever. A plate of multiple shades of palest beige sounds like it shouldn't be beautiful but this truly is. A dessert fit for the shift from the most vibrant colours of autumn to the muted tones of winter. The posset should be cold but the chestnut purée and roasted quinces are at their best just above body temperature.

---

serves 1

---

4 pieces of cream-poached quince *(see below)*

½ tbsp chestnut purée *(p207)*

---

1 large dessert spoon quince posset *(p123)*

---

1 chestnut meringue *(p206)*

½ whole chestnut, peeled

Toss the cream-poached quinces left over from making the posset with some more 1:1 syrup (or quince poaching syrup if you have it) and roast in the oven at 180°C (350°F) for 15–20 minutes until well caramelized. They won't achieve the rosy glow of regular poached quinces but will get darker with beautifully burnished edges.

Put the chestnut purée into a shallow bowl and spread out to the same diameter as your chestnut meringue. Spoon a large dessert spoon of posset on top, followed by 4 thick slices of the warm roasted quince. Top with the chestnut meringue then either grate or shave on the whole chestnut to cover everything.

Raw chestnuts contain high concentrations of tannic acid, which can lead to stomach irritation if ingested in large quantities and should be avoided if you have liver disease, kidney problems and/or intestinal issues. Caution should be observed and you should consult your physician if you have any concerns.

DRIED FRUITS

One day, my dream is to have enough space to dry and store all of the bounteous fruits I come across; to be able to make mincemeat and cakes with fruit that I've preserved myself. Living in London, I'll never be able to recreate the magic of sun-dried Zante currants, figs or golden raisins but maybe I'll be able to get some of the way there. British baking is full of recipes that celebrate currants, raisins and sultanas, products that have been imported since the Middle Ages. The most celebrated and loved of these are for Christmas pudding and mince pies. Although these are very much yuletide recipes, they both benefit from at least a month to mature so start making them well in advance.

Christmas pudding

Recipes for this festive essential are not static; they are made to be tweaked and changed, their ingredients substituted, the details scribbled from one stained family recipe book to another. This version is based on my mother's. She was an excellent but notoriously imprecise cook and this is one of the few reasonably specific recipes she handed down. It's much easier than the long list of ingredients might indicate. Mum was pretty much the only person in our family who liked Christmas pudding back then so I feel she always made it extra special for herself (we were all excited by the Vienetta instead). It may be a trick of the mind but I'm sure there was always a Christmas pudding of indeterminate age in our fridge. No matter when in the year you looked, you would be sure to see a well-wrapped pudding hidden among the jars of condiments and pickles that fridges always accumulate whatever their size. Use this recipe as a framework for your own. Swap in different alcohols, nuts and dried fruits as you wish. I use *nocino,* a green walnut liqueur *(p205),* as it is something I make every year but other homemade spirits would work well too, such as sloe gin or damson brandy. I've served this with clotted cream *(p130),* rich double cream or brandy butter but my favourite way to eat it with a huge scoop of nutmeg ice cream.

makes one 1.2 litre (2½ pint) pudding

55g (2oz) prunes, cut into quarters

20g (scant ¼ cup) dried cranberries

120g (¾ cup) golden raisins

100g (⅔ cup) sultanas

30ml (2 tbsp) brandy, plus extra to serve

40ml (2½ tbsp) *nocino (p205)* or other liqueur

100ml (scant ½ cup) Guinness

40g (⅓ cup) hazelnuts

45g (generous ⅓ cup) pecans

40g (⅓ cup) cooked and peeled chestnuts

75g (5 tbsp) unsalted butter, softened, plus extra for greasing

75g (¼ cup plus 1 tbsp) dark brown soft sugar

30g (2 tbsp) treacle (dark molasses)

2 eggs: 1 whole, 1 yolk

40g (⅓ cup) breadcrumbs

120g (1 cup) wholemeal (whole wheat) flour

¼ tsp mixed spice (apple pie spice)

¼ tsp ground ginger

¼ tsp ground allspice

pinch of salt

25g (2 tbsp) grated carrot

25g (2 tbsp) grated quince

Combine the dried fruits in a large bowl then pour over the brandy, nocino (or other liqueur) and Guinness. Leave the fruit to soak for at least 1 hour or overnight if possible.

Toast the nuts in a dry frying pan over a medium heat until they're smelling fragrant then roughly chop and leave to cool.

Beat the butter, sugar and treacle together until pale and fluffy then mix in the egg and egg yolk until well combined. Add the remaining dry ingredients followed by the carrot, quince and soaked fruit along with its liquid. It will look like a sloppy mess but will smell delicious so all is well. Brush a 1.2-litre (2½-pint) heatproof pudding basin heavily with softened butter and spoon in the mix to around 2–3cm (1in) below the top. Place a disc of baking parchment on top then wrap the whole pudding in baking parchment and secure with string.

Put the pudding in a large saucepan and add boiling water until it comes halfway up the pudding basin. Put the lid on the pan and steam gently for 6 hours, topping up the water as necessary. Once it is cooked it will last a year (or longer) in a cool dry place.

To serve, steam for another 2 hours and turn out onto a plate. Warm 2–3 tablespoons of brandy gently in a pan until it is just steaming. Hit the lights, set the warm brandy on fire and pour it over the pudding.

Mincemeat and quincemeat

Mince pies are the herald of festive cheer here in the UK. They are in the back of my mind as soon as the British apple season starts but I hold out until October when quinces are available to start making the mincemeat, and then until 1 December to bake my first mince pie. If you're not quite that organized (who is really?) then you can make this at any time in the run-up to Christmas. The longer you can give it to rest before baking into pies, the better: I'd suggest at least a couple of weeks. The inclusion of beef mince harks back to a time when mince pies were more about the meat than the fruit. It gives the pies a gentle savoury undercurrent rather than an overtly beefy flavour. The beef and suet also add to the unctuously sticky texture of the mincemeat. The "quincemeat" (a name I wish I could take credit for but which originally came from Nigella Lawson) came out of a need for a meat-free version. The mix of raw and cooked quince gives textural interest, while the addition of dates recreates the sticky quality of the beef and suet. The long, slow roast here helps give the mincemeat a mellow but very rich flavour. Most recipes do not cook out the alcohol beforehand; doing so here really integrates the flavour of the different spirits into the mincemeat and adds complexity. It also smells phenomenal as it bakes. This recipe makes quite a lot of mincemeat but if you're going to all that trouble then I'm sure you're going to want plenty of pies as a reward down the line. I won't judge if you keep the majority for personal consumption.

Mincemeat

makes 2.2kg (4lb 14oz), enough for about 36 pies

400g (14oz) fatty minced (ground) beef

1 whole nutmeg, grated

½ tsp ground cinnamon

½ tsp ground allspice

1 tsp ground ginger

½ tsp ground black pepper

300g (2 cups) Cox or Braeburn apples, coarsely grated

350g (2⅓ cups) sultanas (golden raisins)

350g (2⅓ cups) dried currants

250g (1¼ cups) dark muscovado sugar

200g (7oz) beef suet

zest and juice of 2 oranges

zest and juice of 2 lemons

125ml (½ cup) brandy

125ml (½ cup) rum

50ml (¼ cup) Port

Quincemeat

makes 2.2kg (4lb 14oz), enough for about 36 pies

1 whole nutmeg, grated

½ tsp ground cinnamon

½ tsp ground allspice

1 tsp ground ginger

½ tsp ground black pepper

5g (1 tsp) salt

325g (2 generous cups) apples, coarsely grated

175g (1 generous cup) poached quince, diced *(p122)*

175g (1 generous cup) quinces, peeled, cored and grated

300g (1⅓ cups) dates

350g (2⅓ cups) sultanas (golden raisins)

350g (2¼ cups) dried currants

250g (1¼ cups) dark muscovado sugar

zest and juice of 3 oranges

zest and juice of 3 lemons

125ml (½ cup) brandy

125ml (½ cup) rum

50ml (¼ cup) Port

The methods for the mincemeat and quincemeat are identical except for the first step and the cooling. For the mincemeat, fry or roast the minced beef just enough to give a little colour and to ensure it's cooked through. Add any fat that comes off in the cooking to your mix along with the beef.

Preheat the oven to 120°C (250°F). For both the mincemeat and quincemeat, combine all the ingredients in a large roasting tray and stir well. Bake for 3 hours, stirring every 30 minutes.

Cool the mincemeat over a tray of ice. The fat in the mincemeat will start to solidify around the edges. It is very important to keep stirring the mincemeat as it cools to help evenly distribute the fat throughout the mixture (note: this step isn't necessary for the quincemeat).

Spoon into sterilized jars. Store in the fridge for up to a year. If I have a little mincemeat left at the end of the season I often keep it back to add into the following year's mix as an extra layer of flavour.

Rough puff pastry

Now you've made your mincemeat and it has had a nice long rest for the flavours to get even better acquainted, the time has come to make mince pies. As this is such a rich mincemeat, I don't like to encase it in a short, buttery pastry which works wonderfully for a brighter, more citrussy mix. For this recipe, I love a slightly salty rough puff, which has demerara sugar laminated through it along with the butter to give an extra flakiness. This dough also works brilliantly in a fruit pie or galette.

makes enough for 36 mince pies

300g (2½ sticks) very cold butter, diced

400g (3 cups plus 2 tbsp) plain (all-purpose) flour

5g (1 tsp) salt

2 tbsp demerara sugar, plus extra for sprinkling

1 egg, beaten

Maldon salt, for sprinkling

Gently rub the diced butter with the flour and salt. You can either do this by hand or in a mixer with a paddle attachment. Don't work the butter too much, just coat it in the flour and flatten it into slightly smaller pieces. Make sure you still see defined butter pieces, as these are what will make the pastry puff.

Add 100ml (scant ½ cup) of ice-cold water and mix until the dough has just come together. It will still feel quite rough and shaggy but it gets worked together more with the folding. Shape into a square, wrap tightly in cling film and rest in the fridge for 1 hour. Roll the dough out on a floured surface into a long rectangle roughly 15cm x 40cm (6in x 16in).

Sprinkle on 1 tablespoon of demerara sugar and use a rolling pin to gently press it into the surface. Fold the dough into thirds like a letter. Chill in the fridge for 30–60 minutes then repeat the rolling, sugaring and folding. Keep the folded edge perpendicular to you. That way, you will always roll the dough at 90 degrees to the last direction and it will bake evenly.

After the second letter fold, rest the dough in the fridge for 1 hour (it can happily sit in the fridge for a day or be frozen at this stage). Roll it out to a thickness of 3mm (⅛in) and cut out circles that are 2cm (¾in) wider than the diameter of the holes in a deep muffin tin. Press a pastry circle into each hole and fill generously with the mincemeat allowing roughly 60g (2oz) per pie.

Cut out smaller pastry circles that are the same diameter as the muffin tin holes. Brush the underside of each circle with beaten egg and place on top of the mincemeat to seal the pies. I like to then pinch the edges of the dough together to crimp them.

Brush the tops of the pies with beaten egg and sprinkle with more demerara sugar and a little Maldon salt. Cut a small hole in the top of each pie and bake at 180°C (355°F) for 20 minutes. Leave the pies to cool in the tin for 5 minutes before running a palette knife carefully around the edge to release them. Eat the pies warm, preferably with an equal quantity of clotted cream.

Prune purée

I love using this in a dessert with oats and honey or as a filling for sweet doughs or sandwich cookies. It also works wonderfully served alongside roast pork or duck, or with a game terrine or pâté. Agen prunes are my favourite so try to get them if you can.

makes 250g (9oz)

1 Earl Grey tea bag

200g (7oz) dried pitted prunes

25g (1½ tbsp) honey

fruit vinegar (Riesling, cider or pickling liquor from fruit pickles), to taste

salt, to taste

Put the tea bag in a medium saucepan and pour over 150ml (⅔ cup) of boiling water. Leave to infuse for 5 minutes. Remove the tea bag then add the prunes and bring to a gentle simmer. Cover and cook for about 10 minutes until tender. Pour the prunes and liquid into a blender and process until you have a smooth purée. Taste then season with the honey, vinegar and salt. Keep mixing and tasting after each addition until you have a purée that's well balanced.

CLEMENTINES

Forever the taste of Christmas morning to me, every year without fail there would be a glossy clementine to be found in the bottom of our stockings, along with a bag of chocolate coins. I would eat the reassuringly familiar fruit as I delved through the rest of the treats from Santa (always a new toothbrush and a pair of tights among them). The season for this sweet citrus seems to extend every year but, as a general guide, it starts towards the end of November and ends around March. While clementines are in the same family as mandarins and satsumas, they tend to be a little sweeter with a thinner peel.

Clementine granita

When I was first developing this recipe, I was stuck on the idea that I had to intensify the flavour of clementines, to manipulate them into a greater version of themselves. I tried reducing the juice, roasting or boiling the clementines whole then adding them as a purée. What I realized after multiple failures, and multiple batches that tasted like really cheap orange juice made from concentrate, is that the beauty of clementines is their light, fresh, sweet quality. Cooking or processing them dulled that vibrancy. So here is a granita recipe that fully relies on excellent produce – you really have nowhere to hide. A humbling lesson. This is now the method I would use when making a granita from any of the orange or mandarin family. If you have a refractometer, you'll be aiming for a sugar level of 15°Bx.

makes 650ml (1⅓ pints)

40g (3 tbsp) caster (superfine) sugar

15 clementines

Put the sugar in a bowl then zest 2 of the clementines over it so that you capture all of the escaping oils. Rub the zest through the sugar. Juice the clementines; you should end up with about 600ml (2½ cups) of juice. Whisk the zesty sugar into the juice until it has fully dissolved then pour the mixture into a shallow container and freeze.

Remove from the freezer every hour or two and scrape through with a fork. The sugar is heavier so will naturally freeze on the bottom along with the solids in the fruit, so it is important to keep mixing the granita as it freezes to get an even final product. I like medium-sized ice crystals in this granita, not so fine that it's like snow. Somehow, it captures the light better, showing off the colour of the fruit and giving the granita its own distinct texture.

Clementine leaf cream

Clementine leaves have a subtly green flavour. You need to use quite a few to infuse a cream or custard but leafy clementines are so pleasing, they've almost become the norm, making the leaves easy to source. I like to add a little clementine zest to reinforce the flavour. Unlike fig leaves or blackcurrant leaves, which have such punchy flavours that they can be used without their fruit, clementine leaves work best as a flavour in a clementine-focused dish. A supporting player rather than the star. The test to see if the cream is ready, which I teach every fellow pastry chef, is to ask yourself "does it jiggle like jelly or flow like the sea?". If it flows like the sea, it is not yet done. The Mancunian *chef de partie* in my first kitchen, Natalie, taught me that and it's stuck with me ever since. It works perfectly for custard tarts, jellies or crèmes brûlées.

serves 6

1 litre (4¼ cups) double (heavy) cream

25g (1oz) clementine leaves (about 1 handful)

zest of 2 clementines

50g (4 tbsp) caster (superfine) sugar

175g (¾ cup) egg whites, from about 6 eggs

Heat the cream in a heavy-based saucepan to just under the boil. Crush the clementine leaves gently in your hands then place in a bowl along with the clementine zest. Pour the hot cream over the leaves and zest and leave to infuse overnight. The next day, warm the cream gently then strain out the leaves.

Gently whisk the sugar and egg whites together until just combined but not aerated. Add the warm cream to the egg whites and mix well. Again, this is not about incorporating any air into the mix so go gently. We're trying to create a dense cream like a crème brûlée once it's baked, not an airy mousse. Pass through a chinois or fine sieve and into an ovenproof dish. You'll need something that has a depth of around 5cm (2in). Set the tray inside a larger tray and fill halfway up with hot water to make a water bath. Bake at 110°C (230°F) for 60–90 minutes. When the cream is cooked, it will no longer look liquid when you give the tray a gentle shake but rather have a gelatinous wobble. Let the cream cool to room temperature then chill slightly before serving.

Clementine granita, clementine leaf cream with pumpkin seed oil

I can't take credit for the genius touch of pumpkin seed oil on this dish. That was a James Lowe move mid-service one evening at Lyle's, which transformed this dish from very nice to great. It's important to use Styrian pumpkin seed oil here if you can. It's produced in Austria and Slovenia from Styrian pumpkins and is an incredible dark green, almost black, colour with a beautifully nutty flavour. It's easy to find online and well worth tracking down.

serves 1

1 tbsp citrus sugar *(p147)*

1–2 clementines

1 generous tbsp clementine leaf cream *(p137)*

2–3 tbsp clementine granita *(p137)*

1 tbsp pumpkin seed oil

Make the citrus sugar according to the recipe *(p147)* using a mix of clementine, lemon and citron zests if you can.

To prepare the clementines, cut a thin slice off the top and bottom so that they sit flat. Using a small, sharp knife, carefully cut the peel and outer membrane from the fruit, following its natural shape. Cut through the centre into 4–6 wedges depending on the size of the clementine. Dry the wedges in a dehydrator or low oven for 1½ hours at 60°C (140°F) to intensify their flavour and give a gently chewy texture.

Place a bowl in the freezer to chill 30 minutes before serving. Scoop the clementine cream into the centre of the chilled bowl. Add the semi-dried clementine wedges and sprinkle a little of the citrus sugar on top. Cover everything with the clementine granita. Top generously with more of the citrus sugar and drizzle over the pumpkin seed oil.

LEMONS & CITRONS

Just as rhubarb appears right when we need some brightness – both visually and digestively – the citrus season gets into full swing, too. The sunshine tones of yellows, oranges and reds somehow seem brighter, more intense, due to the grey colour and often grey mood of January. In the UK, they are a reminder of sunnier climes and that the warm shores of the Mediterranean will still be there to be basked in come summer. Even though you'll find lemons in my kitchen throughout the year, they will always feel extra special in winter. There are hundreds of varieties and crosses being grown; it's always exciting to encounter a new variety and see where it leads you in the kitchen. The deeply fragrant lemons from the south of Italy are my go-to for most of the year but my favourite lemon will forever be the Meyer. It was a name I knew from reading American recipes but I had no concept of the flavour or why Meyer lemons were so special until moving to New York. Originally found growing in China, this juicy variety – thought to be a hybrid between the lemon and either an orange or mandarin – was introduced to the United States in the early 20th century. They were a firm fixture during my time at Gramercy

Tavern, which is where I first succumbed to their charms. Meyers are at the gentler end of the lemon scale. Their juice is less acidic than standard lemons and their skin thinner with barely any bitterness. They have a true sunshine tone: a warm yellow with a hint of orange, similar in colour to a ripe quince, which perhaps contributes to my admiration; and a distinct, gently floral smell. I confess to placing them, rather whimsically, in a bowl with quinces in my kitchen when the overlapping seasons permit, enjoying the golden yellows together and revelling in their perfumes. Thankfully, some growers in Europe have started to produce them so we can have the joy this side of the Atlantic from December to early March.

I am often jealous of the sheer number of citrus varieties being grown by specialists in America but then I remember the Mediterranean coast and its truly exceptional producers with their cedros, mandarins, oroblancos and all manner of variants. These recipes are easily adaptable to the different citrus fruit available. As ever, take these techniques and ideas and apply them to whichever interesting examples you find.

Meyer lemon sherbet

Sherbets are somewhere between a sorbet and an ice cream. A base of fruit and milk but without any cream or eggs. In this recipe, the acid of the citrus thickens the milk just as it would in a posset, while the fat in the milk captures the perfume of the Meyer lemon but allows the zippy acidity of the juice to come forward. I love that tension between creamy mouthfeel and vivid acidity. This recipe works with a variety of citrus fruits and flavours – clementine and Darjeeling tea is a particularly winning combination. Just be aware that you need a high acid content to thicken the milk. If you use a fruit that's not as acidic, you'll need to use the same amount of lemon juice as your chosen citrus juice.

makes 1 litre (2 pints)

620ml (2½ cups) whole milk

190g (1 scant cup) caster (superfine) sugar

10g (1 tbsp) Meyer lemon zest, from 7–8 lemons

210ml (1 scant cup) citrus juice (this can be up to 2:1 Meyer:regular lemon)

Combine the milk, sugar and lemon zest in a medium pan. Heat to a simmer to dissolve the sugar and help infuse the flavour of the zest into the milk. Cool to room temperature then chill until the milk is completely cold. If the milk is at all warm, it will split rather than thicken when you add the lemon juice.

Whisk in the lemon juice. Blend the sherbet in batches at high speed until completely smooth. Chill in the fridge for at least 4 hours. Churn in an ice-cream machine then transfer to a container and leave to set in the freezer before serving.

Lemon purée

Anyone who has ever segmented a citrus fruit knows you're left with a huge pile of waste and only a small amount of usable fruit. Since Meyer lemons are so special, I want to get as much from each fruit as possible so whenever I juice or segment one, I keep the peel and trimmings in the fridge until I have enough to make a batch of this purée. Although I've given quantities here, really this recipe is about ratios so work with whatever amount of peel you have. When you cook the blanched peel, you'll fill a pan with 2 parts peel to 1 part sugar before adding enough water to cover. You can then adjust the seasonings accordingly.

1kg (2¼lb) Meyer lemon peel and zest

500g (2½ cups) caster (superfine) sugar, plus extra to taste

50g (3 tbsp plus 1 tsp) unsalted butter, at room temperature

salt, to taste

lemon juice, to taste

Add the peel to a large pan of cold water and bring to a rolling boil. Drain the peel and refresh it in ice-cold water. Return to the pan with more cold water and bring to the boil again before repeating the refreshing and boiling once more. You will have blanched the peel three times in total. This will help to remove any bitterness and start to tenderize it.

Put the drained peel into a clean pan and add the sugar. Pour in enough cold water to just cover. Stir to distribute the sugar and then place a circle of baking parchment (a cartouche) directly on top to keep the peel submerged. Simmer gently until tender; a spoon should easily push through the peel.

Strain the peel, reserving the liquid. Blend at high speed, adding a little of the reserved cooking liquor to achieve a smooth purée. Mix in the butter while it is still warm. The fat helps to mellow the purée and round out any remaining bitterness. You can make this dairy-free by substituting the butter with 50ml (¼ cup) of olive or rapeseed oil but the flavour profile will be slightly different. Season with the salt, sugar and lemon juice. Go slowly, tasting between each addition until you feel it is balanced. Trust your palate.

Preserved lemons

This may seem an odd recipe to find in a book about seasonal British desserts but trust me when I say that preserved lemons are very useful in the sweet world. Finely diced and folded through a lemon purée, crème patissière or ice cream, they add pops of intense flavour as well as a subtle savouriness. They can bring another dimension to citrus dishes which are often all about the balance of sweet and sour. The amount of salt needed depends on the size of your lemons and your jar.

---

organic unwaxed lemons

coarse sea salt

Trim the stem end of the lemons. Stand each lemon vertically and cut a cross three-quarters of the way down so that it opens like a flower. Sprinkle the open lemon with salt. Repeat with all your lemons. Pack them into a sterilized jar, layering with more salt. Squeeze them gently as you press them in to release some of their juices. Make sure the lemons are covered with salt as you reach the top of the jar. Seal and leave somewhere cool for 3–6 months, depending on the size of your lemons – and your patience. To use, rinse under running water to remove any excess salt then discard the flesh; the preserved peel is the real treasure.

Preserved lemon vinegar

You've waited a mere three months for preserved lemons so what's another couple of weeks for this delicious vinegar? This is an amazing seasoning for sweet and savoury dishes. The recipe gives a generous quantity but I use it constantly, whether dressing roasted cauliflower and courgettes, marinating chicken or making these meringues.

---

makes 500ml (2 cups)

2 large preserved lemons

500ml (2 cups) Riesling, Moscatel or apple cider vinegar

Rinse the preserved lemons well under running water to remove any excess salt and pack them into a clean jar. Heat the vinegar to just below a simmer and then pour over the lemons before sealing the jar. Alternatively, you can vacuum seal the lemons and vinegar together in which case there is no need to heat the vinegar first. Leave to infuse for two weeks.

If you want to go even further, you can candy the pickled, preserved lemons. Follow the instructions for the candied Buddha's hand (p145), ignoring the blanching and softening stages.

Preserved lemon vinegar meringue

The vinegar here adds a salty, aromatic quality to the meringue while the acid balances the sweetness from the sugar and helps to stabilize the proteins in the egg white, allowing for a chewy, mallowy centre.

---

makes about 20 meringues

150g (⅔ cup) egg whites, from about 5 eggs

25ml (1 tbsp plus 2 tsp) preserved lemon vinegar

4g (1 scant tsp) salt

300g (1½ cups) caster (superfine) sugar

zest of 1 large lemon

15g (1 heaped tbsp) preserved lemon, diced

Preheat the oven to 120°C (250°F). Combine the egg whites, vinegar and salt in the bowl of a mixer. Whisk at medium speed until soft peaks form. Don't be tempted to turn up the speed or your meringue will be less stable. Add the sugar a third at a time, making sure it's fully incorporated before adding more. Include the lemon zest with the final addition. You should have a thick, glossy meringue. Fold in the preserved lemon. Line two trays with baking parchment or silicone mats and either pipe the meringues into circles or use two dessert spoons to form them into rough quenelles. Make an indent in the centre of each meringue so you have a shallower middle. Bake for 1½ hours until the meringues have a crisp exterior and a mallowy centre.

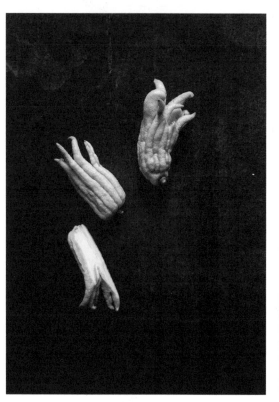

Candied Buddha's hand

You won't forget the first time you see this otherworldly variety of citron with its long, finger-like protrusions. Prized for its highly aromatic peel, the Buddha's hand generally has no juice or flesh. Although it can be zested with a Microplane, I think it works best candied. I love building citrus tarts with the different varieties and textures of citrons and lemons around at the time. Thin coins of Buddha's hand look particularly beautiful on top. This technique can be applied to any form of citrus peel. Cooking times will vary dramatically from fruit to fruit depending on the thickness of the peel. It's important to remember that the peel should be tender before it goes into the syrup and that it needs to remain completely submerged as it cooks.

1 Buddha's hand

250g (1¼ cups) caster (superfine) sugar

Slice the fingers of the Buddha's hand into coins about 3mm (⅛in) thick all the way to the stem. Place in a saucepan, cover with cold water and bring to the boil. Drain, return to the pan and cover with fresh cold water. Bring to the boil then simmer for about 10 minutes over a medium heat until the fruit is just tender.

In a clean pan, combine the sugar with 250ml (1 cup) of water and heat gently to dissolve the sugar. Drain the Buddha's hand and add to the pan. Bring up to a simmer then place a circle of baking parchment directly on top of the fruit and cook over a medium heat for 30–40 minutes. The Buddha's hand should now be translucent and the cooking syrup will have reduced and thickened.

Store the candied fruit in its syrup in the fridge. You can also dry the candied fruit by laying it out on racks and leaving in a cool room overnight before coating it in granulated sugar.

Cedro

After the Meyer, this is the citrus fruit I get most excited about. The cedro (or *cedrat* in French) is a large citron with very thick peel and very little flesh, that looks like a super-sized lemon. What's extraordinary is that the thick peel can be sliced then eaten raw; it lacks astringency or intense bitterness but instead has a sherbetty, zippy flavour. It can commonly be found in Italian mostardas or candied in large chunks. If you want to candy it then follow the instructions as above for the Buddha's hand but bear in mind that each stage will take longer to cook as your fruit is so much larger.

My favourite way to prepare cedros for desserts is to cut them into 1–2mm (1/16in) slices so you get the full cross-section of the fruit. An electric meat slicer is definitely the best tool for the job here as a standard mandoline isn't wide enough. If you do use a mandoline, cut the cedros to a suitable size first. The slices can then be blanched in a 1:1 sugar syrup for 30–60 seconds until just tender. These blanched slices are lovely just as they are alongside a panna cotta, or on top of a Danish, but for even more flavour they can be grilled over charcoal as in the dessert at the end of this section *(p148)*.

Meyer lemon sherbet with preserved lemon meringue

This is definitely a dessert celebrating the acidity and brightness of the fruit. It is sprinkled with a citrus sugar that can be made with a mix of lemon, Meyer lemon, Buddha's hand or whatever special citrus you can get hold of. The double cream hidden in the centre acts as a palate break from the strong flavours through the rest of the dessert. You want a cream that is so thick it doesn't need to be whipped, just spooned in. I like to use Ivy House cream, which is from an extraordinary farm in Somerset that produces the thickest, richest Jersey double cream available. Clotted cream would be a good substitute or any unpasteurized double cream.

for the citrus sugar

140g (¾ cup) caster (superfine) sugar

8g (1½ tsp) salt

12g (1 tbsp plus 1 tsp) citrus zest

Blend all the ingredients together in a spice grinder or mortar and pestle. The sugar will feel wet from all the oils released, which is exactly what you want. Store in an airtight container in the freezer.

serves 1

2 large scoops Meyer lemon sherbet *(p141)*

1 tbsp lemon purée *(p141)*

3 Meyer lemon segments

1 preserved lemon vinegar meringue *(p142)*

½ tbsp double (heavy) cream

1 tbsp citrus sugar *(above)*

The sherbet should be relatively soft for this dish so temper it by transferring to the fridge for 30 minutes until it is sufficiently malleable. Place a 10cm (4in) metal cooking ring in a bowl. Spread the lemon purée in the base of the ring. Cut each lemon segment into two or three pieces and place on top of the purée. Break the preserved lemon meringue into bite-sized chunks and add to the ring. Put the double cream in the centre of the meringue layer then fill the ring with the Meyer lemon sherbet. Flatten off the top to give a level and even surface. Remove the metal ring and generously sprinkle the citrus sugar over the top of the sherbet. You should be able to see the different layers of lemon on the side of this cylindrical dessert.

Grilled cedro with yeast ice cream and puff pastry

This dish is a great example of how a strong repertoire of base elements makes putting a new creation together feel straightforward. The yeast ice cream is also paired with apples in rosemary butter (p99) and the puff pastry is used in two other dishes: one with honey and beeswax ice cream and apples (p170) and the other with brown butter ice cream and marmalade (p183). When we first tasted the grilled cedro slices, the consensus in the kitchen was that they reminded everyone of eating crêpes with lemon. The thin discs with their silky texture and crispy edges mixed with the sweetness from the blanching syrup and the unmistakable lemon flavour were reminiscent of the French classic. That food memory always makes me think of a kitchen filled with the smell of buttery batter. We spent many a Saturday morning making pancakes in my family, with a particular pan and a ladle reserved for that sole purpose. The yeast ice cream conjures up the same buttery smells, so it seemed like the perfect companion to sit alongside the grilled cedro and rich puff pastry.

serves 1

8 slices of blanched cedro (p145)

zest of 1 lemon

lemon juice, to season

preserved lemon vinegar, to season (p142)

2cm (¾in) slice of cooked puff pastry (p199)

1 large scoop of yeast ice cream (p196)

If you don't have access to a charcoal grill, these also work well in a griddle pan over a high heat. Grill the blanched cedro on both sides over a high heat until the edges are slightly charred and they're starting to caramelize. As the slices come off the grill, grate the lemon zest over the top. Season the grilled slices lightly with lemon juice and preserved lemon vinegar to help brighten everything up after the heat of the grill.

Put a shallow bowl or plate in the freezer to chill 30 minutes before serving. Place the slice of puff pastry just off-centre in the dish so that the cut side is facing up and you can see all the beautiful layers. Scoop a large quenelle of yeast ice cream the same length as the puff pastry slice and place it directly alongside. Completely cover the ice cream with the grilled cedro, folding and twisting the slices so that they look like dense, textural petals. The organic appearance of the cedro should be in direct contrast to the linear form of the puff pastry.

BLOOD ORANGES

The product of a natural mutation that developed in oranges grown around the Mediterranean in Italy and Spain, blood oranges get their deep blush of colour from the region's warm days and cold nights. This darker pigmentation is often strongest at the blossom end, which is where you'll find the sweetest part of any fruit. There are three common varieties: Moro, Tarocco and Sanguinello. Moro and Tarocco hail from Italy, while Sanguinello originates from Spain. Moros have a perfect sweet spot in January and February when their skin flushes a deep reddish purple and the balance of sugar and acid is just right. Early Moro oranges tend to be more aggressively acidic so I like to wait a few weeks into January to use them. Taroccos appear from January to April. Flavour-wise, they have a beautiful raspberry note but are less predictably intense in colour. In our January excitement, blood oranges are often paired with the acid-pink forced rhubarb that appears at the same time. Rhubarb and orange are wonderful together but I'm firmly of the belief that each should be celebrated in its own right.

Blood orange sherbet powder

This is a little bit of magic to sprinkle over any blood orange dish. I also like to use it to coat *pâtes de fruit*. When I'm making dehydrated orange wedges, or juicing the fruit for sorbet, I remove the thin zest. Using a good peeler will help you get only the oil-rich top layer and none of the bitter pith. Dry this peel in a dehydrator set to 60°C (140°F) or in a very low oven overnight. It should be completely dry before the next step.

25g (1oz) dried peel *(as above)*
50g (¼ cup) caster (superfine) sugar
5g (1 tsp) citric acid
2g (½ tsp) salt

Combine the ingredients together in a spice grinder or mortar and pestle. Grind until you have a very fine powder. This can be stored in a sealed container and kept for several months somewhere cool and dry.

Blood orange sorbet

This sorbet will be delicious whether your blood oranges are lightly burnished or deep red in colour but will look more dramatic with mid- to late-season fruit that has deeper pigmentation. The addition of the whole fruit blended through the sorbet base helps to give body and an extra pectin boost for a smoother, creamier texture. This recipe also works brilliantly with clementines.

---

makes 1 litre (2 pints)

---

17 blood oranges

170g (¾ cup plus 1½ tbsp) caster (superfine) sugar

---

pinch of salt, to taste

---

lemon juice, to taste

---

citric acid, to taste

Juice all but 2 of the oranges. This should yield about 750ml (3 cups) of juice. Cut the 2 remaining unpeeled blood oranges into rough wedges. Combine the sugar with the orange pieces in a blender or food processor and blend until you have a smooth purée. Whisk this mixture into the juice.

PRO TIP
Alternatively, if you have a refractometer, add two-thirds of the purée then check the sugar level. You are aiming for 25°Bx. Add more of the sugar and orange mix until you reach the correct sugar level; you should need pretty much all the sugary purée.

Taste the sorbet base and season with a small pinch of salt, lemon juice or citric acid if it needs brightening up slightly. Chill, covered, in the fridge for at least 4 hours.

Once the sorbet base is well chilled, pour into an ice-cream machine and churn until frozen. Transfer to a lidded plastic container and keep in the freezer until ready to serve. Transfer the container to the fridge about 30 minutes before serving.

Dehydrated wedges and crisps

Not so much a recipe as a few tips gleaned from many citrus seasons in various pastry sections. Don't try to dehydrate individual segments of citrus; they go crispy and are a disappointment. Instead, go for bigger wedges. The extra mass stops them from disappearing into nothing, and you get a slightly chewy piece of citrus with an intense flavour.

As you'll see from other recipes in this book, I'm a fan of a little chewy bite of fruit in a dessert. Cut the top and bottom off the blood orange so you have flat surfaces to work with. Using a sharp knife cut down the sides of the orange to remove the peel and pith, following the shape of the fruit. You want to remove all the pith but not lose too much of the juicy flesh. Cut into 4–6 wedges, depending on the size of your fruit, going straight through the centre of the segments rather than along the membrane lines. Any membrane left on the outer edge of the wedges can become quite tough once they've been dried. Dry the pieces of blood orange in a dehydrator at 60–65°C (140–150°F) for about 1 hour, or in an oven preheated to 60°C (140°F) for 1–1½ hours. They will have reduced in volume slightly and be dry to the touch. You can carry on dehydrating if you want something with a more dramatic texture.

Now to blood orange crisps. The best way to achieve super-thin citrus crisps is to freeze the fruit before slicing. I would often have a stash of oranges in the freezer ready to slice. If you have a well-sharpened meat slicer, you'll be able to get a perfect, complete slice without this step. Otherwise, you'll end up with raggedy, half slices. Take the oranges from the freezer about 15 minutes before you start to allow them to defrost ever so slightly. Cut off the end of the orange to give a flat surface and then slice 0.5–1mm thick rounds using a mandoline or meat slicer. You can also cut thin slices with a sharp knife, in which case I would chill the oranges until very cold but not quite frozen.

Lay the slices on a dehydrator rack lined with a silicone mat (or you can wrap the tray in cling film to create a flat surface). Dry in a dehydrator at 60–65°C (140–150°F) for 4–5 hours, or in an oven preheated to 60°C (140°F) for 5–6 hours, until completely crisp and brittle.

Blood orange marmalade

I love a soft-set marmalade as part of a citrus dessert. Its flavour is subtly different from using candied, dried or fresh fruit. I pair it with brown butter ice cream (p175) for a dish that tastes like breakfast in all the best ways. For any jam or marmalade making, I always consult *Five Seasons of Jam* by Lillie O'Brien of London Borough of Jam. Lillie often uses lesser-known berries and fruits and pairs them with many of the flavourings you'll find in the *Flowers, leaves & herbs* section of this book, so we speak the same fruity language. If you like jam making or preserving, I can't recommend her book highly enough. The fig leaf and peach jam is utterly heavenly. But back to marmalade; this is based on Lillie's recipe for Seville orange marmalade which yields excellent set, clarity and flavour.

---

makes about 6 x 200g (7oz) jars

1kg (2¼lb) unwaxed blood oranges

1.2kg (10 cups) caster (superfine) sugar

juice of 2 lemons

Remove the green nub left from the stalk of the oranges then add the whole oranges to a deep saucepan with a lid and pour in 1.5 litres (1½ quarts) of water. Bring to the boil then reduce to a gentle simmer for 30–40 minutes. Remove the pan from the heat and leave the oranges to cool in the liquid. I often cook them and then leave them till the next day before starting the next stage.

Remove the oranges from the now cool liquid. Reserve 1 litre (1 quart) of the orange water. Cut the cooked oranges in half and scoop out the flesh. Use a ladle or the back of a spoon to press the flesh through a sieve set over the reserved water to capture as much of the juice as possible. Once you've squeezed out the juice, discard the flesh.

Finely slice the peel (or cut however you desire, though I think a fine shred works best as part of a dessert) and add to a clean preserving pan along with the juicy water, sugar and lemon juice. Bring to the boil and cook for around 20 minutes over a high heat until you reach the setting point of 105°C (221°F). Remove from the heat and leave to rest for 10 minutes to help the peel distribute evenly. Pour into warm, sterilized jars and seal immediately.

Blood orange with olive oil ice cream

The new season olive oil starts to arrive at the end of November and is resplendent in its verdant colour and flavour. It is one of the joyful pick-me-ups you need in winter, just as blood oranges are. This dessert is inspired by a salad of sliced oranges dressed with olive oil and seasoned with salt, which is commonly served after the *primi* in the south of Italy. It cleanses and invigorates your palate after a heavy main course. The candied fennel seeds add little bursts of anise which sit beautifully alongside the berry, citrus of the blood orange. You want a peppery olive oil here, not one with too many bitter, artichoke notes.

for the blood orange and olive oil dressing

makes 200ml (1 scant cup)

juice of 4 blood oranges

100ml (scant ½ cup) new-season olive oil

Pour the blood orange juice into a small saucepan and bring to the boil. Turn down the heat and simmer until reduced by half. Strain the reduced juice, leave to cool and then chill. The ratio for the dressing is 1 part olive oil to 1 part reduced orange juice. Whisk together the two ingredients and taste. Note that it is a split dressing so will not emulsify.

for the crystallized fennel seeds

10g (1 tbsp) fennel seeds

30g (2 tbsp) caster (superfine) sugar

Toast the fennel seeds in a dry frying pan over a medium heat until they start to give off their fragrant aroma. Put the sugar in a saucepan, add 30ml (2 tbsp) of water and bring to the boil until the sugar has dissolved. Stir in the warm fennel seeds and continue cooking over a low to medium heat, stirring constantly until the sugar begins to crystallize. It will turn white and opaque and coat the seeds. If the syrup does not crystallize, sprinkle in a tiny pinch of sugar and the introduction of new crystals will kick-start the chain reaction. Pour the crystallized seeds onto a tray to cool. These will last for months in a sealed container.

serves 1

1 scoop olive oil ice cream *(p181)*

4 pieces dehydrated blood orange *(p153)*

2 tbsp blood orange and olive oil dressing

pinch of crystallized fennel seeds

6–8 blood orange crisps *(p153)*

pinch of Maldon salt

1 tsp blood orange sherbet powder *(p151)*

Place a shallow bowl in the freezer to chill 30 minutes before serving. Scoop a large quenelle of olive oil ice cream into the centre of the bowl. Using a warm spoon, flatten off the scoop, making it wider with a slight indent in the centre. Cut the dehydrated blood orange pieces in half and toss in the dressing. Spoon these on top of the ice cream, allowing the dressing to spill over and pool around the base of the ice cream. Sprinkle a pinch of the crystallized fennel seeds over the blood orange. Don't be heavy-handed with the fennel seeds, you want a subtle surprise every other mouthful not a knockout punch of anise through the whole dish. Lightly crush the blood orange crisps over the dish to cover the fruit then add a few flakes of Maldon salt. Generously dust with sherbet powder.

FORCED RHUBARB

I love fully embracing the warmth and richness of winter desserts throughout December, but January tends to need a fresh approach. Don't get me wrong, I'll use apples and pears as long as the season permits but, come January, there is a gentle shift in people's palates away from the decadence of the festive period to something brighter, cleaner, lighter. Thankfully, this is just when forced rhubarb appears. Unashamedly neon pink, it cheers up the dark first quarter of the year. The best plants are found in the Rhubarb Triangle of West Yorkshire, a nine square-mile area that takes in Wakefield, Morley and Rothwell. The best of the best comes from B. Tomlinson & Son, a family-run business which has been growing rhubarb for four generations. The arrival of its iconic red boxes containing the Harbinger and Arrow varieties excites chefs all over the country. Forced rhubarb plants spend two years outside before being moved to warm, dark sheds where they're tricked into thinking spring has arrived. The crowns of rhubarb use the stored energy in their roots to grow, rather than sunlight, resulting in fruit (ok, technically it is a vegetable) that's very tender and aggressively pink as no green chlorophyll is produced. Walking into those sheds – nondescript buildings set against a nondescript landscape – is wondrous, the warm air filled with a forest of fuchsia stems with acid yellow leaves lit only by candles for the pickers to work by.

Rhubarb juice

The glorious colour of this juice is so joyful. I use it as the poaching liquor for all rhubarb recipes. Forced rhubarb is much more tender than the later outdoor varieties but it can still break a juicer if you're not careful. When a box of rhubarb arrives, my first job is to grade the stalks. Some recipes work best with stalks of a certain size, such as the rhubarb chewies or if you want to make poached strips of a particular width. The fattest stalks are best for finely dicing or juicing.

Divide your stalks into their various uses then trim the leaves as close to the top as possible – the leaves are poisonous so should be thrown away with your food waste. Trim the base of the stem, cutting at an angle so that you are just trimming the edge that has been pulled from the crown. I so often see chefs chopping off huge chunks of rhubarb when they are "trimming" it. It is a beautifully grown and often expensive ingredient so make use of as much of the plant as you can. You can square off the ends of the stalks at this point and add them to the juicing pile.

Chop roughly into 1–2cm (½–¾in) chunks. Cutting it this small prevents the juicer struggling so much with the fibres. Trust me, you'll burn out far fewer motors this way. You can either use an electric juicer here or a blender. If using a blender, pour the resulting pulp into a clean tea towel and squeeze all the juice out through a chinois or fine sieve. Once all the rhubarb is juiced, it will be frothy and a little cloudy. Be sure to really squeeze out the leftover pulp as there will still be a huge amount of juice in there. Set the pulp aside.

Pour the rhubarb juice into a saucepan and bring to just under the boil, then remove from the heat. The impurities will rise to the surface, so either skim them off with a spoon or pass the juice through a fine chinois or sieve lined with muslin. You'll be left with a vivid, clarified juice ready to be seasoned however you wish. As a rule of thumb, you'll get about 700ml of juice from 1kg (2⅔ cups of juice from 2¼lb) of rhubarb.

Rhubarb powder
Use the leftover pulp to make rhubarb powder: simply spread in a thin layer and dry on a very low heat in a dehydrator or oven before blending in a spice grinder.

Rhubarb granita

makes 500ml (1 pint)

400ml (1¾ cups) rhubarb juice

100g (½ cup) caster (superfine) sugar

Whisk the sugar into the rhubarb juice. It will taste slightly too sweet but the sweetness will dull as it freezes. If you have a refractometer, you're aiming for a sugar level of 15°Bx. Pour into a shallow container and freeze.

Remove from the freezer every hour or two and scrape through the granita with a fork. The sugar is heavier so will naturally freeze on the bottom along with the solids in the fruit, so it is important to keep mixing the granita as it freezes so you get an even final product. I like medium-sized ice crystals in this granita, not so fine that it's like snow. Somehow, it captures the light better, showing off the colour of the fruit and giving the granita its own distinct texture.

Rhubarb compôte

The goal here is to cook the compôte hot and fast, then chill it down quickly to preserve the intense colour and avoid it tasting stewed. What you are after here is something that is vibrant both to look at and to taste. The diced rhubarb is barely cooked so retains its texture.

makes 850g (1lb 14oz)

375g (12½oz) trimmed rhubarb, diced into 5mm (¼in) pieces

18g (2¼ tsp) cornflour (cornstarch)

250g (8oz) trimmed rhubarb, thinly sliced

125g (½ cup) rhubarb juice (p156)

75g (⅓ cup) caster (superfine) sugar

Put the diced rhubarb in a bowl, sprinkle on the cornflour and mix to ensure that each piece is well coated.

Next, combine the thinly sliced rhubarb, juice and sugar in a saucepan with a tightly fitting lid. Bring to a rapid boil with the lid on for 3–4 minutes until the rhubarb has completely broken down to a purée. You can speed this along by breaking it apart with a whisk. Mix in the cornflour-coated rhubarb and return to the boil over a high heat for 30–60 seconds. Taste to check the cornflour has cooked out, then immediately remove from the heat. The diced rhubarb will retain its texture and carry on cooking slightly in the residual heat. Pour into a plastic container and chill.

Rhubarb sorbet

This is one of my absolute favourite flavours. The sorbet somehow manages to have a creaminess to it that sits beautifully alongside the natural acidity.

makes 1.5kg (3lb 3oz)

1kg (2¼lb) rhubarb, roughly chopped

500ml (2 cups) rhubarb juice (p156)

350g (1¾ cups) caster (superfine) sugar

Combine the chopped rhubarb, juice and 250g (1¼ cups) of the sugar in a large bowl, cover tightly with cling film and then cook over a gently simmering pan of water for 30–40 minutes.

PRO TIP
Alternatively, if you have a sous-vide machine, vacuum seal the rhubarb mix and cook at 65°C (150°F) for 20–25 minutes until tender.

The goal is to cook the rhubarb in a way that maintains vibrancy and avoids dulled, stewed flavours.

Once the rhubarb is completely tender (you should be able to squash a piece between your fingers), put it in a blender along with its juices and process to a smooth purée. While the rhubarb is still warm, whisk in the remaining sugar. The sorbet base should taste intensely rhubarby and most importantly with just enough sugar to make it delicious. If you have a refractometer, you're aiming for a sugar level of 25°Bx. Chill, covered, in the fridge for at least 4 hours.

Pour into an ice-cream machine and churn until frozen. Transfer to a lidded plastic container and keep in the freezer until ready to serve. Transfer the container to the fridge about 30 minutes before serving.

Poached rhubarb strips

The rhubarb is cut so thin here that it takes very minimal cooking. If you can leave it in the sweetened juice for a few hours to chill before serving you will get a more intense colour.

makes 250g (9oz)

250g (generous ½lb) rhubarb, trimmed and cut into 10cm (4in) lengths

250g (1 cup) rhubarb juice *(p156)*

75g (⅓ cup) caster (superfine) sugar

Slice the rhubarb into 1mm thin strips using either a mandoline or electric slicer. Lay the strips in a plastic container so they're all facing the same way.

Pour the rhubarb juice into a saucepan, add the sugar and bring to the boil. Remove from the heat and pour over the rhubarb strips. Leave to cool to room temperature and then refrigerate. This method also works with 1–2cm (½–¾in) chunks.

Rhubarb chewies

These take about 24 hours to make but are probably one of the best things I came up with at Lyle's, so worth the wait. They're like Haribo Tangfastics but classier. Little chewy, zippy pieces of rhubarb that can – and should – be added to every rhubarb dessert, always.

makes 60

500g (1 generous lb) rhubarb

500ml (2 cups) rhubarb juice *(p156)*

650g (3¼ cups) caster (superfine) sugar

30g (3 tbsp) malic acid

Use rhubarb stems that are 1.5–2.5cm (½–1in) wide; any narrower and they'll dry too fast and become crispy, any wider and you won't get that optimal chew. Cut them into 2cm (¾in) chunks and put in a container that has a lid. Pour the rhubarb juice into a saucepan with 150g (¾ cup) of the sugar and bring to the boil. Note: if you're scaling up, make a syrup that has 30 per cent sugar to juice so 300g (1½ cups) of sugar per 1 litre (1 quart) of juice. It will taste sweet but the rhubarb doesn't sit in the juice for long, so won't have time to absorb much sugar. Pour the just boiling rhubarb juice over the cut rhubarb and cover. Leave to poach for around 30 minutes but start checking after 15 minutes. The edges of the rhubarb will have softened slightly but the pieces should be firm enough for you to pick up and squeeze easily. It will still taste like raw rhubarb at this stage. Drain off the poaching liquor. This can be reused multiple times and then can go into the sorbet or granita base.

Lay the lightly poached pieces in a single layer on dehydrator racks and dry for about 1 hour in a dehydrator set to 50–60°C (120–140°F). Alternatively, dry in a low oven set to 50–60°C (120–140°F). The rhubarb is ready when it no longer feels wet to the touch and is starting to slightly pucker at the edges. Put the remaining sugar in a bowl and stir in the malic acid. Toss the rhubarb into the mix until lightly coated and return to the dehydrator for 2 hours. Repeat the sugar toss two more times, returning it to the dehydrator for 2 hours between each toss. You may have to change the rack after the first toss as it can become very sticky. Leave to dry for a further 5–6 hours after the final toss. The rhubarb should be dry and chewy with a sweet, tangy coating of sugar. Be warned: they'll disappear alarmingly fast.

Rhubarb rice pudding

I always looked forward to the start of the
rhubarb season as this dish would make it
onto the lunch menu. It is a bowl of happiness
and comfort.

serves 1

200ml (1 scant cup) raw or very thick double (heavy)
cream

1–2 tbsp rhubarb compôte *(p158)*

3–4 generous tbsp rice pudding, chilled *(p195)*

6–8 rhubarb chewies *(p159)*

1 tsp rhubarb powder *(p157)*

Gently warm the cream in a small pan until it reaches
45–50°C (113–120°F). Pour it into a bowl and whisk
until it just holds its shape. Spoon the compôte into
the bottom of a small, high-sided bowl. Top with the
rice pudding, followed by the rhubarb chewies. Pipe
or spoon the cream on top to cover the chewies and
rice pudding. Dust generously with rhubarb powder.

PRO TIP
Alternatively, put the warmed cream into a whipped
cream dispenser and twist in one cream whipper
bulb then shake gently to aerate; it should just be
able to hold its shape but not be heavily whipped.

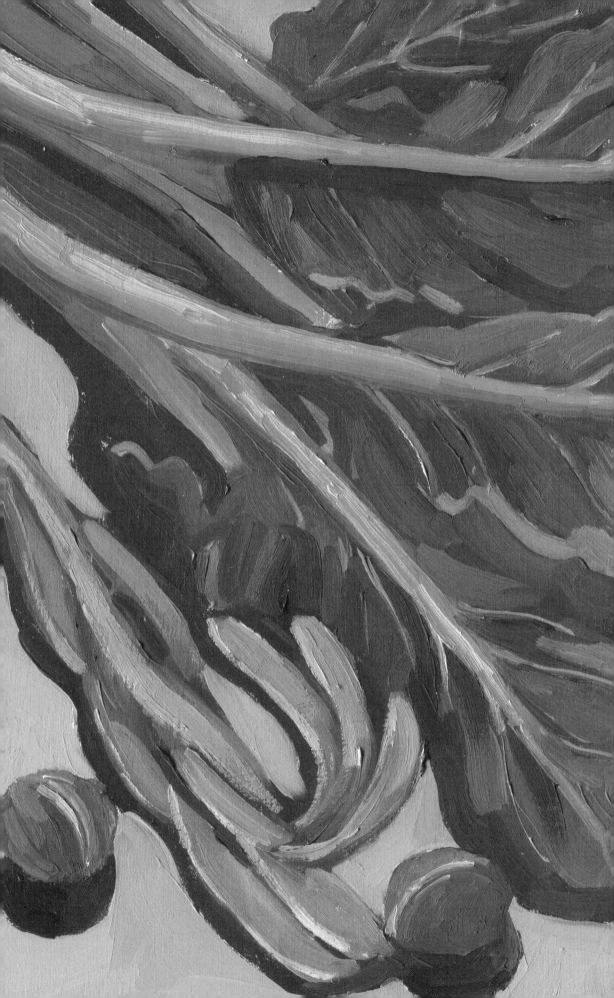

spring

SUGARS

When it comes to any conversation around ethical and short-chain sourcing, sugar is the elephant in the room. The UK was built on the sugar trade and we have caused horrendous harm in search of sweetness; there is no escaping that fact. It is a product that comes from far away but, rather than being considered exotic, is utterly ubiquitous, cheap and plentiful. I believe so strongly in producer relationships and the power they have but I admit I trip up when it comes to sugar. Fairtrade and direct trade sugars are out there but I often wonder if that's enough (in fact, I know it's not). As a commodity ingredient, it feels out of our control, the market determines the price, but we always have our buying power and the ability to enact change on a small scale. It is a start. The real shift would be to wean ourselves off of highly processed sugars, to use other sources of sweetness: honey, fruit molasses, maple and birch syrups. But I think that is a long road and requires a real commitment to reeducating our palates. We are not used to the flavour of sugar but rather its chemical effect on our tongues and energy levels. Start to think of it as a flavour, not just as structure and sweetness. The slow shift can start with the use of unrefined and raw sugars bought from more direct sources and grown in better ways. You can now find Colombian panela sugar in the UK (some brought by sailboat to reduce its carbon footprint), which is a raw cane sugar. It has a very fruity flavour which, when paired thoughtfully, enhances whichever dish it's used in.

Caramel

My first and strongest advice is: do not be afraid. Caramel is not as scary as you think. Anyone who has ever watched a baking show on TV will be convinced that caramel is devilishly difficult to make: it goes wrong, it crystallizes, it's all just too hard. It is *not* the drama it's made out to be. The more you make, the more comfortable you'll get and you will soon realize you are, in fact, in control. Here are some things that will help you on your way:

Choose the right pan and correspondingly sized heat source. You want your sugar to cook quickly so a wide-based pan is a sensible move. Make sure that your hob is heating as much of the pan as you can – the outer edges as well as the centre. The caramel is far less likely to start to crystallize if it's heated evenly throughout. Choose a pan with a light-coloured interior. Non-stick or Teflon-coated pans which are matt black make it more difficult to judge the colour of the caramel. While temperatures are key for many structural properties of sugar, the easiest, quickest and, in my opinion, best way to judge when caramel is done is to use your eyes. Within seconds it can move from slightly too light to perfect to too dark (it's still not scary though, I promise). If you are faffing about with a temperature probe, it can often go over before you can halt the cooking.

There are two ways you can go about caramelizing sugar: with water (wet) and without (dry). With a wet caramel, you add enough water to give a wet sand texture. The sugar crystals dissolve in a liquid first and then caramelize in a liquid, syrup state. There's a danger of crystallization here as any sugar in crystal form that is introduced into the syrup can cause a chain reaction whereby all the sugar tries to return to that crystal state. That's why it's important not to stir the syrup until it has started to caramelize. I like this method when I am doing lots of things at once. I can put the wet caramel on and leave it alone while getting on with another task, coming back to it once it is starting to colour. The more water you add at the start, the longer it will take to evaporate before caramelization occurs. A dry caramel works by transforming the sugar from crystals directly to caramelized liquid. It requires more focus but you are far less likely to get crystallization. You can stir this all the way through (although less frequently at the start). Even if you have some chunks of undissolved sugar as you approach the correct colour, they'll dissolve once you add liquid to the caramel. I like this method for when I want to make a really quick caramel with a smaller volume of sugar and I know I can give it my full attention.

If you are making a dry caramel, go for a moderate heat, take your time and stay in control. If you are making a wet caramel, crank it. While the water is evaporating, you can turn the heat high (I find it rarely crystallizes if it cooks quickly) and then you can turn it down once the mixture starts to caramelize to control how quickly it reaches the perfect colour.

Caramels are very much about personal preference. Do you like them sweeter or with a bitter edge? If you like them sweeter, keep the colour lighter. If you like them bitter, hold your nerve and go darker. If you are using caramel to flavour ice cream, you need to go darker as it will be diluted by the other ingredients so make sure you start with something intense.

This is a good base caramel sauce recipe. It gives a thick, spoonable texture and can easily be adapted to whatever application you choose. I find it helpful to think in ratios to control the outcome and, if necessary, easily manipulate the result. This recipe works as 2:2:1 sugar:liquid:fat. If you want a thinner caramel, use a larger amount of liquid and less butter so a caramel based on 2:3:1 will give you something pourable. If you want to add flavour, infuse the cream before using it to deglaze the pan. This is particularly effective with woody herbs, nuts or coffee. You can also use brown butter or an oil, such as walnut or extra virgin olive oil, as the fat component to change the flavour profile depending on what you want to pair the caramel with.

---

makes 650g (1lb 7oz)

250g (1¼ cups) caster (superfine) sugar

250g (1 cup) double (heavy) cream

125g (1 stick) unsalted butter, diced

5g (1 tsp) Maldon salt

Put the sugar in a clean, high-sided saucepan along with 75ml (⅓ cup) water. Cook over a high heat, swirling the pan to even out the sugar until you have a dark amber caramel. Go as dark as your nerve allows. Remove from the heat and pour in the double cream to deglaze. It will bubble up dramatically which is why it is important to use a high-sided pan. Whisk to make sure all the caramel has been dissolved by the cream.

Add the butter and salt and return to the boil to emulsify the sauce, then whisk well and remove from the heat. Leave to cool slightly before straining through a fine sieve or chinois, then refrigerate.

Fruit caramels

Using fruit juice instead of cream to deglaze the pan will yield a thinner, lighter-textured caramel. My favourite version is with apple juice, as apples and caramel pair so well, but it could easily be adapted to other fruit juices. Choose a fruit whose flavour will be complemented by the caramel rather than overwhelmed by it. Give the juice or unsweetened poaching liquor of pears, plums, blackcurrants or blood oranges a try. I like to reduce the apple juice by half to intensify its flavour before adding it to the caramel, though not all fruit juices will need this step. The base ratio here is 2:1 sugar:liquid so use that as your starting point.

---

makes 575g (1¼lb)

300ml (1¼ cups) apple juice

300g (1½ cups) caster (superfine) sugar

50g (3 tbsp) unsalted butter, diced

4g (1 scant tsp) salt

75ml (⅓ cup) cider vinegar

Pour the apple juice into a saucepan and boil over a medium heat until it has reduced by half. You should end up with roughly 150ml (⅔ cup).

Either make a dry caramel by adding the sugar directly to a hot, clean pan or by adding enough water along with the sugar to create a wet sand texture and heating quickly. Whichever method you choose, you'll need to go dark with the caramel as the bitter edge will combat the sweetness from the fruit juice. If you go by temperature, it should be around 195°C (385°F). Once the caramel gets to the right temperature or colour, remove it from the heat and carefully add the juice. It will bubble up aggressively.

Return to a low heat for 5–10 minutes to dissolve any remaining caramel on the bottom of the pan. Remove from the heat and add the butter and salt, whisking them in well. Once the butter is well emulsified, add the cider vinegar. The latent heat will evaporate the vinegar's abrasive edge leaving you with a gentler sour hit. Strain the caramel then chill.

Whey caramel

A byproduct of cheesemaking, whey is the acidic, lactic liquid that is left behind once the milk has coagulated into curds. In very simplistic terms, the amount of whey drained from the curds will determine the softness or hardness of the cheese produced. It is often treated as waste but some cheesemakers use it to make whey butter or ricotta (Appleby's Dairy in Shropshire and Westcombe Dairy in Somerset are excellent examples). While some cheesemakers and cheesemongers sell whey, you can make it yourself from milk and live yogurt or by straining the liquid from homemade ricotta. This will yield a gentler, more lactic-tasting whey. If you want it to have a slightly funky edge, or be more sour, leave the whey to mature in the fridge for a few days. That sourness is a lovely foil to caramel's inherent sweetness. The whey is all up-front, high notes so I use brown butter to give a nutty finish, which rounds everything out.

---

makes 500g (1lb 2oz)

400g (2 cups) caster (superfine) sugar

200ml (1 scant cup) whey

100g (6½ tbsp) brown butter (p173)

6g (1 generous tsp) salt

Follow the same method as for the basic caramel, deglazing the pan with the whey and then adding the brown butter and salt and mixing until emulsified. I would go slightly lighter on the caramel here. Take it to a medium amber, about 180°C (356°F), before deglazing rather than pushing it right to the edge of bitterness. You want a little sweetness left to balance the whey.

Sugar tuiles

Sugar tuiles are probably the only form of decoration I add to desserts. I enjoy the way they play with transparency and opacity and can provide a hit of texture and flavour. Saying that, I'm not a fan of overly stylized shapes. I think tuiles look their most beautiful broken into irregular shapes.

The recipe utilizes sugar in three forms: liquid glucose, liquid fondant and isomalt (p237). They may be unfamiliar but they are simply sugars with different levels of water, glucose, sucrose and acid. Each one has been treated in a different way to slightly alter its structure and give it distinct properties. The glucose brings the sweet flavour, the fondant adds shine and the isomalt remains transparent even when heated to caramelization temperatures. The base recipe for this is very simple and lasts forever as long as no moisture gets to it. Then the possible flavourings are endless.

150g (⅔ cup) liquid glucose

150g (⅔ cup) pouring fondant (fondant pâtissier)

150g (⅔ cup) isomalt (p237)

Combine the ingredients in a saucepan, adding the glucose first. Place over a medium heat, stirring the mixture to help it melt evenly without caramelizing. It will look thick and chunky to start with but will eventually turn clear as it bubbles away. Cook the mixture to 150°C (302°F). Carefully pour onto a baking tray lined with a silicone mat. It should form a perfectly clear puddle. Leave to cool completely by which point it will have set solid. If you are not using it straight away, it is best to store it in this form as there is less chance of it absorbing any environmental humidity.

Break the tuile mix into smaller pieces (this stage is immensely satisfying but be careful as those shards of sugar are as sharp as glass). Blend at high speed to a fine powder. Store in an airtight container.

Preheat the oven to 160°C (325°F) with no fan or as low a fan as possible. Line a baking sheet with a silicone mat. To get the most even tuiles, use a small sieve or tea strainer to dust the powdered tuile mix onto the tray. If you want a slightly uneven texture, which can look very beautiful, sprinkle the mix by hand but from a height. There is a fine balance between creating a tuile that is very delicate and one that is not so fragile that it shatters in your hand. Bake a couple of practice tuiles to get a feel for how thickly you need to dust on the tuile mix. Too thick and it will be unpleasant to eat.

Bake for 2–4 minutes until the mix changes from opaque powder to melted glass. Keep checking every 30 seconds from the 2-minute mark. Place a piece of baking parchment on a flat work surface (somewhere it will be safe from any splashes of liquid). As soon as you remove the tuile from the oven, flip the silicone mat face-down onto the baking parchment. Leave the tuile to cool for 3–5 minutes and then carefully peel away the silicone mat. Store in an airtight container between layers of baking parchment.

Tuile variations

Now you have the base recipe, you can have a bit of fun. Just bear in mind that any addition to the tuile mix must be completely dry as well as light enough to be supported by the fragile sugar work.

HONEY
Replace 50g (2¼ tbsp) of glucose with 50g (2¼ tbsp) of aromatic honey in the base mix.

FRUIT
Fruit powders are a beautiful addition and help use all of those dehydrated bits of fruit left from poaching or extracting juice. Grind the fruit powder very fine. You can either add the fruit powder when blending the tuile mix or you can dust the powder over the top of a layer of tuile mix before baking. The first option will give you a consistent colour throughout whereas the second will give you a more variegated look. I often sprinkle a little malic or citric acid along with the fruit powder to give a sherbet burst. Rhubarb, blackcurrant, orange or even dried elderflower work particularly well here.

PRALINE
Make a medium amber caramel and pour it over an equal quantity of toasted nuts. Leave to set hard and then grind as fine as you desire. Sprinkle the praline over the top of a layer of tuile mix before baking.

BREADCRUMB
Toast small torn breadcrumbs (or panko breadcrumbs) with a little butter and sugar until caramelized and delicious. Dry in a dehydrator or very low oven. Break up into small shards and sprinkle over the top of a layer of tuile mix before baking.

Honey and beeswax granita

This granita works very much on the same principle as the ice cream *(right)*. Caramelizing the honey first helps to limit the sweetness, as does the milky sourness of the whey, while the beeswax bolsters the bee-ish flavour. I first made this granita to go with an oat mousse, which is why I use oat milk here but you could use all whey or even whey and water. The fattiness of oat milk helps to round out all the flavours, though, so it is my favourite option.

makes 850g (1lb 14oz)
100g (5 tbsp) honey and 30g (1oz) beeswax, or 110g (3½oz) comb honey
485ml (2 cups) oat milk
250g (1 cup) whey

To caramelize the honey and wax, follow the same method as for the honey and beeswax ice cream *(p169)*, using the oat milk and whey to deglaze the pan. Once the honey has dissolved, leave the liquid to cool to room temperature and then transfer to the freezer. Leave it to freeze solid before removing the surface layer of set wax. Any small pieces of wax that are left will get mixed in when you scrape it and will not affect the structure. Use a fork to scrape the granita into fine crystals and then return it to the freezer until ready to serve.

A finer, snowy texture works better here rather than larger crystalline flakes. The small crystals will melt quickly on your tongue communicating the more subtle flavour more immediately. If the granita has been in the freezer for a few days (or longer), run a fork through it again to break it up before serving.

Honey and beeswax ice cream

Honey ice creams are tricky to balance. You want the intense flavour of honey without the finished ice cream tasting overly sweet. One trick is to use a very strong-flavoured honey such as heather, wildflower or chestnut so that you need to use only a small amount. Alternatively, you can caramelize the honey, which takes away some of the sweetness, meaning you can add less and the structure will not be affected. The beeswax reinforces the honey aroma: it provides an initial hit of perfume and then allows the honey sweetness to come through, giving a fully integrated flavour. It's worth seeking out an individual beekeeper's wax for a more nuanced flavour profile. Food-grade beeswax is available online, or make friends with a producer to buy it directly. Alternatively, you can replace both the honey and beeswax with comb honey.

makes 1.6kg (3½lb)

120g (⅓ cup) honey and 30g (1oz) beeswax, or 130g (6½oz) comb honey

400ml (1⅔ cups) double (heavy) cream

800ml (3⅓ cups) whole milk

200g (¾ cup plus 2 tbsp) egg yolks, from about 10 eggs

100g (½ cup) caster (superfine) sugar

5g (1 tsp) salt

Put the honey and beeswax, or comb honey (if using), in a saucepan and warm over a medium heat. Once the wax is melted, turn up the heat and allow the mixture to start caramelizing. It should turn a deep amber; it can be difficult to judge as the colour of honey varies so much. For consistency (and a bit of confidence the first time you make this) use a thermometer. You want the honey and beeswax to reach 150°C (302°F). Once you have achieved the right temperature or colour, pour in the cream followed by the milk. The wax and honey will seize up at this point but return the pan to a low heat for 5 minutes and they will melt into the liquid. Pour into a container and leave to infuse in the fridge overnight.

The next day, the wax should have set into a solid layer on top of the milk and cream. Remove the wax and discard it. Strain the infusion through a chinois or fine sieve to remove any remaining wax then pour into a saucepan and place over a medium heat.

Meanwhile, whisk the egg yolks, sugar and salt together. Once the infusion reaches a rolling boil, remove from the heat and slowly pour about half into the egg yolk mixture, whisking as you go to prevent curdling. Pour the now tempered custard back into the pan with the remaining infusion and mix well. By bringing the milk and cream to a rolling boil first, there should be enough latent heat left in the pan to cook the egg to 82–83°C (180°F) without having to return it to the heat. Check the temperature and if it is below 82°C (180°F), continue to cook the custard on a gentle heat, stirring constantly until it reaches the required temperature. Immediately strain through a fine sieve and leave to cool. Transfer to the fridge and chill for a minimum of 4 hours. Churn in an ice-cream machine then transfer to a container and leave to set in the freezer before serving.

Honey and beeswax ice cream, apple and rapeseed oil

I love this dish with summer or early autumn honey and the first flush of bright autumn apples. You want a honey with a bit of punch. I would avoid lighter acacia or spring honey but buckwheat or heather honey work beautifully here.

---

serves 1

6–8 apple crisps *(p95)*

100ml (1 scant cup) apple, honey and rapeseed oil dressing *(p95)*

1cm (½in) slice of cooked puff pastry *(p199)*

---

1 scoop honey and beeswax ice cream *(p169)*

---

1 tsp rapeseed oil

Cover the apple crisps in the dressing and leave to marinate for 2 hours. You can also combine the apples and dressing and compress in a vacuum sealer in which case you only need to leave them for about 1 hour. The apples should have softened slightly and absorbed the dressing without becoming completely floppy. Strain the apples (you can reuse the dressing for the next batch) and stack them on top of each other. Slice vertically through the centre of the stack to create two piles of half-moons.

Put a plate in the freezer to chill 30 minutes before serving. When assembling this dish, the goal is to create a linear visual with each element compromising a third of the plate. Stand the apple slices upright on the chilled plate, slightly to the left of centre. Lay the cross-section of puff pastry beside the apples. Scoop a large, elegant quenelle of the ice cream and place on the other side of the puff pastry. Drizzle a little rapeseed oil over the top of the ice cream.

FATS

I love all things dairy – milk, cream, butter, yogurt, ricotta, cheeses – and I don't know how you can survive without good olive oil in your kitchen. I surprised myself with how large this section became but it is testament to how important and versatile fats are in my dessert repertoire. Often, I'll build a dish around a fat-based recipe and then adjust the fruit and other elements depending on the time of year. You'll see the olive oil ice cream served with peaches and rosemary in the height of summer, grapes in the autumn and blood oranges in the depths of winter. Ricotta ice cream has to be one of my all-time favourites; it is wonderful paired with a leaf oil like blackcurrant or fig but I also love it scooped alongside grape or plum sorbet. Use this chapter to find the uniting core element of a dessert.

Brown butter

Brown butter is pure alchemy. A simple process of transformation that takes an already delectable product and takes it to another level. It is very easy to make; low effort for high impact.

unsalted butter

Simply dice the butter and add to a light-coloured pan. As when making caramels, you need to judge this by colour so a stainless steel or other pale-hued pan will make it easier to see. Place the pan over a medium heat to melt the butter. If you want to clarify butter, all you need to do is skim the foamy milk solids from the top of the liquid butter once it has fully melted.

To carry on to brown butter, keep the butter over the heat. The water will start to evaporate and the butter will splutter. It will then start to foam up so give it a good whisk at this point to release the butter solids from the bottom of the pan. Those solids will now start caramelizing, the colour will change from golden to brown and the smell will be intoxicatingly nutty.

I like a very dark brown butter but you can go as dark or as light as you prefer. If you are going to fry or cook something in brown butter, then keep it lighter, or if using brown butter as the flavour-driver, you can be a little bolder and go darker. Once the butter has reached the right colour, strain it through a metal sieve into a heatproof container. Brown butter will last for ages; you've removed the milk solids which extends the shelf life so it's something you can always have in the fridge.

Brown butter solids
You'll also be left with a little bit of magic in the caramelized milk solids that you have strained out. Every time you make brown butter, keep the solids back to use in brown butter ice cream or caramelized cream panna cotta (p175).

Shaved brown butter

This recipe is a perfect use of those leftover solids. They are combined with a little more brown butter and icing sugar to create a log that can then be shaved over any dessert. The caramelized, nutty flavour is wonderful with all summery and autumnal fruits, or shave it directly over milk ice cream (p169) or yeast ice cream (p196).

makes 275g (8oz)

50g (3 tbsp plus 1 tsp) brown butter

75g (5 tbsp) brown butter solids (see left)

150g (1 cup plus 2 tbsp) icing (confectioners') sugar

5g (1 tsp) salt

Gently melt the brown butter with the solids in a small saucepan until it is liquid but not hot. Use a whisk to disperse any clumps of caramelized solids. Combine with the icing sugar and salt and mix well. Set the mixture aside for about 30 minutes until it has cooled and started to solidify.

Scrape it out onto a strip of baking parchment and roll it into a log, twisting the ends of the paper to seal it like a giant sweet. Freeze until completely solid. Use a coarse grater or Microplane to shave over desserts.

Brown butter cakes

If you make nothing else in this book, make these. Deservedly legendary, they were served at the end of pretty much every dinner at Lyle's. We'd bake them throughout the evening so we could send them out warm. They are the perfect mix of fudgy centre and crispy edge. If you need further encouragement, I'm pretty sure they secured the love of my life. After my shifts, I would take the leftover cakes to my partner Miles, whom I had just started dating. Four years on, we're still in love and he still asks for brown butter cakes.

In essence, these are like a *financier* but with every component amped up: more butter, more sugar, more salt. The brown butter needs to be really dark for the flavour to make its pronounced impact. For the classic version, add a large handful of lemon thyme to the butter when you put it on to brown. The butter infuses with the bright, herbal flavour as it caramelizes. This works incredibly well with any of the woody herbs: rosemary, sage, bay leaf, winter savoury, so there is plenty of room to play about. You can also substitute different sugars to influence the flavour. At Flor, we would use plain brown butter but then opt for panela sugar to really play up the fudgy, sticky toffee pudding vibe of the cake. Stick to darker, less refined sugars no lighter than demerara for this recipe.

You can bake these as a small two-bite cake to serve as petits fours; as a slightly larger, thinner cake to use as a base for a dessert; or if you spread the mix very thin, it bakes into the crispiest, most beautiful tuile. I like to use the larger cake underneath black figs and fig leaf ice cream or with roasted peaches and almond ice cream. The tuiles make a brilliant shell for an ice cream sandwich. Keep a tub of this mix in the fridge or freezer and scoop out enough batter to bake a couple of mini cakes at a time, whenever you need to show yourself a little love.

for the herb-infused brown butter

250g (2 sticks) unsalted butter, diced

10g (5 or 6 sprigs) any woody herb

Put the butter and herbs in a large, light-coloured saucepan and place over a medium heat. Melt the butter, stirring often. As the water starts to evaporate, the butter will foam up so give it a good whisk to release the butter solids from the bottom of the pan. Continue cooking until it is a very dark, nutty brown. Strain the hot butter through a metal sieve into a metal bowl (it will melt plastic at this point) and leave it to cool to room temperature.

makes 30 mini cakes or 15 larger cakes

160g (⅔ cup) egg whites, from about 6 eggs

255g (1¼ cups) demerara sugar

85g (¾ cup) ground almonds

70g (½ cup plus 1 tbsp) cornflour (cornstarch)

6g (1¼ tsp) salt

170g (⅔ cup plus 1 tbsp) herb-infused brown butter

butter or flavourless oil, for greasing

Whisk the egg whites in a mixer at medium speed until they form medium-stiff peaks; they should be firm but not dry with a slight curl at the tip. Combine the dry ingredients in a large bowl and mix well with a whisk. Fold the whisked egg whites gently into the dry ingredients. Add the cooled, but still liquid, brown butter to the mix one third at a time. Don't worry about knocking too much air from the whites since these are dense cakes by nature. Once all the butter is well incorporated, rest the batter in the fridge for at least 8 hours but preferably overnight. Don't be tempted to skip the resting or you'll end up with overly puffy, uneven cakes.

Preheat the oven to 180°C (350°F). Butter or oil your baking tray very very well. Pipe the batter to fill three quarters of the moulds. At Lyle's, we used a mini cupcake tray and would bake for 16 minutes. For a larger cake, we used 10cm (4in) tart tins and baked for 20 minutes. Leave to cool for 2 minutes before turning out. Serve warm.

Brown butter ice cream

makes 800ml (1½ pints)

400ml (1⅔ cups) double (heavy) cream

400ml (1⅔ cups) whole milk

pinch of salt

200g (¾ cup plus 1 tbsp) brown butter *(p173)*

20g (4 tsp) brown butter solids (optional) *(p173)*

120g (½ cup) egg yolks, from about 7 eggs

120g (½ cups plus 1 tbsp) caster (superfine) sugar

Combine the cream, milk and salt in a large saucepan over a medium heat. Meanwhile, melt the brown butter and solids, if using, together in a small pan so they are liquid but not hot. Whisk the egg yolks and sugar together in a large bowl. Slowly whisk in the liquid brown butter to form a smooth emulsion as if you were making a hollandaise. Once the cream and milk have come to a rolling boil, remove from the heat and slowly pour about half into the egg-yolk mixture, whisking as you go to prevent curdling.

Pour the now tempered egg mix back into the pan with the remaining cream and milk and mix well. By bringing the cream and milk to a rolling boil first, there should be enough latent heat left in the pan to cook the egg to 82–83°C (180°F) without having to return it to the heat. Check the temperature and if it is below 82°C (180°F), continue to cook the custard on a gentle heat, stirring constantly until it reaches the required temperature.

Immediately strain through a fine sieve then chill in the fridge for a minimum of 4 hours. Churn in an ice-cream machine then transfer to a container and leave to set in the freezer before serving.

Caramelized cream panna cotta

I first had brown butter panna cotta at Del Posto in New York when Brooks Headley was the pastry chef. It was absolutely divine and pushed all of my buttons. A celebration of dairy produce, it will sing with a huge range of seasonal fruit. Brooks' recipe takes several days of heating, cooling, heating and setting, which I admit I'm too lazy for. This version keeps the essence of the original but the cream is caramelized rather than the butter so it takes less time. It's quite rich so set the panna cotta in a small bowl or mould to ensure you end up with a balanced dessert.

serves 6-8

700ml (2¾ cup plus 2 tbsp) double (heavy) cream

10g (1 tbsp) brown butter solids (optional) *(p173)*

300ml (1¼ cups) whole milk

30g (2 tbsp plus 1 tsp) demerara sugar

pinch of salt

2½ leaves of gelatine

50g (3 tbsp plus 1 tsp) crème fraîche

Add 200ml (1 scant cup) of the cream to a medium saucepan with the brown butter solids and bring to the boil over a high heat, stirring constantly. The cream will reduce and start to caramelize. Keep reducing and stirring for about 5 minutes until you have a thick, deeply caramel paste. Remove from the heat and pour in the milk to deglaze the pan. It will bubble up so be careful. Whisk to make sure the milk is well mixed with the caramelized cream. Once it's cooled slightly, pour into a container, cover and then chill for 4–5 hours or overnight.

The caramelized cream will have settled as a layer on top of the milk. Remove the thickened layer and pass the milk through a muslin cloth set inside a fine sieve. Combine the infused milk with the sugar, salt and remaining cream in a saucepan and warm gently. Meanwhile, soak the gelatine leaves in cold water for 5 minutes to soften. Remove from the water and squeeze out any excess. Remove the milk and cream from the heat and whisk in the gelatine to dissolve it, followed by the crème fraîche. Pour through a fine sieve again and then into serving dishes. Chill in the fridge for at least 6 hours but preferably overnight.

Goat's whey cajeta

We were very lucky for a couple of years to receive huge buckets of goat's whey from a cheesemaker and farmer we worked with. We weren't sure how to process or use so much of it at first. Luckily, the arrival of the whey coincided with one of Lyle's *The Guest Series* dinners, where we invited chefs from all over the world to come and cook for two nights. They provided amazing opportunities for our team to work alongside some wonderful chefs and learn about cuisines, ingredients and techniques that were completely different to what we did every day in the restaurant. I've rarely met a chef with such a joyful, inspiring and fun spirit as Daniela Soto-Innes, who joined us for *The Guest Series* from Cosme in New York. She wanted to create a dish based around fresh cheese, charred pears and cajeta, a thickened caramel from Mexico traditionally made with condensed goat's milk. Since we had so much goat's whey, I reduced that down instead. It resulted in an incredibly intense paste: salty, sweet and sour all at once. To balance that intensity, I mixed the reduced whey with a caramel sauce so it mellowed out to a beautiful cajeta-style caramel. The resulting dish referenced the plating of the famous mole at Pujol in Mexico City, with concentric circles of burnt pear purée and the goat's whey cajeta topped with a cheese ice cream made with Hay-on-Wye, a fresh goat's cheese. You can use yogurt whey or any cow's milk whey here but the goat's whey will give it a slightly funkier flavour. What is important is to reduce the whey right down so that you are left with an incredibly intense paste that you can then dilute to taste. The reduced whey freezes incredibly well.

for the reduced whey

2 litres (8 cups) goat's whey

Pour the whey into a wide saucepan large enough to allow the liquid to bubble up as it boils. Bring to a rolling boil and continue cooking until it has reduced by about two thirds. Whisk it every now and then to prevent it catching on the bottom of the pan. Turn down the heat so it is now gently simmering and carry on reducing. When it starts to caramelize, stir constantly to prevent it burning (it will splutter so be careful). You may need to change to a smaller pan at this point to prevent it burning. It is ready when it turns a deep caramel colour and, when you drag a wooden spoon along the base of the pan, it leaves a channel that doesn't immediately fill with liquid (as though you were making chutney). You should have approximately 190g (7oz) of reduced whey.

for the caramel

250g (1¼ cups) caster (superfine) sugar

250ml (1 cup) double (heavy) cream

125g (1 stick) unsalted butter, diced

190g (7oz) reduced whey

Add the sugar to a clean, high-sided saucepan. Cook on a high heat, swirling the pan to even out the sugar, until you have reached a dark amber caramel. If you are going by temperature, take it to around 180°C (356°F). Don't go too dark here; the caramel needs a little bitterness but it should still be mellow and sweet. Remove from the heat and deglaze with the double cream. It will bubble up dramatically, which is why it is important to use a high-sided pan. Whisk to make sure all the caramel has been incorporated into the cream.

Add the butter and return to the boil, whisking until it forms a smooth emulsion. Remove from the heat and add the reduced whey. The mixture will have a slightly grainy texture which I rather like but if you want the cajeta to be completely smooth, blend it with a hand-held blender then pass through a fine sieve. Cool and store in the fridge. It is best served at room temperature.

Milk meringue

As a kid, I was always a huge fan of the milk bottle sweets you would get as part of a pick-n-mix selection. This recipe is a definite nod to those milky treats. The meringues have that gently caramelized, condensed milk flavour with a crisp shell and mallowy centre. They are especially good with bright acidic fruits like gooseberry and rhubarb but I also love them with any of the red summer fruits.

makes about 15 meringues

200g (¾ cup plus 1 tbsp) egg whites, from 6–7 eggs

pinch of salt

400g (2 cups) caster (superfine) sugar

50g (6 tbsp) milk powder (non-fat dry milk)

Preheat the oven to 120°C (250°F) with as low a fan setting as possible. Combine the egg whites and salt in a mixer with a whisk attachment. Whisk at medium-slow speed so that you build a strong, stable meringue. Once the whites hold soft peaks, add the sugar one third at a time, whisking well between each addition. Once all the sugar has been incorporated and you have a strong, glossy meringue, gently fold in the milk powder.

Line a baking sheet with baking parchment or a silicone mat. Either pipe the meringue into 6–7cm (2½–3in) domes or use two spoons to scoop quenelles onto the lined trays. Bake for 2–2½ hours. The meringues should be crisp on the outside with a slightly gooey centre. Leave to cool in the oven with the door slightly ajar then store in an airtight container until ready to serve.

Milk ice cream

We were lucky enough at Lyle's to have occasional access to raw milk and, provided we were organized, consistent access to raw cream. Raw, or unpasteurized, milk and cream are always more flavourful and, if they come from a good farm, are totally safe to consume. In the UK, you can buy raw cream in specialist shops but can only purchase raw milk directly from a farm. When we couldn't get raw milk, we would use a raw cream mixed with a good quality pasteurized milk instead. This ice-cream base does not get cooked or heated at all. The goal is to really showcase the pure flavour of the dairy. This is one of the only instances in this book where I recommend using a commercial ice-cream stabilizer to ensure a smooth texture and a softer scoop. Here, it helps facilitate the no-heat recipe, so be sure to buy one that does not need to be heated. Dextrose is a monosaccharide, which means it can hold more water in your ice-cream base than standard sugar (a disaccharide). This ability to grab onto more water molecules per gram will give you a smoother, less icy ice cream that doesn't taste overly sweet.

makes 950g (2lb 2oz)

25g (2 tbsp) caster (superfine) sugar

50g (4 tbsp) dextrose powder

25g (2 tbsp) ice-cream stabilizer (p237)

750ml (3 cups) whole milk

100ml (scant ½ cup) double (heavy) cream

Mix the sugar, dextrose and ice-cream stabilizer together to break up the powders. Combine with the milk and mix well in a blender or with a hand-held blender. Once the sugars have dissolved into the milk, add the cream and mix well.

Leave the ice-cream base to rest in the fridge for a minimum of 4 hours. This is particularly important for texture as it allows the stabilizer to be fully hydrated and the fat to be properly distributed throughout the base. Churn in an ice-cream machine then transfer to a container and leave to set in the freezer before serving.

Vanilla ice cream

Probably the most expensive ingredient in the pastry kitchen, vanilla comes in at around £400–£600 per kilogram. Each flower must be hand pollinated so it's difficult to produce and only grows under specific climatic conditions. The invention of synthetic vanillin made it easy to replace the flavour of this luxurious and pricey and commodity. Vanilla went from being special and scarce to a byword for neutral or basic. I firmly believe that we should only use vanilla as a flavour where it adds substantially to a dish or where the vanilla is really allowed to be the star of the show. It should be the focus of a dish, not just thrown in unthinkingly. I am, however, in no way against the use of good quality bean pastes or extracts. They are often much more affordable and have their uses.

If you are using vanilla pods then be sure to get as much as possible from each one. To make your own extract after using them for an infusion, rinse and dry the pods before adding to a bottle of neutral spirit, such as vodka or grappa. Keep adding spent pods until the bottle or jar is packed and leave somewhere dark to infuse for a few weeks. Or, completely dry the spent pods and grind with a little caster (superfine) sugar to make a powder for dusting Danishes or ice creams.

How you like your vanilla ice cream is a deeply personal choice. At least among pastry chefs. Some prefer the base to be rich from lots of cream and egg yolk, others use more milk and less egg to let the vanilla shine. My preference sits somewhere in the middle: a custard that uses more milk than cream but is still egg yolk-heavy. Then comes the question of which vanilla to use. Try making the same ice cream with pods of different origins so you can taste them side by side, as the variations are hard to distinguish without direct comparison. My favourite by far is vanilla from Tahiti. The fat, juicy, seed-filled pods taste so intense they seem almost fake. Unfortunately, they are also the most expensive as production is limited. Sometimes that super intense flavour (or super high price!) doesn't quite make sense so at The River Café we would use one Tahitian pod for every four from Papua New Guinea. The latter would add a base fruitiness to balance the Tahitian vanilla's floral quality. Vanilla pods can have smoky, fruity, floral or spicy notes depending on their origins. If you pay attention to the vanilla you use, vanilla ice cream should be anything but basic.

To really amp up the flavour, I use another trick I learnt from Daniela Soto-Innes. She threw the whole vanilla pods onto blazing charcoal so they puffed up and their edges became charred. The smell is wholly intoxicating. This way, the beans are easier to scrape, the oils are drawn out and you introduce a gentle smokiness to your infusion. You can achieve a similar result by blowtorching the pods.

makes 1.5 litres (3 pints)	
35g (6–8) vanilla pods	
1 litre (1 quart) whole milk	
300ml (1¼ cups) double (heavy) cream	
170g (scant ⅔ cup) egg yolks, from 9–10 eggs	
150g (¾ cup) caster (superfine) sugar	
5g (1 tsp) salt	

Grill the vanilla pods then slit them down their length and scrape out the seeds with a small knife. Add the seeds and scraped pods to the milk and cream in a saucepan set over a medium heat. Meanwhile, whisk the egg yolks, sugar and salt together. Once the vanilla milk reaches a rolling boil, remove from the heat and slowly pour about half onto the yolk mixture, whisking as you go to prevent curdling.

Pour the now tempered egg mix back into the saucepan with the remaining vanilla milk and mix well. By bringing the milk and cream to a rolling boil first there should be enough latent heat left in the pan to cook the egg to 82–3°C (180°F) without having to return it to the heat. Check the temperature and if it is below 82°C (180°F), continue to cook the custard over a gentle heat, stirring constantly until it reaches the required temperature. Pour the ice-cream base into a shallow container and chill in the fridge for a minimum of 4 hours or overnight.

Strain the infused custard through a fine sieve. Churn in an ice-cream machine then transfer to a container and leave to set in the freezer before serving. Rinse the spent vanilla pods in water and leave to dry before finding a second life for them.

Baked cream

This recipe comes from northern Italy where egg yolks are always in demand but egg whites are forever in excess. It works on the same principle as a classic set custard made with yolks – where the protein from the eggs provides a gentle set once cooked – but uses the whites instead. The result is lighter and the cream flavour more pronounced. Use the most decadent cream you can get your hands on; unpasteurized or raw cream works perfectly here. Try substituting the sugar with an equal amount of maple syrup or honey, or adding mahlab *(p237)* when serving it with poached plums. Infuse the cream with vanilla to pair with strawberries or rhubarb, or with citrus zest or spices or any leaves (fig, herbs, blackcurrant, clementine), that suit the dish you are building.

serves 8

1kg (4¼ cups) rich double (heavy) cream

50g (3½ tbsp) caster (superfine) sugar

180g (⅔ cup) egg whites, from about 6 eggs

Heat the cream in a saucepan over a medium heat to just below the boil. If you are flavouring it, pour the hot cream over your flavouring, cool, then leave to infuse overnight in the fridge. The next day, warm the cream gently and strain out the infused ingredient.

Preheat the oven to 110°C (230°F). Mix the sugar and egg whites together, not to aerate them but just to combine the ingredients and break up the whites. Add the warm cream to the egg whites and mix well. Again, this is not about incorporating any air into the mix so go gently. Pass through a fine sieve or chinois and pour into a shallow baking dish.

Set the dish inside a larger baking tray and fill with enough water to come halfway up the outside of the dish. Bake for 60–90 minutes. When the cream is cooked, it will no longer look liquid when you give the tray a gentle shake but rather have a gelatinous wobble. It should resemble a dense, thick cream like a crème brûlée. Leave to cool to room temperature then chill slightly before serving.

PRO TIP
If you have a Rational or combi oven *(p236)*, cook on the combi setting at 90°C (195°F) with 60 per cent moisture and fan speed 3 for 45 minutes–1 hour.

Ricotta ice cream

I've gone through many recipes for ricotta ice cream. The best ones are always those that contain at least 40 per cent ricotta. Because it has a really high protein and milk solid content, ricotta is an ideal ingredient for ice cream. Those proteins and solids help to capture air and give a silky smooth texture. If you reduce the percentage of ricotta to make a more fluid base, you will have to add sugar or milk powder to replace the ricotta's naturally beneficial qualities. Essentially, you're making more work for yourself. Ricotta's flavour is gentle but it's in its creamy, slightly grainy texture that it truly shines. I love that texture transformed into ice cream. For me, the best ricotta comes from Westcombe Dairy in Somerset, where they make it with the whey left over from Cheddar production. It is a wondrous expression of the milk, animals and land it comes from. This recipe also works beautifully with fresh buffalo or sheep's milk ricotta.

makes 800ml (1½ pints)

150g (¾ cup) caster (superfine) sugar

500g (16½oz) fresh ricotta

25ml (1½ tbsp plus ½ tsp) lemon juice

small pinch of salt

Combine the sugar with 150ml (⅔ cup) of water in a saucepan, whisk well and place over a medium heat. Stir occasionally until the sugar is completely dissolved, leave to cool then chill thoroughly.

Once the syrup is completely chilled, add the lemon juice, then blend in the ricotta until it is smooth and season with a little salt. Churn in an ice-cream machine then transfer to a container and leave to set in the freezer before serving.

Yogurt mousse

This is a great base for any fresh or poached fruit throughout the year. The acidity of the yogurt is less cloying than a classic mousse, bavarois or whipped cream. Thickening the milk with cornflour stabilizes the mousse, keeping it light even after the other elements are added. It works brilliantly with poached or roasted fruit folded through, or when combined with a thickened fruit purée to create a fool. I love this with gooseberries, apricots, tayberries or rhubarb. If you pair it with a flavoured meringue that complements your chosen fruit, then you have an instantly harmonious dessert without too much effort or thought.

serves 6

110ml (scant ½ cup) whole milk

40g (3½ tbsp) caster (superfine) sugar

15g (2 tbsp) cornflour (cornstarch)

500g (2 cups) thick plain yogurt

250ml (1 cup) double (heavy) cream

Whisk together the milk, sugar and cornflour in a saucepan. Place over a medium heat and continue whisking gently until the mixture comes to the boil and has thickened. Pour into a shallow container and chill completely in the fridge.

Combine the milk mixture with the yogurt in a food processor and blend until completely smooth. Whip the double cream until it holds medium peaks and gently fold through the thickened yogurt. Leave to set in the fridge before using.

St Jude ice cream

Cheese ice cream can be a challenging concept. I have tasted some really quite unsuccessful examples over the years. The danger is always that the funk of the cheese will overpower the sweet lactic qualities that give it balance. St Jude is a small individual, mould-ripened cow's milk cheese from Suffolk produced by one of the loveliest women in British cheesemaking, Julie Cheyney. Originally inspired by St Marcellin, it owes its rich, buttery flavours and moussey texture to the beautiful milk from Fen Farm Dairy's cows. You can use other cheeses in this recipe but make sure they are young and of a similar style. Don't be put off by the use of Ultratex; it's a thickening agent derived from maize that will give the ice cream just the right consistency.

makes 800ml (1½ pints)

600ml (2½ cups) whole milk

110g (3½oz) St Jude or other young cow's milk cheese

40g (2 tbsp plus 2 tsp) liquid glucose

20g (1 tbsp plus 2 tsp) caster (superfine) sugar

5g (1 tsp) Ultratex *(p237)*

The simplest recipe around. If the cheese is slightly mature then remove the rind first. Combine the ingredients in a blender and process until smooth. Churn in an ice-cream machine then transfer to a container and leave to set in the freezer before serving.

Olive oil ice cream

Many moons ago, before I was a chef, I read about someone putting olive oil and a sprinkle of salt on vanilla ice cream and thought it sounded very odd. How far I have come. I would (and do) happily pour a drizzle of olive oil over most ice creams (it goes particularly well with vanilla, wild fennel or nectarine) so it seemed logical to use it to flavour ice cream. I wouldn't use the most expensive, rarest oil you have in the ice-cream base; I'd rather drizzle that over the top. Do use a good extra virgin oil, though. I like something quite peppery and punchy. Be generous with the salt; remember you are seasoning to help intensify the flavour.

makes 1.2 litres (2½ pints)

500ml (2 cups) whole milk

300ml (1¼ cups) double (heavy) cream

25g (2 tbsp) condensed milk

generous pinch of salt

120g (½ cup) egg yolks, from 6–7 eggs

100g (½ cup) caster (superfine) sugar

220ml (1 scant cup) extra virgin olive oil

Combine the milk, cream, condensed milk and salt in a large saucepan and place over a medium heat. Whisk the egg yolks and sugar together in a large bowl. Slowly whisk in the olive oil in a thin stream to emulsify it with the egg yolks as if you were making mayonnaise.

Once the milk and cream come to a rolling boil, remove from the heat and slowly pour about half into the yolk mixture, whisking as you go to prevent curdling. Pour the now tempered egg mix back into the pan with the remaining milk and cream and mix well. By bringing the milk and cream to a rolling boil first, there should be enough latent heat left in the pan to cook the egg to 82–83°C (180°F) without having to return it to the heat. Check the temperature and if it is below 82°C (180°F), continue to cook the custard on a gentle heat, stirring constantly until it reaches the required temperature.

Immediately strain through a fine sieve and chill in the fridge for a minimum of 4 hours. Churn in an ice-cream machine then transfer to a container and leave to set in the freezer before serving.

Olive oil and ricotta cake

This cake is everything you want from an olive oil cake: damp and rich. This was originally based on a cherry, ricotta and olive oil cake by Leticia Clark in her beautiful book *La Vita è Dolce*. My sous-chef at The River Café, Bella, took it and created a peach version with polenta, which was incredible. This is stripped back even further to just the oil and ricotta. I've upped the olive oil slightly to make it heady with that flavour. Use an oil that is bright and fruity. This cake will take really well to any fruity additions: stone fruits, citrus, grapes or even herbs like wild fennel or rosemary would be great here. Simply chop the fruit into bite-sized pieces and fold through the batter at the end.

makes 1 x 25cm (10in) cake or 15 mini cakes

275ml (1 cup plus 2½ tbsp) extra virgin olive oil

4 eggs

250g (1¼ cups) caster (superfine) sugar

250g (8oz) fresh ricotta

200g (1¾ cups) ground almonds

100g (¾ cup) polenta (or stoneground cornmeal)

2 tsp baking powder

1 tsp salt

2 tbsp demerara sugar

butter or flavourless oil, for greasing

Preheat the oven to 170°C (340°F). In a large bowl, whisk the olive oil and eggs together. You don't need to create volume, just make sure they are well combined. Beat the sugar and ricotta together until smooth and add to the eggs and oil. Finally, add the dry ingredients, except the demerara sugar, and mix well.

I like to make these as mini, petit four-sized cakes but you can bake this as a single layer in a 25cm (10in) springform cake tin. Whatever you decide, grease the tin well, line the base with baking parchment then pour in the batter and sprinkle with the demerara sugar. Bake for 15–20 minutes for mini cakes or 45 minutes–1 hour for a 25cm (10in) cake.

Brown butter ice cream, puff pastry and marmalade

I'm sure every pastry chef has an idea for a dish that they carry with them from job to job through their career. Mine was a dish with the flavours of toast and marmalade. Ever since reading about brown bread ice cream, I was determined to create a dish that tastes like breakfast. Interestingly, I have never been a sweet toast person; it's strictly toast and Marmite for me, never jam. You can't make a dessert out of toast and Marmite though... Brown bread ice cream is a real classic of the St John dessert menu, a masterclass in how to write a perfectly formed and concise list. As Lyle's had so much in common with St John, both owners having spent formative time there, I felt it would be a little too close to the bone to do a brown bread ice cream. Instead, I tried an ice cream made with yeast to make the most of its brioche-y character but it wasn't quite as comforting as I wanted. Brown butter ice cream quickly became the answer. Paired with marmalade (I originally made a kumquat version) and a slice of puff pastry, this dish was finally starting to hit all of those toasty, buttery, jammy notes I had been hoping for. The final shavings of brown butter solids and the bright green, orange flavour of the tagetes leaves turned this dessert into one of my very favourite spring dishes at Lyle's.

Place a rimmed plate in the freezer to chill 30 minutes before serving. Scoop a large quenelle of brown butter ice cream to the left of the dish. Use a hot spoon to flatten the right side of the quenelle down onto the plate. Add a spoonful of marmalade on top of the flattened side of the ice cream. Place the puff pastry to the right of the marmalade. The puff pastry and ice cream should sandwich the marmalade. Scatter the shaved brown butter over the dish. Place a couple of tagetes leaves on the ice cream and pastry and lastly scatter over the picked petals.

serves 1

1cm (½in) slice of cooked puff pastry (p199)

1 large scoop brown butter ice cream (p175)

1 dessert spoon blood orange marmalade (p153)

20g (1½ tbsp) shaved brown butter (p173)

2–3 tagetes (marigold) flowers, petals and leaves picked

Milk meringue with tayberries and yogurt mousse

This dish is ideal with any berry, especially gooseberries, or you could try it with rhubarb. The meringue can be tooth-achingly sweet but is balanced by the acidity of the yogurt mousse alongside the wild-tasting berries.

serves 1

2–3 tbsp yogurt mousse *(p180)*

250g (8oz) tayberries, plus 4–5 perfect tayberries, to serve

1 milk meringue *(p177)*

Make the yogurt mousse according to the recipe *(p180)*, adding 100g (3½oz) of tayberries to the yogurt as you blend it with the thickened milk so that the fruit is puréed through the base. Add the remaining tayberries along with the whipped double cream and fold through so that you get larger pieces of slightly crushed berries.

Use a sharp knife to cut the top off the meringue and divide it into three rough pieces. Place the base of the meringue in a shallow bowl or plate and spoon the tayberry and yogurt mousse on top. Scatter the tayberries over the mousse then cover some of the mousse with the top of the meringue.

CHOCOLATE

It took me a long time to get excited about chocolate desserts. They fall into the trap of feeling too easy. People will order a chocolate dessert even while announcing that they are not a dessert person. At Lyle's, and to an extent at The River Café – restaurants that were built around seasonality and using what is best at that moment – chocolate felt out of place. It is a constant. Once it arrives in your kitchen, it does not change, does not develop in flavour, so what is exciting about it? There has typically been a disparity between the efforts we go to in sourcing well-grown, ethically and sustainably produced fresh ingredients and the minimal thought that we put into ordering chocolate via a dry store company. Thankfully, that is changing. There has been a shift from treating chocolate as a commodity to respecting it as an ingredient with a story and a personality to be drawn out: with *terroir*. Find chocolate makers who are working directly with growers across their ranges; who are actively trying to benefit the skilled people doing the hard business of growing and fermenting the beans; who are aiming to not only reduce but reverse the environmental impact the industry has had. Choose a producer with clear and traceable sourcing credentials if you are going to use chocolate. After the chocolate maker has met all of those criteria, then you can focus on finding the flavour profile you love.

Personally, I go for chocolates that embrace the natural acidity of cocoa and that work to balance that throughout the range. It is only when I started to be introduced to – and taste – these chocolates that a dessert built around chocolate started to sound exciting to me.

For someone who isn't that into chocolate desserts, I have a lot of thoughts on the subject. Being able to temper chocolate is a skill that all pastry chefs should have but it's not one I practise all that often as my career has moved forward. Chocolate should be celebrated in a dish, not used to sculpt or form a garnish. Don't let it become a superfluous addition. It takes great skill to make a perfect shiny bonbon but I often find their flavours ill-conceived: the fillings still need to complement the chocolate they are encased in. If you do make bonbons, make sure they deliver something special in that one mouthful. Some of my favourites are filled with caramels: those made from yeast or whey work particularly well.

Finally, I would urge caution when pairing chocolate with fruit; they can so easily clash. I want to say "don't do it" but that is my palate, and you need to find what you like best. I believe it's better to celebrate the individual ingredients rather than diminish them by putting them together.

Chilled chocolate mousse

This mousse is designed to be intensely chocolatey with as little as possible to dilute the flavour. It relies on a whipped cream dispenser (p237) to aerate it rather than the traditional whisked eggs or cream. The addition of water may seem odd but it allows the mix to reach an ideal viscosity without introducing more dairy flavour or fattiness. I love using a really bright, acidic chocolate and cocoa powder in this recipe, particularly when pairing it with buckwheat ice cream. If you can find them, single-origin cocoa powders that really showcase all those fruity, acidic notes are perfect for this mousse.

serves 4–6

175g (¾ cup) double (heavy) cream

1g (⅛ tsp) salt

20g (2½ tbsp) cocoa powder

130g (4½oz) chocolate, 70–85 per cent cocoa solids

You will need a half-litre whipped cream dispenser and two whipper bulbs for this recipe. Combine the cream, salt and cocoa powder in a saucepan with 175ml (¾ cup) of water. Bring to a simmer, whisking to incorporate the cocoa. Break the chocolate into small pieces in a bowl and pour the hot cream mixture over. Let it sit for 2 minutes to melt the chocolate then use a whisk to incorporate it into a smooth, well-emulsified mix. Leave to cool to 45–50°C (113–122°F).

PRO TIP
If using a Thermomix, put all the ingredients into the jug, set the temperature to 50°C (122°F) and blend until smooth and well emulsified.

Pour into a cream dispenser charged with two whipper bulbs and shake really well. When you start to spray, the mousse should hold its shape; if it does not, shake some more. Spray the mousse into containers and chill immediately. Leave to set in the fridge for at least 3 hours. You can set the mousse in the dish it will be served in, or set a larger portion you can scoop from as you serve. A smaller, deeper container is better than a larger, shallower one.

Warm chocolate mousse

Another mousse that uses a whipper (p237) for aeration but this uses both egg whites and cream to create a mousse that coats your palate and embraces the rich fattiness and opulence of chocolate. I prefer a darker chocolate for this recipe, one that's verging on bitter. A chocolate that is 80 per cent-plus cocoa solids and has a flavour profile that lists smoke, tobacco, toasted nuts, and/or caramel in its tasting notes is what you're after.

serves 4–6

140g (4½oz) chocolate, 80 per cent cocoa solids or higher

140g (½ cup plus 1 tbsp) double (heavy) cream

120g (½ cup) egg whites, from about 4 eggs

You will need a half-litre whipped cream dispenser and two whipper bulbs for this recipe. Break the chocolate into small pieces and place in a heatproof bowl. Set the bowl over a saucepan of simmering water, making sure it doesn't touch the water. Gently melt the chocolate, stirring frequently.

Meanwhile, warm the cream until it is just starting to steam. Take the chocolate off the heat and pour the warmed cream over it. Use a rubber spatula to mix them together to form a smooth ganache. Add the egg whites (no need to whisk them first) and mix well to combine. The mixture will thicken and then relax into a smooth liquid as you stir in the egg whites. If you are not serving the mousse immediately, you can chill this mix and then rewarm it over a bain-marie just before you serve it.

Pour into the cream dispenser and charge with two whipper bulbs. Shake well. When it is ready, the mousse will just hold its shape when piped out.

Cocoa husk ice cream

Cocoa husks are the thin shells around the cocoa bean that are removed before the beans are roasted. Often sold as tea, they have the rich, fragrant top notes of chocolate without the tongue-coating richness. Chocolate ice cream is tricky to get right. The fat content from the cocoa butter in chocolate messes with the ice cream's structure, so using enough to give the right flavour can result in a hard, chalky ice cream. You can get around this by using cocoa powder instead to deliver the chocolate hit but it still results in a dense, tongue-coating ice cream. Cocoa husk ice cream delivers the nostalgic chocolate flavour as well as the perfect structure and texture.

makes 1 litre (2 pints)

750ml (3 cups) whole milk, plus extra for topping up

75g (⅔ cups) cocoa husks

100ml (½ cup) double (heavy) cream

100g (½ cup) caster (superfine) sugar

2.5g (½ tsp) salt

25g (3 tbsp) cornflour (cornstarch)

Warm the milk to just below a simmer then pour it over the cocoa husks in a large bowl. Leave to infuse in the fridge overnight. Strain through a fine sieve and really squeeze out the cocoa husks. Discard them once they have given up all their liquid.

Weigh or measure the infused milk. You will have lost a little with the cocoa husks so top it back up to 750ml (1½ pints) with some extra milk. Pour it into a saucepan, add the cream, sugar and salt and warm over a medium heat.

In a small bowl, combine 2 tablespoons of the warming liquid with the cornflour and mix until smooth. Pour back into the main pan and mix well. Continue to cook until the liquid has thickened and has just come to a gentle boil. Taste the ice-cream base to make sure the cornflour has been cooked out and none of the flouriness remains. Strain into a clean bowl and chill in the fridge for at least 4 hours or overnight. Churn in an ice-cream machine then transfer to a container and leave to set in the freezer before serving.

Chocolate cake

Every pastry chef or chef – in fact, just everyone – needs a standout flourless chocolate cake in their repertoire. Restaurant reputations have been made on the strength of this dish alone and some have become the stuff of legend: The River Café with its chocolate nemesis; Zuni Café with its gâteau victoire. I can't promise to help you achieve that anointed status but I can promise you a very, very delicious cake. This recipe is based on the grilled chocolate cake from Estela in New York. There, the finished cake is given a blast under the grill to give it a crackly top and then paired with black sesame ganache and whipped cream. It is well worth a visit to their beautiful dining room for that dish alone.

serves 8

flavourless oil, for greasing

225g (1 cup plus 2 tbsp) light brown soft sugar

250g (2 sticks) unsalted butter, diced

pinch of salt

450g (16oz) chocolate, 85 per cent cocoa solids

6 eggs

This cake is baked in a bain-marie so that it cooks very gently, giving a super soft yielding texture. Preheat the oven to 160°C (320°F). Line the base of a 20cm (8in) springform cake tin with baking parchment and brush the sides with oil. Wrap the base of the tin in foil and place in a larger baking tray that is at least as deep as the cake tin.

Combine the sugar, butter, salt and 160ml (⅔ cup) of water in a saucepan and place over a low heat to melt the butter. Break the chocolate up into small pieces and put in a large bowl. Once the butter has melted and the sugar has dissolved, pour the contents of the pan over the chocolate. Leave it to stand for 1 minute and then stir well to melt the chocolate. You should end up with a smooth and glossy ganache.

Whisk the eggs in a mixer at medium speed. When they are ready, they will have tripled in volume and the whisk will form a ribbon trail on the surface of the mixture when you pull the whisk out. Fold the eggs into the chocolate mixture then pour the batter into the prepared tin.

Pour water from a just-boiled kettle into the baking tray so that it comes halfway up the outside of the cake tin. Cover the whole tray loosely with foil and bake for around 40 minutes. The cake is ready when the edges have pulled away from the sides of the tin and there is no wobble in the centre. Remove from the oven and take off the foil cover. Leave it to sit in the hot water for 15 minutes before removing it from the tray and allowing it to cool completely in the tin. I love this served with whipped cream that has been lightened with crème fraîche or a large scoop of the cocoa husk ice cream *(left)*.

PRO TIP
If you have a Rational or combi oven, cook the cake at 110°C (230°F) with 100 per cent moisture and fan speed 3 for 1½ hours.

Buckwheat ice cream, chocolate mousse and caramel

The mutual earthiness of buckwheat and chocolate means they sit perfectly alongside each other; the same is true for rye and chocolate. Replacing some of the white flour in any cake, brownie or biscuit with buckwheat flour will give a deeper, gently nutty flavour, particularly if you toast the buckwheat flour first. It is essential for the balance of this dish to use an acidic, fruity chocolate in the mousse. Although, you can adjust the amount of acidity in the dish by adding a little vinegar to the caramel if your chocolate is not punchy enough.

for the caramel

makes 650g (1lb 7oz)

250g (1¼ cups) caster (superfine) sugar

250ml (1 cup) double (heavy) cream

125g (1 stick) unsalted butter, diced

15g (1 tbsp) Maldon salt

Put the sugar in a clean, high-sided saucepan and pour in 75ml (⅓ cup) of water. Cook over a high heat, swirling the pan to even out the sugar, until you have a dark amber caramel. Go as dark as your nerve allows. Remove from the heat and pour in the double cream. It will bubble up dramatically which is why it is important to use a high-sided pan. Whisk to make sure the caramel has combined with the cream.

Add the butter and salt and return to the boil. Use a whisk to mix the caramel and ensure it is emulsified. Leave to cool slightly before straining through a fine sieve or chinois and refrigerating.

serves 1

1 large scoop buckwheat ice cream (p193)

1 generous tsp caramel

pinch of Maldon salt

1–2 tbsp chilled chocolate mousse (p193)

2–3 shards buckwheat tuile (p193)

The caramel is best served at room temperature for this dish but the mousse should stay chilled.

Place a bowl in the freezer to chill 30 minutes before serving. Scoop a large quenelle of buckwheat ice cream and place slightly off-centre in the bowl. Make a small indent in the top of the ice cream and fill with the caramel. Sprinkle the Maldon salt on top. Add a large spoonful of chocolate mousse. Cover the mousse with the shards of buckwheat tuile, positioning them so that they are parallel to the work surface and appear to be floating.

GRAINS

Thinking of flour as a flavour ingredient rather than just a means to an end has been utterly transformative for me as a pastry chef. It's no longer: "what do I need this ingredient to do?" but "how do I want it to taste?" In the same way that I learned over and over that fruit tastes exponentially better when it's well-grown and freshly picked, I began to apply that thinking to other base ingredients in the pastry chef's larder. I have been really lucky to work alongside chefs, cooks and bakers whose passion for grains has been utterly evangelical and captivating. They taught me to taste the differences between varieties and between growing regions. They introduced me to the incredible flavour of freshly milled flours and to growers who have been putting flavour first for decades. I'm really excited for the pastry chefs and bakers coming through today's kitchens who are educated and excited about different grains and flours. In the UK, Hodmedod's is a great and very accessible source of freshly milled flours and grain varieties. Go and speak to your local artisan bakery too; they'll often sell you a bag of flour and talk to you about how to use it.

I really enjoy building a dessert around a grain or cereal. This can take many forms: as an infusion in an ice cream or mousse; as the texture in a shortbread or pastry; or as one of my all-time favourites, rice pudding. Many of the recipes here are adaptable to different grains and flours. The buckwheat ice cream will work really well with rye grain or toasted rice. The puff pastry and milk bread can happily accommodate other flours as part of the mix. There is space to have some fun and use the grains and cereals that you love. Wherever the recipes instruct you to toast the grain, be sure to toast it very well. The flavour will be all the better for it.

Buckwheat ice cream

It may sound a bit wholesome and not especially tasty, but buckwheat ice cream is quite the opposite. It captures the wonderfully earthy, malty qualities of the grain. The only heat applied to this ice cream is the hot, toasted buckwheat added to the cold milk. I think the lack of cooking helps to keep the flavour fresh and clean, but still with great depth and a lovely light feel. To create a thickened milk without cooking, I use Thick & Easy or Ultratex (p237) in the base. Don't be put off by the names; they are modified starches which will give your ice cream a beautifully smooth texture.

makes 750g (1lb 10oz)

160g (1 cup) buckwheat (buckwheat groats)

600ml (2½ cups) whole milk

80ml (⅓ cup) double (heavy) cream

30g (2 tbsp) caster (superfine) sugar

40g (3 tbsp) liquid glucose

16g (1½ tbsp) Thick & Easy or 8g (2½ tsp) Ultratex

small pinch of salt

Put the buckwheat in a baking tray or roasting dish and toast in a preheated oven at 200°C (400°F) for 35–45 minutes until the grains are well coloured and smell deliciously nutty. This takes longer than you think so don't be tempted to take it from the oven when it is still pale. Once the buckwheat is deeply golden, put it into a lidded container with the cold milk. Chill the infusion in the fridge overnight.

By the next day, the milk should have taken on the gentle pinkish-grey colour of the buckwheat. Break it up using a hand-held blender. Strain the infusion through a fine sieve, pressing the buckwheat to extract as much of the milk as possible.

Combine the infused milk with the cream, sugar, glucose, thickener and salt in a blender. Blend at medium speed until thick. Let the ice-cream base rest in the fridge for a minimum of 4 hours. Churn in an ice-cream machine then transfer to a container and leave to set in the freezer before serving.

Buckwheat tuile

This is adapted from the tuile recipe I learnt in college: the kind of tuiles that are designed to be stencilled into shape and then moulded into some kind of sculpture while hot. Not really my vibe visually but a solid recipe for a crisp addition to a dessert. Make the brown butter as dark as you can; it will deliver more flavour that way.

makes 540g (1lb 3oz), or about 3 sheets

150g (⅔ cup) dark brown butter (p173)

150g (1 cup plus 2 tbsp) buckwheat flour

150g (1 cup) icing (confectioners') sugar

90g (generous ⅓ cup) egg whites, from about 3 eggs

small pinch of salt

Preheat the oven to 170°C (340°F). Warm the brown butter in a small saucepan so that it is liquid and just warm but not hot. Sift the flour and sugar together and put in a mixer along with the brown butter and the remaining ingredients. Beat with a paddle to a thick, smooth batter.

Line a baking sheet with a silicone mat and pour on the tuile batter while it is still warm (it is trickier to spread once it has cooled). Use an angled palette knife to spread it as thinly and evenly as possible. You should get about three trays from this mix. Bake for 8–10 minutes until the tuiles are dry and evenly browned. Once they have cooled, flip them over and peel away the silicone mat. Store between layers of baking parchment in an airtight container.

Buckwheat shortbread

Buckwheat flour is excellent in shortbread. For one thing, buckwheat loves butter. It is also gluten-free so there is never any worry about overworking the dough so it becomes tough. It will always be beautifully short and delicate.

makes 25 biscuits

110g (¾ cup) buckwheat (buckwheat groats)

230g (1½ cups) buckwheat flour

5g (1 tsp) salt

230g (2 sticks) unsalted butter, at room temperature

110g (generous ½ cup) demerara sugar

Preheat the oven to 170°C (340°F). Toast the buckwheat in the oven until it starts to brown and smells deliciously nutty. Leave to cool before roughly crushing in a food processor or in a mortar and pestle. The aim is to introduce a coarse texture to the shortbread so you want to break up the buckwheat roughly, not crush it to a powder. Combine with the buckwheat flour and salt and set aside.

Beat the butter and sugar together in a mixer, food processor or by hand until well combined. You are not looking to cream or aerate the butter, just to make sure the two ingredients are well incorporated. Add the dry ingredients and mix to combine. Line a baking sheet with baking parchment and place an 8cm (3in) ring mould in one corner. Weigh 25g (about 2 tbsp) of dough and press into the ring mould to create an even layer. Remove the ring and repeat with the remaining dough, keeping the shortbreads evenly spaced. Alternatively, press the dough into one large cake tin or baking tray.

Bake until golden, so 12–14 minutes for individual shortbreads, or 20–25 minutes for one large one. Leave to cool completely on the baking sheet then carefully transfer to an airtight container to store. These are incredibly short and therefore very delicate so be gentle when handling them.

Oat biscuit

This is utterly addictive. The recipe was given to me by a colleague when I was working in New York. He had spent time in the UK and had come to embrace our national obsession with biscuits, particularly the Hobnob. It is a buttery, shattering biscuit that has just the right mix of salt and sugar. This recipe will make any oats taste great but will be even better when you use exceptional oats. I like to roll the dough super-thin and bake it pressed between heavy baking trays. You get sheets of biscuit to crumble up or break into shards as required. It works equally well if you roll the dough slightly thicker, chill it and cut into rounds for a more traditional shape. These are perfect for ice-cream sandwiches. Or go the whole hog and dip one side in melted chocolate. The rolled dough lasts really well in the freezer and can be baked from frozen.

makes 6 sheets

450g (3 sticks plus 6 tbsp) cold unsalted butter, diced

400g (2 cups) demerara sugar

300g (3⅓ cups) rolled (old-fashioned rolled) oats

300g (1½ cups) plain (all-purpose) flour

15g (1 tbsp) salt

15g (1 tbsp) bicarbonate of soda (baking soda)

Put the butter and sugar in a mixer and beat at low speed until well combined. You are not looking to cream or aerate the butter, just to make sure the two ingredients are well incorporated. Add the remaining ingredients and mix to combine.

Roll the dough out very thinly between two sheets of baking parchment. You should be able to see through it when you hold it up to the light. Chill the rolled-out dough in the fridge or store in the freezer to bake at a later date.

Preheat the oven to 180°C (350°F). Cut the dough to the desired shape and lay it onto trays lined with baking parchment or a silicone mat, or sandwich the sheet of dough (still between the baking parchment) between two heavy baking trays. Bake for 10–13 minutes until crisp and golden. If you have baked it in a sheet, remove the top tray and piece of parchment so that it does not steam while cooling. Once completely cool, store in an airtight container.

Oat mousse

Think of this as an oat custard that can either be aerated to make a mousse or churned into an ice cream. Use the most flavoursome oats you can get your hands on. The oats produced by Pimhill Farm in Shropshire make you realize just how delicious an ingredient oats can be. Rolled oats or pinhead oatmeal work here.

for the infusion

75g (5 tbsp) unsalted butter

450g (15oz) rolled or pinhead oats (old-fashioned rolled or steel-cut)

1.5 litres (1½ quarts) whole milk

250ml (1 cup) double (heavy) cream

Preheat the oven to 180°C (350°F). Melt the butter (cultured butter will give you an extra flavour boost if you have it) and mix through the oats. Spread the buttery oats into a thin layer on a baking tray and bake for 30–40 minutes. They should smell deeply toasty and have taken on a deep honey colour when they are done. If the oats aren't well toasted, they will soak up a lot more of the liquid and won't impart as strong a flavour. Leave them to cool to room temperature.

Pour the milk and cream into a bowl or lidded container and add the cooled, toasted oats. If the oats are too warm, they will release more of their starch into the liquid and the mix will become porridgy. Infuse overnight in the fridge.

250g (1¼ cups) caster (superfine) sugar

5g (1 tsp) salt

60g (6 tbsp) Thick & Easy *(p237)*

Strain the oats through a sieve or a piece of muslin, squeezing out as much of the liquid as possible. The oats can be eaten for breakfast (try them with some fruit in a Bircher muesli). Pour the infusion into a blender and add the sugar, salt and Thick & Easy. Blend at medium speed until the mixture thickens. If making ice cream, chill the base for a few hours before churning in an ice-cream machine. For a mousse, pour into a whipped cream dispenser *(p237)* and charge with 1 whipper bulb. Shake well. The mousse should just hold its shape when you dispense it.

Rice pudding

When I lived in New York, my treat when I was missing home would be a tub of rice pudding from the local fancy supermarket. It's my comfort food. I love it cold and straight from the can or warm from the oven with that caramelized edge. I have made many different versions over the years: enriched with butter, yolks and mascarpone at Gordon Ramsay's Pétrus; in huge batches at Gramercy Tavern, with custard folded through at the end in a show of decadence. My favourite is a relatively simple recipe based on the one I was taught by Miro Uskokovic at Gramercy Tavern. The vanilla is important: either use a fat, juicy pod (I like Tahitian) or splash out on vanilla bean paste. It should taste heady with floral vanilla.

serves 4–6

1 vanilla pod or ½ tsp vanilla bean paste

650ml (2¾ cups) whole milk, plus extra to finish

325ml (1⅓ cups) double (heavy) cream

90g (scant ½ cup) caster (superfine) sugar

pinch of salt

70g (⅓ cup) pudding rice (short-grain white rice)

Slit the vanilla pod lengthwise and scrape out the seeds. Put the seeds and pod (or vanilla bean paste) into a saucepan with the milk, cream, sugar and salt. Bring to a rolling boil, whisking to help disperse the vanilla. When the milk and cream are boiling, whisk in the rice and immediately reduce the heat to a gentle simmer. Cook over a low heat for about 40 minutes, stirring every now and then to make sure it cooks evenly and doesn't catch on the bottom of the pan. After about 30 minutes, start tasting. When it's ready, the rice will be tender. Grains of rice will start to appear on the surface of the pudding in the centre of the pan but there will still be a ring of liquid around the outside.

Pour into a shallow container, cover with a layer of cling film placed directly onto the surface and leave to cool to room temperature. Transfer to the fridge for 30 minutes then stir in some extra milk until you have a gently spoonable texture. Go slowly adding the milk as you want to keep that luscious thickness. Chill completely.

Yeast ice cream

This tastes like the smell of a loaf of still-warm brioche fresh from the oven. Dreamy. Sweet and somehow buttery, it captures that bakery scent in ice cream form. I use this in lots of different dishes: with apples, milk bread and caramel; with puff pastry and grilled cedro lemon. It provides a perfect French-toasty base for fruit. You first allow some of the milk to ferment with the yeast and then use that yeasty milk to create a custard.

for the yeast-infused milk

200ml (1 scant cup) whole milk

30g (2 tbsp) caster (superfine) sugar

50g (1¾oz) fresh yeast, or 20g (2 tbsp) dried active yeast

Combine the milk and sugar in a saucepan and warm over a gentle heat until it reaches body temperature or 35–40°C (95–104°F) on a thermometer. Remove from the heat and whisk in the yeast. Cover the pan and leave somewhere warm for 30–45 minutes. The milk should become very frothy and smell intensely yeasty and fermented. It will bubble up a lot so be sure to use a large enough pan.

makes 2 litres (4 pints)

1 litre (1 quart) whole milk

800ml (3⅓ cups) double (heavy) cream

240g (1 cup) egg yolks, from about 12–13 eggs

230g (1 cup plus 2½ tbsp) caster (superfine) sugar

5g (1 scant tsp) salt

Combine the yeast-infused milk with the milk and cream in a large saucepan. Place over a medium heat and bring to a rolling boil. Meanwhile, whisk the egg yolks, sugar and salt together.

Once the milk and cream mixture reaches a rolling boil, remove from the heat and slowly pour about half onto the yolks, whisking as you go to prevent curdling. Pour the now tempered egg mixture back into the saucepan with the remaining milk and cream and mix well. By bringing the milk and cream to a rolling boil first there should be enough latent heat left in the pan to cook the egg yolk to 82–83°C (180°F) without having to return it to the heat. Check the temperature and if it is below 82°C (180°F), continue to cook the custard over a gentle heat, stirring constantly until it reaches the required temperature. Immediately strain through a fine sieve and leave to cool.

Transfer to the fridge and let the ice-cream base rest for a minimum of 4 hours. Churn in an ice-cream machine then transfer to a container and leave to set in the freezer before serving.

Yeast caramel

This caramel works on the same principle as the ice cream. The cream is warmed with the sugar and yeast and allowed to ferment briefly. I have added some sourdough levain (starter) here because it is something I always have around and it brings an extra layer of flavour. If you don't have any, just up the fresh yeast to 30g (1oz). The cream will taste almost unpleasantly strong after it has fermented; that's ok, it needs to be powerful for the flavour to carry through once the caramel has been added. The intense heat of the caramel should be enough to halt any fermentation in the cream but return it to a rolling boil after deglazing to be sure. I have used this caramel to fill chocolates and pastries, or you could try adding it to a chocolate dessert.

for the fermented cream

450ml (1¾ cups) double (heavy) cream

25g (2 tbsp) caster (superfine) sugar

50g (3 tbsp) mature sourdough levain (optional)

20g (¾oz) fresh yeast or 8g (3 tsp) dried active yeast; if not using the levain, 30g (1oz) fresh yeast or 12g (4 tsp) of dried active yeast

Combine the cream and sugar in a large saucepan and warm over a gentle heat until it reaches body temperature or 35–40°C (95–104°F) on a thermometer. Remove from the heat and whisk in the yeast and levain (if using) or the larger quantity of yeast if you don't have any levain. Cover the pan and leave somewhere warm for 30–45 minutes. The cream should become very frothy and smell intensely yeasty and fermented. It will bubble up a lot so be sure to use a large enough pan.

makes 950g (3½ cups)

300g (1½ cups) caster (superfine) sugar

150g (1 stick plus 2 tbsp) unsalted butter, diced

3g (½ tsp) salt

Either make a dry caramel by adding the sugar directly to a hot, clean pan or by adding a little water along with the sugar and heating quickly (p165). Whichever way makes you feel comfortable. You're aiming for a caramel that's medium-dark amber. This will allow a bit of sweetness to carry through to balance the savouriness of the levain. If it's too dark, it will become excessively bitter and will overwhelm the yeasty flavours. If you go by temperature, it will be around 180°C (356°F).

Once the caramel gets to the right temperature or colour, remove it from the heat and carefully add the fermented cream. It will bubble up aggressively. Return to a low heat for 5–10 minutes to dissolve any remaining caramel on the bottom of the pan. Remove the pan from the heat and whisk in the butter and salt until well combined. Strain the caramel through a fine metal sieve or chinois and leave to cool completely before using.

Puff pastry

I spent a lot of time working out this puff pastry recipe at Lyle's. The goal was to create a puff that was incredibly high so we could cut a beautiful cross-section from it that was packed with delicate layers. I wanted it to be crisp yet tender and intensely buttery. It also needed to be hand-laminated (where alternating layers of butter and dough are pressed together) and achievable by the non-pastry chefs who worked on the section with me. The first year we did this, it was on the lunch and dinner set menu in December, the busiest time of the year. I had to make it every single day to keep up with demand. I had really strong arms after a month of hand laminating this much dough. All that repetition gave me this recipe and technique so it was worth the aching arms.

You want a mix of strong and plain flour (bread flour and all-purpose) here. Strong flour gives support so you can bake a tall piece of pastry and the soft plain flour helps to keep it tender. The dough isn't rested for long between folds so if you used only strong flour, you would have a really elastic dough that would constantly spring back as you rolled it out. You want flours that will allow for more extensibility (stretch) with a bit of elastic tension (spring back). Saying this, if you want to play about with different kinds of wheat, grains or wholegrain flours, I heartily encourage it. Bear in mind that wholegrain flours will need more water and that you always want that balance of extensibility and elasticity. The vinegar helps to stop any oxidation of the flour through the long rolling and folding process, keeping the dough from going grey. This is particularly helpful if you are using stoneground flours as they tend to oxidize a bit quicker. The vinegar and the cream contribute to the tenderness of the crumb, too.

The first step is to make the dough, or *détrempe*, which needs to rest for at least an hour but preferably overnight. Towards the end of the resting time, you can make the *beurrage* (the butter block). The key to any form of lamination is the temperature and plasticity of the butter. It needs to be cool but malleable, so I like to prepare the butter block about an hour before I plan to start lamination. I work flour into the *beurrage* to give a little more flexibility; it improves the plasticity and

means you don't have to be quite so precise with the temperature. This is helpful if you are making this in a kitchen where temperatures are highly variable.

for the dough

400g (3 cups) strong bread flour
220g (1¾ cups) plain (all-purpose) flour
16g (1 tbsp plus ½ tsp) salt
60g (5 tbsp) caster (superfine) sugar
30g (2 tbsp) unsalted butter, melted and cooled
10ml (2 tsp) white wine vinegar
70ml (5 tbsp) double (heavy) cream

Combine the dry ingredients in a bowl. Combine the wet ingredients in a separate bowl along with 260ml (1 cup plus 2 tbsp) of water. Mix the dry and wet together by hand to form a rough dough. You don't need to work it too much. It will feel slightly dry but should come together and have no patches of flour left. Form into a ball, cover and rest in the fridge for at least 1 hour or overnight.

for the *beurrage*

620g (5 sticks plus 1½ tbsp) cold butter, diced
180g (1¼ cups) strong bread flour

Put the butter in a mixer with a dough hook and work at medium-low speed until it is smooth and no lumps remain. The hook prevents the butter from being beaten too heavily and becoming aerated. Add the flour and continue mixing until it forms a homogenous mass. Spread this mix between two pieces of baking parchment to form a 16 x 16cm (6½ x 6½in) square block. Chill for 30 minutes–1 hour. The dough and *beurrage* should be at a similar temperature and consistency when you start the first fold.

Use a knife to score a cross into the dough, cutting no more than halfway through. Push the four petals out and down from the centre with a rolling pin. Roll out the dough on a well-floured surface. The goal is to roll so that you have four flaps and a slight mound in the centre. This mound should match the size of the *beurrage*, 16 x 16cm (6½ x 6½in). Brush any excess flour from the dough and place the *beurrage* in the centre. Enclose the four flaps of pastry over the butter to seal it in. You want the dough to be tightly surrounding the *beurrage* with no air pockets.

Use a rolling pin to firmly tap the length of your block and widen it out slightly to about 20cm (8in). Roll the block with firm, even strokes so that it forms a rectangle about 45cm (18in) long. Keep your rolling even throughout the length and make sure it stays straight. You can be generous with how much flour you use when rolling. Brush off any excess flour and gently fold the top of the dough into the centre followed by the base so that they meet in the middle. Fold the dough in half and you should have what looks like a book of dough. This is your first book fold. Wrap in cling film and chill for at least 1 hour.

Unwrap the dough and turn it so that the long seam is on the left and perpendicular to the edge of the work surface. Roll firmly and evenly until it is 45–50cm (18–20in) long again. Use plenty of flour to prevent any sticking but be sure to brush off the excess before completing the fold. Trim the ends of the dough a little if they are uneven. Repeat the book fold as before and rest for 1 hour in the fridge. Repeat this whole process one more time so that you have now completed three book folds. The dough will now feel smooth and should show clear layers when you cut through to trim the ends before folding.

Once you have completed three folds, rest the dough for 1–2 hours. With the seam horizontal and parallel to the edge of the work surface, roll the dough until it is 20cm (8in) long. Only use a lengthwise rolling action. Once the dough is the correct length, turn it by 90 degrees so that the seam is now on the left and is perpendicular to the edge of the work surface. Roll the dough lengthwise again until it is about 60cm (24in) long. You should end up with a piece of pastry that is 20 x 60cm (8 x 24in) and about 1cm (½in) thick. Again, it is important to use firm, even movements when rolling. Cut into two pieces, lay on trays lined with baking parchment and freeze for 30–45 minutes. It should be really, really cold but not fully frozen.

Preheat the oven to 200°C (400°F). Remove the dough from the freezer and use a sharp knife to trim about 1cm (½in) off the edges. Try to cut down with one clean motion so that you are not tearing or pinching any of the layers. This will mean that you

get a clean, even rise. Cut the pastry into blocks of 8 x 18cm (3 x 7in) and space out on baking trays lined with parchment or silicone mats.

Put in the oven and immediately turn down the heat to 140°C (285°F) and bake for 3½–4 hours. Do not open the oven door, particularly for the first 1½ hours as the pastry could collapse. The pastry is cooked through when it is deeply golden and feels light when you lift it. Leave to cool completely on a wire rack before storing in an airtight container. The dough freezes well: after the final book fold, wrap it in a double layer of cling film and store in the freezer. Defrost in the fridge before rolling and baking.

Milk bread

Pastry chefs have a tendency to think that brioche is the king of enriched doughs and use it any time the opportunity presents itself. I love brioche (I really do) but sometimes its super-charged butteriness can make it too dominant a component in a dish. In these cases, Japanese milk bread is your best friend. Super fluffy, soft and gently enriched, it has a slightly tighter crumb that makes it ideal for soaking up lots of flavour. French toast or *pain perdu* made with milk bread is my go-to. The extra fluffy, stretchy quality of milk bread is achieved by cooking a small amount of the flour with milk and water to make a paste that is then mixed into the main dough. This is called *tangzhong,* a method Japanese bakers borrowed from the Chinese technique for making soft and springy buns. This dough is endlessly versatile: it can be baked as loaves, buns or works really well when filled and rolled.

makes 2 loaves

for the *tangzhong*

45g (⅓ cup) strong bread flour

120ml (½ cup) whole milk

Put the flour and milk in a saucepan along with 120ml (½ cup) of water and whisk together. Cook over a medium heat, stirring constantly until the mixture has thickened to the texture of crème pâtissière or a thick custard. Leave it to cool to room temperature.

for the dough

28g (1oz) fresh yeast or 11g (1 tbsp) dried active yeast

225ml (1 scant cup) whole milk

3 eggs: 2 whole, 1 yolk

25g (2 tbsp) condensed milk

650g (5 cups) strong bread flour

120g (½ cup) caster (superfine) sugar

8g (2 tsp) salt

120g (1 stick) unsalted butter, softened

flavourless oil, for greasing

Dissolve the yeast in the milk and add the whole eggs and condensed milk. Put all the dry ingredients in a mixer and add the cooled *tangzhong* (see left). Mix at medium speed for 10–15 minutes until it comes together to form a cohesive dough. Leave to rest in the bowl for 5 minutes.

Turn the mixer back on and add the butter one third at a time. Mix for a further 10 minutes until you have a beautifully glossy dough. Transfer to a lightly oiled container, cover with a clean tea towel and leave for 2–3 hours until it's doubled in volume.

Divide the dough in two and shape into loaves by tightly rolling into a log. Place into oiled loaf tins and cover with a damp cloth. Leave somewhere warm to prove until doubled in volume again.

Preheat the oven to 180°C (350°F). Beat the egg yolk and dilute with a little water then brush on to the risen loaves to glaze them. Bake for 35–40 minutes. Turn out of the tins and leave to cool. This bread freezes extremely well but it's also irresistible when warm and freshly baked so it won't always make it to the freezer.

Oat mousse, honey granita and prune purée

I come over all patriotic when it comes to oats. They grow very well in Scotland (they're not averse to the cooler temperatures and consistent rain) so feature prominently in our cooking and baking traditions. From savoury uses – such as in haggis – to sweet – as in the classic mixture of oats, cream, honey, whisky and raspberries that is cranachan – oats feature throughout the Scottish cooking canon. I don't think there is a better smell than toasty, buttery oats. This dessert captures and celebrates that aroma, mixing it with honey in a nod to cranachan.

serves 1

2 x 8cm (3in) rounds of oat biscuit *(p194)*

1 dessert spoon prune purée *(p135)*

100g (½ cup) oat mousse *(p195)*

2 tbsp honey and beeswax granita *(p168)*

Spread the oat biscuits with a thin layer of prune purée to form a sandwich. Pipe a kiss of prune purée into the bottom of a bowl. Cover with the oat mousse and place two generous spoonfuls of granita next to the mousse. The idea is to use the oat and prune sandwich to scoop up the mousse and granita so you get all the flavours and textures with each mouthful.

NUTS

The nut harvest starts in spring with green or unripe almonds and walnuts and continues through into autumn. Green nuts are a beautiful addition to a dish and show a more delicate flavour than ripe nuts. They are picked before the shell has formed inside the fruit so they have a subtle, milky sweetness. Green almonds can be eaten whole when very young; later the fruit can be snapped open and the almond within peeled of its thin skin, which becomes rubbery and unpleasant once it's developed. With roasted mature nuts, it turns papery and can simply be rubbed off. To get the best from green walnuts takes a little more work: they can be candied, pickled or turned into a magical liqueur.

Come August, it's time for cobnuts and young hazelnuts to be picked from the orchard – or "plat" in the case of cobnuts. The south east of England is covered in cobnut plats, often forgotten, but laden with nuts to harvest. As the year wears on, the young, milky nuts give way to dried, buttery nuts as our palates seek out the warmer, richer flavours they supply. Finally, chestnuts appear in November along with the new-season walnuts.

Nuts supply endless possibilities in the pastry kitchen. A nut ice cream makes a perfect base on which to build a fruit dessert, such as almond ice cream with stone fruits. Then there are classic pairings such as walnuts with pears, apples or quinces; or hazelnuts with bright summer berries. Nuts also have a natural affinity with chocolate, coffee and many alcohols as they share so many of the same flavour compounds. They are an excellent supporting act to so many ingredients but don't be scared to make them the star. It feels only fitting to get excited about whichever nut is in season and really show it off. Be picky about where you source your nuts from. Many nut trees are incredibly thirsty (particularly almonds), so can be detrimental to the land they're planted on in large, commercial farms. Agroforestry projects provide a brilliant and sustainable way to grow and harvest nuts. Often planted in rows alongside other crops, they help to reduce soil erosion and water stress, and increase biodiversity. Well-grown nuts, to put it very simply, taste much better. Buy nuts in small quantities and be sure to store them somewhere cool to stop them going rancid. They contain high levels of oils (which is what makes them so delicious) so are prone to deterioration if not stored well. You can keep them in the freezer if you have a particularly warm kitchen (and a big enough freezer).

Green walnut liqueur

The royal parks of London are excellent places to find walnut trees; Hyde Park in particular has avenues of them. They are the kind of tree, like figs, that you start to see everywhere as soon as you notice one. You need to start fighting the squirrels for green, unripe walnuts in June. You are traditionally meant to pick them (as a barefoot maiden) on the eve of the feast of St John the Baptist on 24 June but, if you don't happen to be a maiden, or if you have a thing for wearing shoes, you just need to make sure you pick the walnuts before the shell starts to form inside. Green walnut liqueur – or *nocino* – is cut from the same cloth as other medicinal, herbaceous Italian *digestivi* like *amaro*. I never fully understand the more abrasive examples but *nocino* is gentler than the rest. It is beautiful in fruit cakes, Christmas puddings, poured over ice creams or paired with chocolate or coffee flavours. You don't need to use an expensive spirit here, any supermarket own-brand will serve you well. The spicing of *nocino* comes down to personal preference. I like to keep it simple with half a vanilla pod and some coffee beans but half teaspoons of whole spices like peppercorns or cloves, or the thinly pared peel of half a lemon or orange, will also work well.

makes 1 litre (2 pints)

30 green walnuts

500g (2½ cups) demerara sugar

1 tsp coffee beans

½ vanilla pod, peel of ½ lemon or orange, ½ tsp of black peppercorns, cinnamon, cloves or mace (optional)

1 litre (1 quart or 33.8 fl oz bottle) vodka or grappa

Cut the walnuts into quarters. Green walnuts will stain your hands and chopping board a deep green-black, so wear gloves when cutting and immediately wash your chopping board to prevent permanent stains. Tip the quartered walnuts into a clean and sterilized 2-litre Kilner jar or similar storage jar (or two 1-quart jars). Add the sugar, coffee beans and any spices or citrus peel you are using. Clip or screw the jar shut and give it a good shake. Leave it to sit in a sunny spot for 1 day. The sugar will start to draw out and mix with the green-black liquid from the walnuts to form a syrup.

Add the vodka or grappa and give it another good shake. Leave the jar in its bright, sunny spot for 6 weeks giving it the occasional shake. You can then either strain and decant the liqueur into sterilized bottles or, like me, keep the preserved green walnuts in their boozy bath. Either way, it is time for it to rest somewhere dark until winter. It gets more mellow and rich the longer it is left.

Chestnut meringue

Now for the purists among you, chestnuts are not technically a nut but this is the chapter in which they sit most comfortably. These meringues are in essence a chestnut macaron but were never served as a sandwiched pair. Instead, I would make one larger meringue and serve it on top of a quince posset. The mixture of shattering shell and fudgy centre is a textural pleasure that shouldn't be confined to perfect French pâtisseries or petits fours at the end of a meal in a Michelin-starred restaurant. The trick with macarons – and therefore with this meringue – is to fold the final mixture to make it slack enough to pipe perfectly smoothly but not so much that it becomes a puddle. A matter of a couple of folds can make all the difference. Go slowly; you want to achieve a batter that is starting to get glossy and shiny and that just holds its shape when you pull a ribbon of batter across the surface.

For the ground chestnuts in this recipe, peel and finely grate 5–6 peeled raw chestnuts. Toast in an oven preheated to 180°C (350°F) for about 10 minutes until dry then leave to cool. Grind the dried chestnuts to a fine powder in a spice grinder or mortar and pestle.

whites and continue whisking at medium speed for 3–5 minutes until the meringue is aerated and glossy but hasn't cooled completely. The residual heat will help to dissolve the sugars in your nut paste, giving the finished meringues a crisp, shiny exterior.

Gently fold the egg whites into the chestnut mixture one third at a time. You can be more aggressive folding in the first third to make sure it is completely smooth but be more gentle with the remainder. The best tool for this is a plastic pastry scraper. You are aiming for a slight gloss and for the batter to be liquid enough to flow while still holding its form. A drop of batter should hold for about 5 seconds before it melts back into itself.

Preheat the oven to 160°C (325°F). Pipe the meringue into roughly 5cm (2in) diameter circles onto a tray lined with baking parchment. Tap the tray to flatten the meringues and tap out any air pockets. Let the piped meringues sit for about 20–30 minutes at room temperature so that they form a skin, just as you would for macarons; when you touch them gently, they should no longer feel wet or sticky. Bake for 16–18 minutes. When they are cooked, they should peel easily from the parchment but still have a slightly soft middle. Leave to cool completely and store in an airtight container.

---

makes 16 meringues

35g (¼ cup) ground almonds

35g (⅓ cup) ground chestnuts, toasted (above)

130g (1 cup) icing (confectioners') sugar

80g (5 tbsp plus 1 tsp) egg whites, from about 3 eggs

80g (⅓ cup plus 1 tbsp) caster (superfine) sugar

Combine the ground almonds and toasted ground chestnuts with the icing sugar in a food processor and whizz until very fine. Tip into a large bowl and add 45g (3 tbsp) of egg whites to make a thick, smooth paste.

Combine the caster sugar with 25ml (1 tbsp plus 2 tsp) of water in a saucepan and place over a medium heat to make a syrup. Whisk the remaining egg whites in a mixer at medium speed until soft peaks form. As soon as the syrup reaches 116°C (240°F), pour it in a steady stream into the egg

Chestnut purée

I've used this to top chocolate cakes, fill croissants and as part of various plated desserts. It's just absolutely divine whatever you decide to use it for. You can go to the trouble of cooking and peeling your own chestnuts if you have access to great fresh ones but I tend to use chestnuts that have already been cooked and peeled that come vacuum sealed.

makes 500g (1lb 2oz)

200g (6½oz) cooked and peeled whole chestnuts

25g (2 tbsp) brown butter (p173)

200ml (1 scant cup) whole milk

pinch of salt

1 tsp light muscovado sugar

50g (3 tbsp) double (heavy) cream

Combine the chestnuts, brown butter and milk in a saucepan over a medium-low heat. Cook for about 20 minutes until the chestnuts start to get soft and a little mushy. Pour into a blender and process to a smooth purée. It looks like a lot of milk but as the chestnuts break down they thicken the liquid so don't worry. Taste the purée once it is smooth and season with the salt and sugar. Taste and check it again, adding more sugar or salt as required. Finally, blend in the cream to finish.

Frangipane

A good frangipane recipe is an incredibly useful thing to have at your disposal. The differences come down to application and personal preference. I like a slightly coarser texture where you really taste the nuts and butter. As for different uses, I love hazelnut frangipane made with a light muscovado sugar to go with plums; almond to go with pears or quince; a mix of walnut and almond made with demerara to go with apple. Try playing about with your choice of nuts and sugars to create the flavour profile you want. Toasting the nuts will add more depth but don't toast more than 50 per cent of them or the end result will be greasy. For a sturdier, cakier mix, add a little flour along with the nuts. Using ready-ground nuts will give a drier mix (they absorb more of the melting butter) and a more consistent texture. This recipe makes enough to fill a shallow 33-cm (13-in) tart case or a deeper 30-cm (12-in) case.

250g (1⅔ cups) nuts

pinch of salt

250g (2 sticks) unsalted butter, softened

250g (1¼ cups) caster (superfine) sugar

3 eggs

40g (4½ tbsp) plain (all-purpose) flour (optional)

Grind the nuts with the salt in a food processor until fine then set aside. Mix the butter and sugar in a food processor, mixer or by hand until well combined, You are not looking to aerate the butter and sugar, just to cream them together. Overbeating will give a puffier final product. Mix in the eggs followed by the ground nuts and flour (if using). The frangipane will keep in the fridge for 3–5 days but let it to come up to room temperature before you pipe or bake it.

If you are baking the frangipane in a pastry shell, first blind bake the pastry, leave to cool and then fill with the frangipane and fruit and jam. For a gluten-free option, forgo the pastry and flour and bake the frangipane in an ovenproof dish brushed with soft butter and dusted with demerara sugar. Bake at 150°C (300°F) for about 1½ hours, depending on the depth of your dish. This lower, slower bake will give you a more even final product.

Vanilla and hazelnut cookies

I use these in the raspberry ice-cream sandwiches but I like to keep a stash in the freezer at all times. They're based on Ravneet Gill's chocolate chip version. She knows what she's talking about when it comes to cookies and biscuits so they are beautifully textured. The hazelnut flavour is really important so use the best you can. Whole vanilla pods may seem extravagant but they help make these cookies truly special. The walnut and almond cake from The River Café uses whole pods in the same way and it's my favourite cake to make – and eat – there. If you can't stretch to pods, use a generous teaspoon of vanilla bean paste.

makes 25 cookies

50g (½ cup) ground hazelnuts

180g (1½ cups) blanched hazelnuts

140g (1 stick plus 2 tbsp) unsalted butter, softened

3g (½ tsp) salt

140g (¾ cup) light brown soft sugar

110g (½ cup) caster (superfine) sugar

2 vanilla pods, finely chopped

1 egg

200g (1¾ cups) plain (all-purpose) flour

4g (¾ tsp) bicarbonate of soda (baking soda)

3g (generous ½ tsp) baking powder

Toast the ground and blanched hazelnuts in the oven at 180°C (350°F) for 10–15 minutes until deeply golden with an intense aroma. Leave to cool. Mix the butter, salt and sugars together until just combined. Add the vanilla pods to the butter and sugar along with the egg and mix well. Roughly chop the cooled nuts so you have a mix of large and small chunks. Sift together the flour, bicarbonate of soda and baking powder then stir in the hazelnuts. Add to the wet ingredients and mix well. Use an ice-cream scoop to form balls of cookie dough or weigh out 35g (2 tbsp) per cookie and roll into balls. Chill the shaped cookies overnight or freeze for later use.

Preheat the oven to 160°C (325°F). Space the cookies out on a baking tray lined with baking parchment and bake for 12–15 minutes. You can bake these straight from the freezer.

Walnut shortbread

This is the same as the buckwheat shortbread recipe (p194) but the buckwheat and flour have been swapped for toasted walnuts and rye flour. You don't have to reinvent the wheel with every dish you put on a menu: trust the recipes you have and adapt the flavours to suit the seasonal ingredient. I like this version of the shortbread with autumnal fruits; the earthy flavours pair beautifully with apples, pears, pumpkin and quince. I use a small ring mould here to create individual shortbreads but you can press the shortbread mix into one large cake tin or tray instead.

makes 25 x 8cm (3in) biscuits

110g (1 cup) walnuts, shelled

230g (1¾ cup) rye flour

5g (1 tsp) salt

230g (2 sticks) unsalted butter, softened

110g (½ cup plus 1 tbsp) demerara sugar

Preheat the oven to 170°C (340°F). Spread the walnuts out on a baking tray and toast in the oven for 7–10 minutes until they're starting to brown and smell deliciously nutty. Leave them to cool before crushing roughly in a food processor or mortar and pestle. The aim is to introduce a coarser texture to the shortbread so you want to break up the nuts, not crush them to a powder. Combine with the rye flour and salt and set aside.

Beat the butter and sugar together until combined; you're not trying to aerate the mixture, just make sure the ingredients are evenly incorporated. Add the dry ingredients and mix to combine. Weigh 25g (1½ scant tbsp) of dough and press into an 8cm (3in) ring mould and repeat with the remaining dough. Bake for 12–14 minutes until golden. Leave to cool completely on the tray then carefully transfer to an airtight container to store. These are incredibly short and therefore very delicate so be gentle when handling them.

Vegan almond ice cream

You need a really high-powered blender for this ice cream. I tried many, many times in my ok-but-not-great blender at home and could never quite get the nuts totally smooth. This ice cream works best in a Pacojet (p236) as the extra blending abilities give the silkiest results but it will churn well in an ice-cream machine. We would make sure to have a stock of this in the freezer at all times at Lyle's which we could churn to order. It meant that I wasn't having to prepare a vegan dish daily and then waste produce if it wasn't needed. If you want to go the extra step with this ice cream then you can make your own almond milk. Soak blanched almonds in cold water overnight at a ratio of one part nuts to two parts water. The next day, blend the nuts and water together and squeeze through a muslin cloth to extract as much liquid as possible. You can also make this base with hazelnuts and hazelnut milk.

makes 1kg (2¼lb)

30g (2½ tbsp) caster (superfine) sugar

10g (1 tbsp) tapioca flour

15g (1 tbsp) ice-cream stabilizer (p237)

800ml (3⅓ cups) almond milk

75g (⅓ cup) liquid glucose

150g (1 cup) blanched almonds

pinch of salt

Mix the sugar, tapioca flour and ice-cream stabilizer together then whisk into the almond milk. Put the mixture in a large saucepan along with the glucose. Cook over a medium heat, stirring well until it reaches 75°C (167°F).

Meanwhile, toast the almonds in an oven preheated to 200°C (400°F) for 15–20 minutes. They should be deeply golden and glossy from releasing their own oils. Add the hot nuts to the hot milk, leave to cool slightly then infuse in the fridge overnight.

The next day, pour into a blender and process until very well combined. Churn in an ice-cream machine then transfer to a container and leave to set in the freezer before serving.

Nut ice cream

Like the vegan almond ice cream, you need a high-powered blender for this. Use this base recipe to make any nut-flavoured ice cream. I always like to have a rotation of hazelnut, almond and walnut going throughout the year: hazelnut to serve with the first of the summer berries; almond in the late summer to pair with stone fruits; and walnut in the autumn and winter to offset a warm chocolate mousse or pears. The important thing here is to toast the nuts really well to get the maximum flavour from them. If you make this ice cream with walnuts then blanch the toasted walnuts in boiling water and refresh in cold water twice to remove any bitterness. This will yield the cleanest, most pure-tasting walnut ice cream.

makes 1kg (2¼lb)

750ml (3 cups) whole milk

100ml (scant ½ cup) double (heavy) cream

50g (3 tbsp) liquid glucose

25g (3 tbsp) caster (superfine) sugar

10g (1¼ tbsp) tapioca flour

150g (1 cup) nuts, skinless

Put the milk and cream in a large saucepan along with the glucose. Mix the sugar and tapioca flour together then whisk into the milk and cream. Cook over a medium heat, stirring well until it reaches 75°C (167°F).

Meanwhile, toast the nuts in the oven at 200°C (400°F) for 15–20 minutes. They should be deeply golden and glossy from releasing their own oils. Add the hot nuts to the hot milk, leave to cool slightly then infuse in the fridge overnight.

The next day, pour into a blender and process until very well combined. Churn in an ice-cream machine then transfer to a container and leave to set in the freezer before serving.

Warm chocolate mousse with walnut ice cream and green walnut liqueur

This is definitely a grown-up chocolate dessert. It is rich and intense and one of my absolute favourites. The flavours work beautifully together. Any dessert that combines hot and cold, particularly when it comes to chocolate, is a win in my book. The warm mousse covers the walnut ice cream with its centre of green walnut liqueur. As you eat it, you dip through the mousse, getting hits of boozy *nocino* and the cold, clean-tasting ice cream.

serves 1

1 large scoop walnut ice cream *(p209)*

1 tbsp green walnut liqueur *(p205)*

4–5 generous tbsp warm chocolate mousse *(p187)*

30g (3 tbsp) walnuts, toasted and finely chopped

½ preserved walnut from making walnut liqueur, cut into thin matchsticks *(p205)*

Place a deep, high-sided bowl in the freezer to chill at least 30 minutes before serving. Scoop a large ball of the ice cream into the chilled bowl and make a deep well in the centre. Fill the well with the green walnut liqueur. Cover the whole thing with the warm chocolate mousse. Sprinkle the chopped walnuts over the mousse and lay the matchsticks of preserved walnuts artfully on top.

Cobnut ice cream with raw cobnuts

If the chocolate and walnut dessert is all about rich, intense flavours, this dish is positively austere. And I do mean austere as a positive. Traditionally grown in Kent, cobnuts are a variety of hazelnut harvested from mid-August to October and are most revered when eaten young and fresh rather than dried. They are milky and delicately flavoured early in the season and that is precisely what this dish celebrates. We would pick crates and crates of them every year as the season rolled around. They are labour-intensive to crack and peel: their green husks need to be removed, then the shells cracked and the thin, unpleasant-tasting skin around the nut peeled away. Once you've done all that, store them in cold water until ready to use. The method for this ice cream differs slightly to account for the increased expense and effort of securing cobnuts.

for the cobnut ice cream

makes 1kg (2¼lb)

750ml (3 cups) whole milk

100ml (scant ½ cup) double (heavy) cream

50g (3 tbsp) liquid glucose

25g (2 tbsp) caster (superfine) sugar

10g (1¼ tbsp) tapioca flour

150g (1 cup) blanched hazelnuts

100g (⅔ cup) cobnuts, peeled

Use the same method as for the nut ice cream (*p209*) using the hazelnuts to infuse the milk. Once the milk has infused, strain to remove the hazelnuts (you can reroast them and use in another recipe; they will have an ever so slightly milky note in their next incarnation), and blend in the cobnuts before churning the base.

serves 1

1 scoop cobnut ice cream

10–12 cobnuts, peeled

small pinch of Maldon salt

1 tsp cobnut or hazelnut oil

Place a bowl in the freezer to chill at least 30 minutes before serving. Use either a very sharp knife or mandoline to thinly slice the cobnuts vertically to show their full shape. Place a perfect quenelle of just churned cobnut ice cream into the centre of the frozen bowl. Use a clean spoon to gently flatten the top of the ice cream then cover the surface with the slices of cobnuts so that they overlap like scales. Sprinkle on the salt and finish with a drizzle of the nut oil.

OUTDOOR RHUBARB

There is a break in the season around March or April when the last of the forced rhubarb has been harvested and the outdoor rhubarb has not quite reached maturity. My favourite time to use outdoor rhubarb is towards the end of April, through May and into the beginning of June. It is a lovely precursor to the first of the strawberries that arrive later in the month as the sun really begins to shine. Outdoor rhubarb doesn't always get the same fanfare as its more brazen sister, forced rhubarb. It is not as tender nor as luminous as the earlier season rhubarb but has other qualities worthy of your attention. Since it is more robust, it can stand up to more fierce heat and longer cooking times, making it perfect in galettes, pies and crumbles. It also tends to have a fruitier flavour compared to the acidic, vegetal qualities of forced rhubarb. Look out for varieties that deliver that fruity hit like Raspberry Red or Fulton's Strawberry Surprise. They have a deeper magenta-red colour rather than the dayglow pink. You can apply the same techniques from the forced rhubarb chapter here though you may need to adjust the sugar slightly.

Rhubarb juice

The juice of outdoor rhubarb carries the dramatically deep colour of the fruit. To make it, first wash and trim the rhubarb then cut it into 1–2cm (½–¾in) pieces. The tougher fibres of this rhubarb will make a juicer work very hard so it is worth spending the time cutting it into smaller pieces first. You can use a blender if you don't have a juicer and then just squeeze the pulp through a clean tea towel or muslin to extract the juice. Whichever method you use, once you have collected the juice, transfer it to a saucepan and bring to the boil and then strain through a sieve lined with muslin. When you initially juice the rhubarb, it will look much duller and murkier than the forced rhubarb juice but it brightens instantly once it has been brought to the boil and strained to clarify it.

Poached rhubarb

Poaching is a gentle way to cook fruit while maintaining its structure and shape. By cooking it in its own juice, you can deepen and reinforce the essential flavour. I keep outdoor rhubarb in larger pieces for poaching than forced rhubarb. It requires a bit more sugar to penetrate the fibres and season the stalks all the way through.

makes 500g (1lb 2oz)

500g (1 generous lb) trimmed rhubarb

500g (2 cups) clarified rhubarb juice

250g (1¼ cups) caster (superfine) sugar

Preheat the oven to 160°C (325°F). Cut the rhubarb into 3–5cm (1–2in) lengths and place in a single layer in an ovenproof dish. Put the juice and sugar in a saucepan and bring to the boil then pour over the cut rhubarb. Cover the fruit with a piece of baking parchment (a cartouche) and poach in the oven for 15–20 minutes. The rhubarb should be tender but not falling apart; a knife or skewer should slide in with little resistance. Leave to cool to room temperature before refrigerating; it will continue to cook in the poaching liquor as it cools. The longer it stays in its liquor, the more the colour will deepen.

Rhubarb jelly

All of that wonderful poaching liquor needs a purpose and this is an excellent use for it. It is the colour of rubies and utterly delicious. The ratio of gelatine to liquid given here will result in a soft-set but stable jelly. If you want it firmer so you can set it in a mould and then turn it out, increase the gelatine to 10 leaves per litre (quart) of liquid.

makes 1kg (2¼lb)

7 leaves of bronze grade gelatine

1 litre (1 quart) poaching liquor from making poached rhubarb or rhubarb chewies (p159)

caster (superfine) sugar, to taste

Break the gelatine leaves in half and soak them in iced water for 5 minutes to soften. Make sure the water is very cold as you don't want the gelatine to start melting before it is fully hydrated.

Warm the poaching liquor and taste to see if it needs more sugar. Bear in mind that it will taste less sweet when it is cold than when it is warm. Once the liquid is well seasoned and approaching a simmer, remove from the heat. Squeeze any excess water from the gelatine and add it to the hot rhubarb liquor. Never add gelatine to a boiling liquid as this will affect its setting ability. Whisk gently to make sure all the gelatine is dissolved.

I like to set this in a plastic container and then take slightly broken spoonfuls when I am plating a dish but you can set it in individual dishes if you prefer. To speed setting, chill the rhubarb jelly in a bowl sitting in an ice bath until it is just starting to thicken. Pour the jelly into your chosen container and refrigerate for about 4 hours until set.

Roasted rhubarb

If you are going to roast fruit, always do it at high heat. You want to make the most of turning on the oven to caramelize the top of the fruit in a way you never can on the stove. If you cook it at too low a temperature, the fruit will steam and poach in its own juices, turning to mush before you have time to achieve that glorious caramelization. This is the one time with rhubarb where I think adding extra flavourings benefits the fruit. A spent vanilla pod or dash of bean paste mixed with the sugar will add an extra dimension, while a few strips of orange peel with a squeeze of juice will pump up the fruitiness.

outdoor rhubarb, cut into 5cm (2in) batons

caster (superfine) sugar

vanilla pod, vanilla bean paste, orange peel, rosemary, star anise or wild fennel, to flavour

Weigh the rhubarb and multiply by 0.15 or 0.2 to work out how much sugar you need. You want between 15 and 20 per cent, depending on how sweet you like your rhubarb (1 cup of sugar weighs 200g, or nearly 7oz). Combine the sugar with the flavouring of your choice in a large bowl then add the rhubarb and toss it all together.

Preheat the oven to 200°C (400°F) and leave the rhubarb to macerate while the oven heats. Tip the macerated rhubarb into a roasting tin so that it's tightly packed in a single layer. Roast for 8–10 minutes. The rhubarb should be tender and lightly caramelized but still holding its shape.

Raspberry Red rhubarb jelly with vanilla ice cream and oat biscuit

I was never a fan of jelly and ice cream as a child but I still feel the strong pull of the collective nostalgia for this classic combination. The textural mix of wobbly jelly, silky ice cream and crunchy oat biscuit is pure pleasure.

serves 1

1 large shard of oat biscuit *(p194)*

1 large scoop vanilla ice cream *(p178)*

2 generous spoons rhubarb jelly *(p215)*

4–5 chewy rhubarb pieces *(p159)*

Put a shallow bowl in the freezer to chill 30 minutes before serving. Break off a small piece of oat biscuit and crumble it into the bottom of the chilled bowl. Place a large scoop of vanilla ice cream on top. Put two generous spoons of jelly around one side of the ice cream (you can break the jelly up slightly so it is not a solid piece). Top with the pieces of chewy rhubarb. Break a large piece of oat biscuit and press it gently on top so that the ice cream is hidden but the jelly and chewies are showing.

FLOWERS, LEAVES & HERBS

The first heralds of spring are the unfurling leaves and tentative blossom buds. The weather may still be a bit miserable, and the days short, but the hope of a new season found in the flourishing growth is always exciting. While we wait for the sun to shine and the fruit to ripen, there is much flavour to be found from young leaves, blossoms and herbs. Abundant cherry blossoms are calling out to be picked and preserved so that when the cherries finally ripen we have the blossoms' delicate almond notes to pair them with. The magnolia trees that are the first truly spectacular blossoming can be captured in sugar, both their delicate ginger flavour and palest pink hue.

Next appears the true harbinger of summer, elderflower. As the sun shines and the temperature warms, the elderflower bursts forth, releasing its intoxicating perfume around the city and countryside and decorating both with its delicate blooms. It comes in with the outdoor rhubarb and the first of the strawberries; heavenly and fortuitous combinations.

As the weather warms further, we begin to get the wild fennel, chamomile and heat-loving herbs like lemon verbena. The flavours they provide are punchier, their intensity increasing with that of the sun. I love chamomile with apricots and verbena with blackcurrants. If you are fortunate enough to grow your own, or have access to a fruit farm, you'll know the joy of the leaves and blossoms before – and along with – the ripening fruit. Many leaves carry the top notes of the fruit they belong to without any of the jammy, sugary qualities. Fig and blackcurrant leaves are the best examples of this. I cover these in their respective chapters but the same principles can be applied. A few

fruit leaves added to a poaching liquor or ice-cream base will reinforce the flavour in a more aromatic manner.

Many herbs are available throughout the year. Thyme, sage, rosemary and bay are all easily adapted for sweet uses. Lemon thyme will always be a firm favourite from my years at Lyle's but I think bay has gradually moved its way to the top of my list. Bay leaf custard is surprisingly delicious; try pairing it with oranges or rhubarb. There are also the seasonal herbs that come in the spring and summer. Tagetes or marigold can have a beautifully gentle apple and orangey note to them – what a combination! Anise hyssop carries a delicate aniseed flavour that is stunning with peaches. Geranium, sweet cicely, pineapple weed, lemon balm: there are so many herbs to pick, grow and play with to complement the fruit in your dessert. It's really all about tasting and exploring to find out what you like.

Many of the recipes here use infusions to capture the delicate scents and flavours found among the spring blossoms. The principles are all easily transferable to other flowers and leaves. If you swap the herb or flower I have used for another, make sure to keep tasting as you go to find that perfect level of flavour intensity. Different infusions need different amounts of time to get the best from the ingredient. Our cities are covered with edible plants and flowers; trust me, once you know what you're looking for you'll start to see things to pick everywhere. I would recommend going with someone who knows what they are doing or using a good foraging guide. There are many blooms that smell glorious but aren't safe to eat so always check if you are picking something new.

Preserved cherry blossom and leaves

Cherry blossom, or *sakura*, is a traditional flavour in Japan where the spectacular ornamental cherry trees are celebrated every spring. If you ever see *sakura* tea (or *sakura* anything to be honest), it's worth buying. The pastel pink flowers have been salted, pickled and dried to bring out the incredible almond flavour. The preserved blossoms are used to flavour sweets, cakes, even Kit Kats in Japan, while the young leaves are seen wrapped around *mochi* (sweet rice cakes) and other confectionery.

I went to Maynards Fruit Farm in East Sussex to pick young blackcurrant leaves one spring and happened to arrive on a day when the cherry trees were in full bloom. Though not quite as resplendent as the showy ornamental trees, they were still a beautiful sight. There are many varieties of ornamental and fruiting cherry trees to be found in our cities; I tend to pick from the cherry orchard on the farm so that I can be 100 per cent sure of what I am getting. Not all of the pink blossoming trees will be cherry so, as always, make sure you know what you've foraged before you consume it. Cherry blossoms do contain traces of toxic compounds; the salting helps to break them down but it's best not to consume large quantities. The amounts used in these recipes are fine.

---

cherry blossom and young leaves

salt

cider or umeboshi vinegar

Pick flowers that are on the cusp of full bloom. Completely open ones will fall apart in the preservation process, so look for those whose buds have just opened and the puffy white flowers have begun to emerge. Separate the blossom into individual leaves and whole flowers with minimal stalk. Weigh the flowers and leaves together and divide the figure by two to calculate the salt required, for example, you'll need 50g (¼ cup) of salt for 100g (3½oz) of flowers. Sprinkle the salt through the flowers and leaves and toss gently to coat them. Transfer to a jar and place a weight on top of the flowers to gently push them down. I use a ziplock bag filled with water for this. Leave in a cool place for 1 week. The smell will already be intense when you open the jar.

Rinse the excess salt from the blossoms by placing them in a sieve under cool running water for a few minutes. Allow the water to drain off and then weigh the flowers and leaves again. You want to pickle the blossoms in 5 times their weight in vinegar. For example, for 100g (3½oz) of flowers, add 500g (2 cups) of vinegar. Return the flowers and leaves to a clean jar and pour over the vinegar. Store somewhere cool and dark for at least 1 week before using.

You can remove the blossoms from the vinegar at this point and dry them gently. They can then be used to infuse a cream, custard or other liquid, or ground into a powder. Try dressing cherries with a splash of the vinegar, add it to a meringue base or in any number of savoury dishes. I love using the leaves to wrap around small cakes in a nod to *sakura mochi*, as in the cherry blossom steamed sponge (*p52*).

Magnolia syrup

The first of the dramatic blossoms to appear in spring, magnolia could feel almost gaudy if it weren't for its elegant flowers. They range from palest creamy white to intense fuchsia with different blushes along the way. What makes the trees look so striking is the fact that the flowers appear before the leaves. I had read a vague note about them tasting like ginger, which sent me off in search of a tree I could nab a few flowers from. It felt like a true revelation the first time I bit into a petal. Although the flavour will differ slightly depending on the pigmentation of the flower, as a general rule, magnolia has the flavour of young ginger: slightly spicy with a beautiful floral quality. The whiter flowers tend to have more citrussy, cardamom notes while the deeper fuchsia flowers get spicier and more gingery. Try to pick buds that are younger and have only just opened and avoid any that have started to brown on the edges.

---

makes 1 litre (2 pints)

150g (¾ cup) caster (superfine) sugar

100g (2–3) magnolia flowers

7g (1 tsp) citric acid

Combine the sugar with 750ml (3 cups) of water in a saucepan. Bring to a rolling boil over a medium heat until the sugar has dissolved. When the syrup is boiling, add the whole magnolia flowers. Return to a rolling boil and add the citric acid. Immediately transfer to a shallow container then chill over ice or in the fridge. I like to leave the flowers in the syrup as they have a pleasingly ethereal quality. Store chilled. This is superb poured over ice cream, used to dress or poach fruit, or added to a drink.

Elderflower custard

This is a very rich, egg yolk-heavy custard.
I love to use it with either outdoor rhubarb or
gooseberries for a dish inspired by a classic
floating island. The accompanying meringue
is very sweet so the sugar levels in the custard
are relatively low. If you want to use it for a
less sweet dish then you can up the sugar.

makes 700g (1lb 10oz)

125ml (½ cup) double (heavy) cream

375ml (1½ cups) whole milk

160g (⅔ cup) egg yolks, from about 9 eggs

40g (3 tbsp) caster (superfine) sugar

small pinch of salt

2–3 heads of elderflower

Combine the cream and milk in a medium saucepan
set over a moderate heat. Meanwhile, whisk the egg
yolks, sugar and salt together. Put the elderflowers
in a bowl, place a fine sieve inside it and sit the bowl
in an ice bath.

Once the milk and cream reaches a rolling boil,
remove from the heat and slowly pour about half
into the yolk mixture, whisking as you go to prevent
curdling. Pour the now tempered egg mix back into
the saucepan with the remaining cream and milk
and mix well. By bringing the milk and cream to a
rolling boil first there should be enough latent heat
left in the pan to cook the egg to 82–83°C (180°F)
without having to return it to the heat. Check the
temperature and if it is below 82°C (180°F), continue
to cook the custard over a gentle heat, stirring
constantly until it reaches the required temperature.
Immediately strain the custard over the elderflowers
and leave to infuse for an hour. Strain the cooled,
infused custard and discard the elderflowers then
transfer to the fridge to cool completely.

Elderflower cordial

This drink feels so quintessentially British to my mind. Elderflower grows prolifically from the north to the south of our fair isle, though I'd have to wait a few extra weeks for it to appear in Glasgow than I do now I'm in London. I use elderflower cordial in drinks, to gently sweeten strawberries and gooseberries and also as the liquor in summer puddings. Elder grows along hedgerows, canals, scrub and wetlands, often accompanied by stinging nettles. The foamy blooms appear from late May and can be found through till July. May often brings some gloriously sunny days in the UK and they happily coincide with great flushes of blooming elderflowers. You want to pick from trees that are not on busy roads or near traffic and at least one metre from the ground. It is best to pick early on a sunny, dry day. Elderflower's aroma can vary from pleasantly honeyed to a slight ammonia-like whiff of cat's pee over the course of a hot day, so keep sniffing as you go to make sure you are gathering only the sweetest smelling blossoms. Pick the heads that still have some flowers just opening as these will carry the most aromatic pollen. Use scissors to cut cleanly and with as little branch as possible, then process as soon as you can.

makes 1.2 litres (2½ pints)
15 large elderflower heads
200g (1 cup) caster (superfine) sugar
2 lemons

I prefer a 20 per cent syrup for cordials, for example 200g (1 cup) of caster (superfine) sugar to 1 litre (1 quart) of water. It provides a gentle sweetness that won't overpower the delicate flavours, nor do you have to add extra citric acid to balance any overt sweetness and aid storage.

Inspect the elderflower heads carefully and remove any small bugs. If you do need to wash it, gently dip the flowers into some very cold water and shake off; don't immerse the whole heads or leave them to soak as you'll lose a lot of the aromatic pollen. Slice the lemons thinly and add to the prepared elderflower in a bowl. Combine the sugar with 1 litre (1 quart) of water in a large saucepan and bring to the boil to dissolve the sugar. Remove from the heat and pour over the elderflower and lemon. Leave to infuse in the fridge overnight before straining and bottling in clean, sterilized bottles.

Store in the fridge for up to 1 month. This elderflower cordial won't last quite as long as higher sugar recipes, so if you want to store it for longer, transfer to a plastic container and freeze.

You can use the spent elderflower heads to create a powder. Simply dehydrate them in a low oven or dehydrator and grind to a powder in a spice grinder or mortar and pestle. It is not the most beautiful of colours but still has a bright floral flavour.

Elderflower vinegar meringue

I often add vinegar to meringues. I enjoy the slightly chewy texture it gives as well as the balance it brings to a normally tooth-achingly sweet dessert. In this case, the amount of vinegar is much larger than normal so requires a more stable meringue. An Italian meringue works best and, rather than baking as a piped or scooped shape, it's spread thinly and dried at a low temperature. The resulting meringue sheets fizz and dissolve on your tongue, leaving behind the strong elderflower perfume.

for the elderflower vinegar

20ml (1 tbsp plus 1 tsp) elderflower cordial

100ml (scant ½ cup) cider vinegar

1 large head of elderflower

Warm the cordial and vinegar together in a small saucepan over a gentle heat until steaming but not boiling. Pour over the elderflower and leave to infuse for at least 2 hours before straining into a bottle. If you can infuse it for longer, the flavour will develop further. I always have a bottle in my cupboard for savoury as well as sweet uses.

for the meringue

90g (generous ⅓ cup) egg whites, from about 3 eggs

180g (¾ cup plus 2 tbsp) caster (superfine) sugar

60g (¼ cup) elderflower vinegar

Preheat the oven to 100°C (210°F) and line a baking sheet with baking parchment or a silicone mat. Place the egg whites in the clean bowl of a mixer and whisk at slow-medium speed.

Meanwhile, combine the sugar with 40ml (2½ tbsp) water in a small saucepan and bring to the boil. When the syrup reaches 116°C (240°F), turn the mixer up to a higher speed and whisk the egg whites until they form soft peaks. When the syrup reaches 120°C (248°F), take it off the heat and quickly and confidently pour it in a steady stream into the egg whites, continuing to whisk at high speed. For an Italian meringue, you want to hit 121°C (250°F); if you pull your syrup off the heat at 120°C (248°F) the temperature will continue to rise by that final degree on your way to the mixer. Once all the syrup has been added, turn the mixer down to medium. Continue to whisk for a further 10–15 minutes while it cools and stabilizes. It will now be thick and glossy. Pour in the vinegar and whisk until combined.

Use an angled palette knife to carefully spread a thin, even layer of meringue 2–3mm (⅛in) thick onto the lined baking sheet. Bake in the oven for 2–4 hours until it is completely dry and peels cleanly from the baking parchment. If you have a dehydrator, you can line the racks (either by wrapping in cling film or with a silicone mat) and dry the meringue at 65°C (150°F) for 2–3 hours. Store in an airtight container between layers of baking parchment.

Wild fennel ice cream

Fennel pollen is quite pricey when you buy it dried but in the height of summer, wild fennel can be found all over. It grows quickly and prolifically and is classified as an invasive plant. Coastal areas are particularly good places to find it but I've had great harvests from sunny east London scrublands, too. It smells heady with anise and has very distinct umbrella-shaped clusters of bright yellow flowers. The blossoms will eventually turn to seeds so always make sure to leave some on any plant you pick from. I am not a particular fan of liquorice or strong anise flavourings but wild fennel has a gently sweet, more minty, citrussy quality that I love. This ice cream is excellent with any stone fruit. You can play around and try different herbs and flowers in the base. Chamomile, lilac, elderflower and pineapple weed will all work here, just keep tasting the cooling custard to check when the flavour is right for you.

makes 1.5 litres (3 pints)

8 large heads wild fennel

800ml (3½ cups) whole milk

400ml (1¾ cups) double (heavy) cream

170g (generous ⅔ cup) egg yolks, from 9–10 eggs

100g (½ cup) caster (superfine) sugar

3g (½ tsp) salt

The base for this ice cream is an infused crème anglaise: hot custard is poured over the wild fennel and left to infuse as it cools. Place the fennel heads in a bowl set in an ice bath. Combine the milk and cream in a large saucepan and bring to a rolling boil.

Meanwhile, whisk the egg yolks, sugar and salt together. Once the milk and cream reaches a rolling boil, remove from the heat and slowly pour about half into the yolk mixture, whisking as you go to prevent curdling. Pour the now tempered egg mix back into the pan with the remaining milk and cream and mix well. By bringing the milk and cream to a rolling boil first, there should be enough latent heat left in the pan to cook the egg to 82–83°C (180°F) without having to return it to the heat. Check the temperature and if it is below 82°C (180°F), continue to cook the custard over a gentle heat, stirring constantly until it reaches the required temperature. Immediately pour it over the fennel heads and infuse for 30 minutes, taste and leave for a further 10 minutes if the flavour is not yet strong enough.

Strain the chilled custard through a chinois or fine sieve into a container and refrigerate for at least 4 hours or overnight. Churn in an ice-cream machine then transfer to a container and leave to set in the freezer before serving.

Lemon verbena semifreddo

This may seem like a lot of steps but the outcome is more than worth it. A semifreddo is, in essence, a frozen mousse so it's lighter in texture than ice cream. I love to set this in a terrine then serve it in slices. You can even set different flavours on top of each other to create a layered effect. For the opening of Flor, we made a Neapolitan-style semifreddo with layers of peach, tayberry and lemon verbena. It was beautiful on the plate and, most importantly, beautiful to eat. Try rippling rhubarb or gooseberry compôte through when you pour it into the mould, or adding a layer of raspberries or diced peach in the middle.

serves 8

600g (2½ cups) double (heavy) cream

10g (tiny bouquet) lemon verbena, leaves picked

80g (⅓ cup) egg whites, from about 3 eggs

250g (1⅓ cup) caster (superfine) sugar

80g (⅓ cup) egg yolks, from 4–5 eggs

120g (½ cup) crème fraîche

flavourless oil, for greasing

Warm the cream in a small saucepan until it is steaming but not boiling and add the lemon verbena. Immediately pour into a bowl set in an ice bath. Once the cream is cold, strain it and discard the verbena.

Next, put the egg whites into the bowl of a mixer with a whisk attachment. Put 125g (⅔ cup) of the sugar into a small saucepan with 50ml (¼ cup) of water. Place over a high heat. When the syrup reaches 110°C (230°F), turn the mixer to medium speed to start whisking the whites until they form soft peaks. When the syrup reaches 120°C (248°F), take it off the heat and turn up the mixer. Quickly and confidently pour the syrup in a steady stream onto the egg whites, continuing to whisk at high speed. Once all the syrup has been added, reduce to medium speed and carry on whisking until the meringue has cooled completely.

Meanwhile, combine the egg yolks and remaining sugar in a metal bowl set over a saucepan of simmering water (bain-marie) to make a sabayon. Whisk the yolks and sugar over a gentle heat until they are light and pale; when you lift the whisk out, it should leave a ribbon trail that holds on the surface of the mixture before melting back in. Remove from the heat and leave to cool slightly.

Combine the chilled infused cream with the crème fraîche in a bowl and whisk until it holds soft peaks. Gently fold in the sabayon. Once the sabayon is mostly incorporated, add the meringue mix in two stages. Fold gently but firmly to maintain all of the volume with no lumps of meringue or cream.

Lightly oil a loaf tin or terrine and line with a double layer of cling film so that it overhangs the sides of the tin. Pour in the semifreddo and give the tin a gentle tap to make sure there are no air pockets. Freeze overnight. To serve, turn the tin upside down to release the semifreddo. Cut 2cm (¾in) slices, then remove the thin strip of cling film and serve on chilled plates. You can store slices of semifreddo between layers of baking parchment in an airtight container in the freezer.

Poached meringue with elderflower custard and outdoor rhubarb

The classics are classics for good reason; just think of peach melba or *tarte tatin*. For me, floating islands sit proudly in that group too. In its original form, a poached meringue on top of custard, drizzled with a bitter caramel that hardens as it cools. There's a glorious play of textures between the unctuous custard, light meringue and crisp caramel. This version sticks to those three contrasting elements but introduces fruit into the mix, too. The poached meringue sits in a pool of floral custard on top of a sharp compôte of fruit and is topped with a crisp sugar tuile flavoured with rhubarb. Play around with seasonal versions throughout the year. Try a bay leaf custard with Tarocco blood oranges in winter, or anise hyssop custard with cherries or chamomile custard with apricots in the height of summer.

for the poached meringue

200g (generous ¾ cup) egg whites, from 6–7 eggs

100g (3½ tbsp) caster (superfine) sugar

2g (½ tsp) egg white powder (optional)

pinch of elderflower powder *(p223)*

This is in essence a French meringue. The egg white powder adds a little extra protein and strength, which helps the meringue last longer through a restaurant service so if you don't have it, don't worry. Start whisking the egg whites at medium-slow speed. This will help build a more stable meringue with a tight texture so don't be tempted to whack it up to high. Combine the sugar with the egg white powder (if using). Once the whites form soft peaks, add half of the sugar and keep whisking until it's well incorporated. Add the remaining sugar and whisk until you have a stiff and glossy meringue. Fold through the elderflower powder.

Set up a stovetop steamer, bringing the water inside to a gentle simmer. Lightly oil 8cm (3in) ring moulds and place on a plate small enough to fit inside the steamer basket. Pipe the meringue into the moulds so it is about 2cm (¾in) high, making the top as flat and even as you can. Place the plate inside the steamer, put the lid on and steam for 6–10 minutes until the meringues are firm and well risen. If you have a steam oven, cook the meringues for 6 minutes at 75°C (165°F). Once the meringues are cooked, remove from the steamer and slice off the top so you have an even cylinder. These are best eaten within a few hours.

serves 1

1 x 10cm (4in) sugar tuile with rhubarb powder *(p167)*

1 dessert spoon rhubarb compôte *(p158)*

1 poached meringue

50g elderflower custard, chilled *(p222)*

1 elderflower head, to serve (optional)

Bake the sugar tuile as a circle 2cm (¾in) wider than the meringue so that it will look like it is floating over the dish. Use a wide shallow bowl for this dessert. Place a dessert spoon of the rhubarb compôte into the centre of the bowl and flatten it to form an even surface. Gently slide the meringue on top. Pour the elderflower custard around the meringue. You want to make sure you have ample custard with every spoonful of meringue and compôte. Place the sugar tuile directly on top of the meringue and sprinkle with individual elderflowers picked from the flower head.

Ricotta ice cream with magnolia syrup

One of the prettiest dishes I've made. At Lyle's, we were in the habit of simply pairing ricotta ice cream with a delicious oil, such as fig leaf, blackcurrant or new-season olive oil. Then I learnt about magnolia as a flavour, so it seemed a natural progression to pair it with magnolia syrup. The ricotta ice cream provides a delicate sweet-savoury base to showcase the gingery spice of the liquor. It has enough body from the high percentage of ricotta to provide textural contrast to the thin syrup even as it melts. Use a buttery, gently peppery olive oil here. The magnolia needs to remain the star; the oil should just bolster it. I'm never a huge fan of tableside theatrics but this dish really does look best when the magnolia syrup and oil are poured into the bowl as it's served.

serves 1

1 large scoop ricotta ice cream *(p179)*

small pinch of Maldon salt

magnolia petals, to serve

2 tbsp chilled magnolia syrup *(p220)*

1 tsp extra virgin olive oil

Place a small bowl in the freezer to chill 30 minutes before serving. Scoop a large quenelle of ricotta ice cream into the chilled bowl and place just off-centre. Sprinkle on some Maldon salt and lay one or two magnolia petals beside the ice cream. Combine the magnolia syrup and olive oil (they will remain split). Pour the syrup and oil into the bowl next to the ice cream.

INDEX

Page numbers in *italics* refer to main entries

A

almond milk: vegan almond ice cream 209
almonds
  almond and fig cake *82*, 83
  olive oil and ricotta cake 181
apple juice
  apple, honey and rapeseed dressing 95
  fruit caramels 166
apples 94–101
  apple crisps 95, *98*, 99, 170, *171*
  apple sorbet with Calvados or cider 96
  brown butter-poached russet apples 96, *97*, 100, *101*
  mincemeat 132–33
  quincemeat 132–33
apricots 56–63
  apricots poached in chamomile 58

B

beef: mincemeat 132–33
beeswax
  honey and beeswax granita 168
  honey and beeswax ice cream 169, 170, *171*
berries
  late-summer pudding *70*, 71–73
  summer pudding *70*, 71–73
biscuits
  buckwheat shortbread 194
  oat biscuits 26, *27*, 104, *105*, 194, 216, *217*
  vanilla and hazelnut cookies 208
  walnut shortbread 208
blackcurrant leaves
  blackcurrant leaf ice cream 42, *44*, 45
  blackcurrant leaf oil 43
  blackcurrant leaf sugar 43
  blackcurrant leaf vinegar meringue 42
blackcurrants 40–47
  blackcurrant cordial 41

blackcurrant powder 41
late-summer pudding *70*, 71–73
poached blackcurrants 41, *44*, 45
blood oranges 150–55
  blood orange marmalade 153
  blood orange sherbet powder 151
  blood orange sorbet 152
  blood orange with olive oil ice cream 154, *155*
  dehydrated wedges and crisps 153
bread, milk 201
breadcrumb tuiles 168
brown butter 173
  brown butter cakes 174
  brown butter ice cream 175, *182*, 183
  shaved brown butter 173
buckwheat
  buckwheat ice cream *190*, 191, 193
  buckwheat shortbread 100, *101*, 194
  buckwheat tuile 193
  cherry and buckwheat clafoutis 51
butter
  brown butter 173
  brown butter cakes 174
  brown butter ice cream 175, *182*, 183
  brown butter-poached russet apples 96, *97*, 100, *101*
  rosemary butter emulsion 95, *98*, 99
  shaved brown butter 173

C

cajeta, goat's whey 86, *87*, 176
cakes
  almond and fig cake *82*, 83
  brown butter cakes 174
  chocolate cake 189
  corn cake 85
  olive oil and ricotta cake 181
Calvados, apple sorbet with 96
candied Buddha's hand *144*, 145
caramel 165–66
  apple caramel *98*, 99

buckwheat ice cream, chocolate mousse and caramel *190*, 191
caramelized cream panna cotta *118*, 119, 175
fruit caramels 166
goat's whey cajeta 176
whey caramel 116, *117*, 167
yeast caramel 197
cedro *144*, 145
  grilled cedro with yeast ice cream and puff pastry 148, *149*
chamomile, apricots poached in 58
cheese
  goat's cheese and cherry tart *54*, 55
  pears, oats and goat's cheese 104, *105*
  St Jude ice cream 180
cherries 48–55
  cherry and buckwheat clafoutis 51
  cherry and goat's milk sherbet 50
  cherry granita 49
  goat's cheese and cherry tart *54*, 55
  pickled cherries 49, 52, *53*
cherry blossom
  cherry blossom steamed sponge with sweet and pickled cherries 52, *53*
  preserved cherry blossom and leaves 219
chestnuts
  chestnut meringue 126, *127*, 206
  chestnut purée 207
chewies, rhubarb 159
chocolate 186–91
  chilled chocolate mousse 187, *190*, 191
  chocolate cake 189
  cocoa husk ice cream with warm Passe Crassane pear *106*, 107
  warm chocolate mousse 187, *210*, 211
Christmas pudding 129–31, *130*
cider, apple sorbet with 96
citrons 140–49

clafoutis, cherry and buckwheat
51
clementine leaf cream 137, 138,
139
clementines 136–39
  clementine granita 137, 138, *139*
cobnut ice cream with raw
  cobnuts 212, *213*
cocoa husk ice cream *106*, 107,
188
compôtes
  cherry compôte *54*, 55
  gooseberry compôte 25
  rhubarb compôte 158, 160, *161*
cookies
  raspberry ice-cream sandwich
  32, *33*
  vanilla and hazelnut cookies
  208
cordials
  blackcurrant cordial 41
  elderflower cordial 223
corn cake 85
  corn ice cream with
  caramelized corn cake and
  whey cajeta 86, *87*
cranberries: Christmas pudding
  129–31, *130*
cream
  baked cream 38, *39*, 68, *69*, 179
  blackcurrant leaf ice cream 42
  brown butter ice cream 175
  caramel 165–66
  caramelized cream panna
  cotta *118*, 119, 175
  clementine leaf cream 137, 138,
  139
  fig leaf ice cream 81
  gooseberry fool 25
  hay-infused cream *34*, 35
  honey and beeswax ice cream
  169
  lemon verbena semifreddo 225
  quince posset 123
  strawberries and cream 22, *23*
  tayberry fool 30
  wild fennel ice cream 224–25
  yeast caramel 197
  yeast ice cream 196
crisps, rehydrated apple 95, *98*,
99
croutons: apple crisps with
  rosemary butter, yeast ice

cream, croutons and apple
  caramel *98*, 99
currants
  late-summer pudding *70*, 71–73
  mincemeat 132–33
  quincemeat 132–33
  summer pudding *70*, 71–73
custard
  elderflower custard 222, *226*,
  227
  hay custard and tayberry tart
  34, 35

D

dairy-free strawberry ice cream
  20
damson stone vinegar fudge 91
damsons 88–93
  damson ice cream 90, 92, *93*
  damson jelly 89
  damson leather 90
dates: quincemeat 132–33
dressing, apple, honey and
  rapeseed 95
dried fruit 128–35
  Christmas pudding 129–31, *130*
  mincemeat 132–33
  quincemeat 132–33
  see also individual types of fruit
drinks
  blackcurrant cordial 41
  elderflower cordial 223
  green walnut liqueur 205

E

eggs
  baked cream 179
  brown butter ice cream 175
  chestnut meringue 206
  chocolate cake 189
  clementine leaf cream 137
  elderflower custard 222
  elderflower vinegar meringue
  224
  fig leaf ice cream 81
  honey and beeswax ice cream
  169
  milk meringue 177
  poached meringue with
  elderflower custard and
  outdoor rhubarb *226*, 227

sage meringue 116, *117*
  vanilla ice cream 178
  wild fennel ice cream 224–25
elderflower
  elderflower cordial 223
  elderflower custard 222, *226*,
  227
  elderflower vinegar meringue
  224
emulsion, rosemary butter 95,
  98, 99

F

fats 172–85
fennel: wild fennel ice cream
  224–25
fennel seeds, crystallized 154
fig leaves
  fig leaf ice cream 81, *82*, 83
  fig leaf oil 80
figs 76–83
  almond and fig cake *82*, 83
  fig jam 77
  fig leather 77
flowers 218–29
fools
  gooseberry fool 25, 26, *27*
  tayberry fool 30
frangipane 207
fruit
  fruit caramels 166
  fruit leathers 67, 77, 90
  fruit tuiles 168
  stone fruit sorbet 60, *62*
  see also dried fruit *and*
  individual types of fruit
fruit leathers
  damson leather 90
  fig leather 77
  plum leather 67
fudge, damson stone vinegar 91

G

glucose: sugar tuiles 167–68
goat's cheese
  goat's cheese and cherry tart
  54, 55
  pears, oats and goat's cheese
  104, *105*
goat's milk: cherry and goat's
  milk sherbet 50

goat's whey cajeta 86, *87*, 176
gooseberries 24–27
  gooseberry compôte 25
  gooseberry fool 25, 26, *27*
  red gooseberry sherbet 26
grains 192–203
  see also individual types of grain
granita
  Chasselas grape granita 111
  cherry granita 49
  clementine granita 137, 138, *139*
  honey and beeswax granita 168, 202, *203*
  mulberry granita 37, 38, *39*
  rhubarb granita 157
grapes 108–13
  Chasselas grape granita 111
  grape powder 109
  Nebbiolo sorbet 109, 112, *113*
  roasted Fragola grapes 110

H
hay custard and tayberry tart *34*, 35
hazelnuts: vanilla and hazelnut cookies 208
herbs 218–29
  see also individual types of herb
honey
  honey and beeswax granita 168, 202, *203*
  honey and beeswax ice cream 169, 170, *171*
  honey tuiles 168

I
ice cream
  blackcurrant leaf ice cream 42, *44*, 45
  blood orange with olive oil ice cream 154, *155*
  brown butter ice cream 175, *182*, 183
  buckwheat ice cream *190*, 191, 193
  cobnut ice cream with raw cobnuts 212, *213*
  cocoa husk ice cream *106*, 107, 188

corn ice cream with caramelized corn cake and whey cajeta 86, *87*
dairy-free strawberry ice cream 20
damson ice cream 90, 92, *93*
fig leaf ice cream 81, *82*, 83
honey and beeswax ice cream 169, 170, *171*
loganberry ice cream 30
milk ice cream 177
mulberry ice cream 37
nectarine ice cream 60
nut ice cream 209, *210*, 211
olive oil ice cream 61, *63*, 112, *113*, 181
pumpkin ice cream 115, 116, *117*
raspberry ice-cream sandwich 32, *33*
ricotta ice cream 46, *47*, 179, 228, *229*
St Jude ice cream 100, *101*, 180
strawberries and cream 22, *23*
sweetcorn ice cream 84
vanilla ice cream 178, 216, *217*
vegan almond ice cream 209
wild fennel ice cream 224–25
yeast ice cream *98*, 99, 196
infusion, mulberry leaf 38

J
jams
  fig jam 77
  raspberry jam 32
jelly
  damson 89
  rhubarb jelly 215, 216, *217*
juice, rhubarb 156

L
late-summer pudding *70*, 71–73
leathers, fruit
  damson leather 90
  fig leather 77
  plum leather 67, 68, *69*
leaves 218–29
lemon verbena semifreddo 225
lemons 140–49
  lemon purée 141
  Meyer lemon sherbet 141, *146*, 147

preserved lemon vinegar 142, *143*
preserved lemons 142
liqueur, green walnut 205, *210*, 211
loganberries 28–35
  loganberry ice cream 30
  semifreddo 31

M
magnolia syrup 220, *221*
  ricotta ice cream with magnolia syrup 228, *229*
maple-roasted pumpkin *118*, 119
marmalade, blood orange 153
  brown butter ice cream, puff pastry and marmalade *182*, 183
meringues
  blackcurrant leaf vinegar meringue 42, *44*, 45
  chestnut meringue 126, *127*, 206
  elderflower vinegar meringue 224
  milk meringue 177, 184, *185*
  poached meringue with elderflower custard and outdoor rhubarb *226*, 227
  preserved lemon vinegar meringues 142, *143*, *146*, 147
  sage meringue 116, *117*
milk
  blackcurrant leaf ice cream 42
  buckwheat ice cream 193
  cobnut ice cream with raw cobnuts 212, *213*
  cocoa husk ice cream 188
  fig leaf ice cream 81
  honey and beeswax ice cream 169
  Meyer lemon sherbet 141
  milk bread 201
  milk ice cream 177
  milk meringue 177, 184, *185*
  nut ice cream 209
  oat mousse 195
  olive oil ice cream 181
  pumpkin ice cream 115
  red gooseberry sherbet 26
  rice pudding 195
  St Jude ice cream 180

sweetcorn ice cream 84
vanilla ice cream 178
wild fennel ice cream 224–25
yeast ice cream 196
mincemeat 132–33
mousse
chilled chocolate mousse 187,
190, 191
oat mousse 195, 202, *203*
warm chocolate mousse 187,
210, 211
yogurt mousse 180, 184, *185*
mulberries 36–39
mulberry granita 37, 38, *39*
mulberry ice cream 37
mulberry leaf infusion 38

N

nectarines 56–63
nectarine ice cream 60
nuts 204–13
frangipane 207
nut ice cream 209
see also individual types of nut

O

oat milk: honey and beeswax
granita 168
oats
damson ice cream with warm
oat sponge and whisky 92, *93*
oat biscuits 26, *27*, 104, *105*,
194, 216, *217*
oat mousse 195, 202, *203*
oils
blackcurrant leaf oil 43
fig leaf oil 80
olive oil
olive oil and ricotta cake 181
olive oil ice cream 61, *63*, 112,
113, 154, *155*, 181
oranges 150–55
blood orange marmalade 153
blood orange sherbet powder
151
blood orange sorbet 152
blood orange with olive oil ice
cream 154, *155*
dehydrated wedges and crisps
153

P

panna cotta, caramelized cream
118, 119, 175
pastry
puff pastry *198*, 199–200
rough puff pastry 135
peaches 56–63
peaches poached in white wine
and bay 58
roasted peaches 59, 61, *63*
pears 102–107
chewy pears 103
cocoa husk ice cream with
warm Passe Crassane pear
106, 107
pear sorbet 103, 104, *105*
pickled cherries 49, 52, *53*
plums 64–73
fruit leather 67, 68, *69*
late-summer pudding *70*, 71–73
plum sorbet 67
poached plums 66
possets
quince posset 123, 126, *127*
praline tuiles 168
prunes
Christmas pudding 129–31, *130*
prune purée 135, 202, *203*
puff pastry *198*, 199–200
brown butter ice cream, puff
pastry and marmalade *182*,
183
grilled cedro with yeast ice
cream and puff pastry 148,
149
pumpkin seed oil 138, *139*
pumpkins 114–19
maple-roasted pumpkin *118*, 119
pumpkin ice cream 115, 116, *117*

Q

quinces 122–27
pickled quinces 123
poached quinces 122
quince posset 123, 126, *127*
quincemeat 132–33

R

raisins: Christmas pudding
129–31, *130*

rapeseed oil, honey and
beeswax ice cream, apple
and 170, *171*
raspberries 28–35
late-summer pudding *70*, 71–73
raspberry ice-cream sandwich
32, *33*
raspberry red rhubarb jelly with
vanilla ice cream and oat
biscuits 216, *217*
semifreddo 31
summer pudding *70*, 71–73
rhubarb 156–61, 214–17
poached rhubarb 214
poached rhubarb strips 159
rhubarb chewies 159
rhubarb compote 158, *226*, 227
rhubarb granita 157
rhubarb jelly 215, 216, *217*
rhubarb juice 156, 214
rhubarb powder 156
rhubarb rice pudding 160, *161*
rhubarb sorbet 158
roasted rhubarb 215
rice pudding 160, *161*, 195
ricotta
olive oil and ricotta cake 181
ricotta ice cream 46, *47*, 179,
228, *229*
rosemary
rosemary butter emulsion 95,
98, 99
rosemary tuile 61, *63*
rough puff pastry 135

S

sage meringue 116, *117*
St Jude cheese ice cream 100,
101, 180
semifreddo 31
lemon verbena semifreddo 225
raspberry ice-cream sandwich
32, *33*
sherbet
blood orange sherbet powder
151
cherry and goat's milk sherbet
50
Meyer lemon sherbet 141, *146*,
147
red gooseberry sherbet 26, *27*
shortbread

buckwheat shortbread 100, *101*, 194
walnut shortbread 208
sorbet
  apple sorbet with Calvados or cider 96
  blood orange sorbet 152
  Nebbiolo sorbet 109, 112, *113*
  peach sorbet 61, *63*
  pear sorbet 103
  plum sorbet 67, 68, *69*
  rhubarb sorbet 158
  stone fruit sorbet 60, *62*
  strawberry sorbet 21
sponges
  cherry blossom steamed sponge with sweet and pickled cherries 52, *53*
  damson ice cream with warm oat sponge and whisky 92, *93*
stone fruit sorbet 60, *62*
strawberries 18–23
  chewy dried strawberries 19
  dairy-free strawberry ice cream 20
  strawberries and cream 22, *23*
  strawberry granita 21
  strawberry ice cream 20
  strawberry juice 19
  strawberry sorbet 21
  summer pudding *70*, 71–73
sugars 164–71
  blackcurrant leaf sugar 43
  caramel 165–66
  fruit caramels 166
  sugar tuiles 167–68
  whey caramel 167
sultanas
  Christmas pudding 129–31, *130*
  mincemeat 132–33
  quincemeat 132–33
summer pudding *70*, 71–73
  late-summer pudding *70*, 71–73
sweetcorn 84–87
  corn cake 85, 86, *87*
  sweetcorn ice cream 84, 86, *87*
syrup, magnolia 220, *221*

T

tarts
  goat's cheese and cherry tart *54*, 55
  hay custard and tayberry tart *34*, 35
tayberries 28–35
  hay custard and tayberry tart *34*, 35
  milk meringue with tayberries and yogurt mousse 184, *185*
  semifreddo 31
  summer pudding *70*, 71–73
  tayberry fool 30
thyme, baked cream, mulberry granita and 38, *39*
tuiles
  buckwheat tuile 193
  rosemary tuile 61, *63*
  sugar tuiles 167–68
  tuile variations 168

V

vanilla
  vanilla and hazelnut cookies 32, *33*, 208
  vanilla ice cream 178, 216, *217*
vegan almond ice cream 209
vinegar
  blackcurrant leaf 42
  damson stone vinegar fudge 91
  elderflower vinegar meringue 224
  preserved lemon vinegar 142, *143*
vodka: green walnut liqueur 205

W

walnuts
  green walnut liqueur 205, *210*, 211
  walnut shortbread 208
whey
  goat's whey cajeta 176
  honey and beeswax granita 168
  whey caramel 116, *117*, 167
whisky, damson ice cream with warm oat sponge and 92, *93*
white wine: peaches poached in white wine and bay 58

Y

yeast
  yeast caramel 197
  yeast ice cream *98*, 99, 148, *149*, 196
yogurt
  gooseberry fool 25
  yogurt mousse 180, 184, *185*

FURTHER READING

> "Read with the mind-set of a carpenter looking at trees." Terry Pratchett

Reading about and around food has made me a better chef. It has kept me inspired and creative through the monotony of kitchen work and the long exhausting hours and days. When I feel stuck for inspiration, I sit down with a stack of the following books and just read. I rarely try to replicate directly from any of these titles but reading them will throw light on a flavour combination I haven't explored; a casual mention of a technique will spark an idea for how to prepare a fruit that's coming into season; or just the simple act of reading about someone else's excitement for an ingredient will help me remember my own. These are the books I return to most often and that have had the biggest impact on my cooking.

Desserts

Brooks Headley, *Brooks Headley's Fancy Desserts*, WW Norton & Company, 2014

Claudia Fleming and Melissa Clark, *The Last Course*, Random House, 2001

Judy Rodgers, *The Zuni Cafe Cookbook*, WW Norton & Company, 2003

Lindsey Remolif Shere, *Chez Panisse Desserts*, Random House, 1985

Nancy Silverton, *Desserts*, Harper Collins, 1986

Nigella Lawson, *How To Be A Domestic Goddess*, Vintage Publishing, 2000

Philip Howard, *The Square: Sweet*, Absolute Press, 2018

Ravneet Gill, *The Pastry Chef's Guide*, Pavilion Books, 2020

Fruit

Alan Davidson, *Fruit: A Connoisseur's Guide and Cookbook*, Mitchell Beazley, 1991

Alice Waters, *Chez Panisse Fruit,* Harper Collins, 2002

Edward A Bunyard, *The Anatomy of Dessert*, Modern Library, 2006

Jane Grigson, *Jane Grigson's Fruit Book*, Penguin Books, 2000

Kate Lebo, *The Book of Difficult Fruit*, Picador, 2021

Miranda York, *The Food Almanac,* Pavilion, 2020

Nicole Rucker, *Dappled*, Avery, 2019

Ice cream

Dana Cree, *Hello, My Name Is Ice Cream*, Clarkson Potter, 2017

Francisco J Migoya, *Frozen Desserts*, John Wiley & Sons, 2008

Kitty Travers, *La Grotta Ices*, Square Peg, 2018

Preserving

Diana Henry, *Salt, Sugar, Smoke*, Mitchell Beazley, 2012

Lillie O'Brien, *Five Seasons of Jam*, Kyle Books, 2018

Pam Corbin, *Preserves: River Cottage Handbook No 2*, Bloomsbury, 2008

Reference

Harold McGee, *McGee On Food & Cooking,* Hodder & Stoughton, 2004

Niki Segnit, *The Flavour Thesaurus*, Bloomsbury, 2010

Darra Goldstein, *The Oxford Companion to Sugar and Sweets,* Oxford University Press, 2015

For the joy of the writing

Diana Henry, *How To Eat a Peach*, Mitchell Beazley, 2018

MFK Fisher, *The Art of Eating*, Picador, 1983

Nigella Lawson, *How To Eat*, Vintage Classics, 1998

Nigella Lawson, *Feast*, Chatto & Windus, 2004

Richard Olney, *Simple French Food*, Grub Street, 2003

Samin Nosrat, *Salt Fat Acid Heat*, Canongate, 2017

Simon Hopkinson, *Roast Chicken and Other Stories*, Ebury Press, 1999

Tamar Adler, *An Everlasting Meal*, Scribner Book Company, 2012

Wendell Berry, *The Farm*, Counterpoint Press, 1995

USEFUL TOOLS & INGREDIENTS

You can make most of the recipes in this book without the need for specialist equipment but there are a few machines and gadgets that will make life a little easier and your desserts more consistent.

Dehydrator
You can use your oven as a dehydrator, setting it to as low as possible and opening the door occasionally to release any moisture. Ideally you're looking for 50–60°C (122–140°F). However, ovens are not designed to work at such low temperatures efficiently. Dehydrators are fairly cheap and are a really useful addition to the kitchen of any fruit picker or preserver. If I find myself short on time to prep a glut of fruit then the dehydrator is my greatest friend.

Digital kitchen scale
This will allow you to weigh everything with a greater degree of accuracy than weighted scales or volume measurements. I often cite very small weights for ingredients such as salt or malic acid. A jewellery scale is incredibly useful here as it measures milligrams. It's also very small so won't take up space in an already jam-packed kitchen.

Ice-cream machine
Don't bother trying to churn ice cream by hand. I have used both Sage and Cuisinart machines when testing recipes for this book. I much prefer a machine that freezes as it churns rather than one that requires you to pre-freeze the bowl. Living in London, I'm used to small fridges and even smaller freezers with no room for a bowl. When I have friends over, I put the ice cream on to churn as we sit down to eat so it's ready by dessert time. I highly recommend this tactic; freshly churned ice cream is such a treat. If you don't have an ice-cream machine, I point you instead towards the semifreddo and granita recipes. They'll be delicious and work perfectly without one.

Instant read digital thermometer
Having one of these will make you a much more consistent cook. Trust me when I say a custard can look just as cooked to a trained eye at 78°C (172°F) as it does at 82°C (180°F) but the texture won't be as silken and you won't have cooked the egg out properly. I use it mostly to confirm readiness rather than trusting it above my own instinct.

Microplane grater
These do the job better than any other kind of grater. I have three that I use throughout the book: a fine zester for citrus; a coarse grater for nuts; and a shaver for chestnuts or goat's cheese.

Muslin or cheesecloth
I use these interchangeably but cheesecloth has a slightly more open weave. Use a double layer to help strain and clarify any liquid beautifully. You can use a J-Cloth or clean tea towel instead.

Refractometer
Instead of relying on a recipe or your own perception of sweetness, a refractometer allows you to instantly read the sugar level in a liquid or purée. I can't recommend having one enough for creating sorbets and granitas with great textural consistency no matter what fruit you use. You can buy them for as little as £20. As a general rule, I like sorbets in the range of 22–25°Bx and granitas at 12–15°Bx.

PROFESSIONAL EQUIPMENT
Throughout this book, I've included tips for anyone working in a professional kitchen, or for skilled home cooks looking to up their dessert game. Here's what I find invaluable in a restaurant environment:

Blender
The better your blender, the better your final product. A high-speed Vitamix will quickly purée any fruit to silky smoothness reducing any time where oxidation could occur. For flavoured oils such as fig leaf or blackcurrant leaf, a Vitamix or Nutribullet works perfectly. Don't try them in a Magimix or Robot Coupe or you'll end up with a lot of washing up. A Thermomix is even fancier (and pricier). It has heat settings so you can blend at a fixed temperature for a set period. I love using one to create beautiful emulsions and they're great at low speed for making ganaches.

Pacojet
Not something I would ever expect a home cook to have; at Lyle's and Flor we used a Pacojet for our ice creams. They are great for small kitchens as they don't take up much space and allow you to churn small amounts. The recipes in this book should all work well in a Pacojet as well as in an upright churner. For sorbets, reduce the sugar in all of the recipes down to 22°Bx for Pacojet. You'll need to churn more often but you can reduce the sugar as you don't need the structure to be as stable.

Rational oven
Found in the majority of professional kitchens, these ovens are still a bit like magic. You can bake, steam or do a combination of the two with extremely accurate temperature control across the full scale of heat. I have made sure to give cooking instructions for a Rational oven wherever appropriate. The

combination (or combi) setting introduces steam so is perfect for gentle baking. Use it wherever you would normally use a bain-marie, such as with the baked cream *(p179)* or chocolate cake *(p189)*.

Whipped cream dispenser
A cream whipper will allow you to create aerated creams, custards and mousses. It aerates using nitrous oxide gas that you introduce into the sealed dispenser. The bulbs are inexpensive but are an age-protected product.

SPECIALIST INGREDIENTS
You don't need to be a chef to get your hands on these specialist ingredients; they can easily be found online. Just try to buy small quantities so you don't pack your kitchen full of powders that you use only a few times a year.

Acids
I often use citric or malic acid to season fruit. Both can be found easily online or through specialist suppliers. In general, you'll only ever need small amounts so it is better to buy less, more frequently. There are two rules when using acids: firstly, use the acid most closely related to the fruit you are using, so citric for citrus and malic for anything apple, pear or quince-related; secondly, go lightly, tasting constantly as you add more. Use them to highlight flavours, not overwhelm them (it can tip very quickly). The exception to the second rule is when using malic acid in combination with sugar for a Haribo Tangfastic effect which I love. Ascorbic acid will prevent fruit oxidizing and discolouring. It's typically found in chemists where it's sold as vitamin C powder.

Cocoa husks
Cocoa husks are the thin skin around the cocoa bean that is removed during winnowing before the beans are roasted. They are often sold online as cocoa husk tea – just be sure it contains 100 per cent cocoa shells and nothing else. Otherwise, it's worth finding a bean-to-bar chocolate maker nearby to see if they will sell you some of their waste husks.

Freeze-dried sweetcorn
This is available in both whole kernel and powdered form from health food shops and online. If you have a spice grinder, buy whole kernels and grind them as you need them as they'll keep their flavour for longer.

Fresh yeast
Your best bet for finding fresh yeast is through small independent or health food shops. If you can't get

your hands on it, simply multiply the amount of fresh yeast in a recipe by 0.4 to give the required quantity of dried active yeast. Osmotolerant dried yeast is the best to use for enriched doughs.

Ice-cream and sorbet stabilizers
I try to use these only where I really need them and to keep quantities to a minimum. They generally contain different blends of naturally derived substances like guar gum, locust bean gum, iota carrageenan and dextrose so they aren't some mysterious mix of chemicals to be feared. They will give your ice creams a smoother texture and a finer ice structure. For a thorough breakdown of ice-cream stabilizers and sugars, I would recommend *Hello, My Name Is Ice Cream*, by Dana Cree.

Mahlab
This aromatic spice is made from the seeds of a species of cherry tree; the flavour tastes like bitter almond. It's most often found in Middle Eastern cuisines. If you can track it down, you can use it in any recipe that uses the flavour of plum stone, apricot kernel or cherry pit.

Sugars
Isomalt is derived from sugar beet. It is not very sweet tasting but is able to withstand high temperatures without caramelizing. I use it in the sugar tuile recipe to keep the finished tuiles colourless and transparent. Liquid fondant is useful for creating glossy glazes. I use it along with isomalt and glucose in the sugar tuiles. Dextrose and glucose taste less sweet than granulated sugar (sucrose) but as they are monosaccharides (single molecules) rather than disaccharides (two joined molecules) like sucrose, they can hold twice as much water. This means that in your ice cream you can create a less sweet flavour while improving the texture if you replace some of the sucrose with glucose or dextrose.

Thick & Easy and Ultratex
These are instant thickeners that I like to use to add body to mousses or ice creams that I don't want to apply heat to. They are modified maize starches and are easily available online. Unromantic but they are useful ingredients.

General note
I use UK large eggs (US extra large) throughout. Salt is fine sea salt unless otherwise stated. I've given electric fan oven temperatures for all recipes, except those with specific Rational or combi instructions.

ACKNOWLEDGEMENTS

My first thank you has to go to Ravneet Gill. You gave me the push to start writing this book and have consistently cheered me on through the whole process. Your genuine desire for your successes to raise up those around you is so special. Thank you for sitting me down that morning and giving me direction again.

Working at Lyle's made me the chef I am today and I owe a huge amount to all the people I worked with there. Thank you James Lowe for really spurring me on and giving me the space to learn. Chris Trundle for always wanting to have a conversation about the next delicious thing – you really gave me the confidence to trust my own judgement. Also, Tom McParland, Jack Coghlin, Will Blank, John Ogier and the many other chefs from my time there.

In the same breath, I have to thank our restaurant suppliers as well as those who have helped to source the ingredients for the photoshoots and recipe testing for this book. Tom Maynard of Maynards Fruit Farm: thank you for always pointing out the good trees and teaching me about fruit. The beautiful farm your family has created has been one of my biggest culinary influences. Ana Morris at Natoora; Rick Hansult and Yvonne Yeoh at Neal's Yard Dairy; Joanna Brennan at Pump Street Chocolate: I'm grateful to all of you.

Everyone at The River Café who has tasted, tested and listened to me talk about this book. Particularly my *dolci* team of Bella, Lara, Rochelle, Marin and Amy, who have had to put up with many anxious monologues. You have been incredibly supportive and stepped up whenever I needed some extra time. Also a big thank you to Sian Wyn Owen, Joseph Trivelli and Ruthie Rogers for your help, encouragement and book advice.

Cassie Sciortino for being my unofficial editor. You were the first person to read every word I wrote and gave me confidence even when I felt like I wasn't writing anything good. Thank you for always making sure I sounded like myself, my dear friend. I have to thank my greatest pastry support network: Christine Lisa, Gezina Plumb, Cathleen Hall, Jessie King, Marissa Negro and Cassie. I feel so lucky to have found such an incredible group of colleagues and friends. Our #Pastrychella chats have got me through so much.

I am blessed with multiple groups of extraordinary female friends both professionally and personally: Emma Swift, Helen Evans, Rav Gill and Terri Mercieca, Alex Bell, Cerys Galbraith, Amy Roch, Amy Murphy, Kate Whisker, Ellie Doney and the Evoo Club. Your encouragement, advice and friendship throughout this process and beyond mean so much to me. Likewise, the women of my family have always been my greatest support: Ellie, Lydia, Helen and Elspeth, I am proud to be a Barclay sister. Thank you also to the men in the family, particularly my cousins Archie and Jim, for testing and eating many of my recipes!

The biggest thanks go to the team of people who have taken this book from an idea to a beautiful reality. Thank you for seeing the potential and helping me realize the vision. Caitlin Leydon, Stephanie Milner, Bess Daly, Amber Dalton and Kiron Gill. I'm so proud of what we have produced together. Thank you Kim Lightbody, Rachel Vere, Hanna Miller and Tamara Vos for making the shoot days calm and fun, and creating the most beautiful images. Thank you Erika Lee Sears for the stunning cover and title art works.

Lastly, thank you Miles. You washed up, ate so much ice cream, stopped me spinning out completely on more than one occasion and didn't complain once as I slowly occupied more and more of the flat with books, a freezer and ice-cream machines. Thank you for cheering me on and always giving me the love and hugs I need. x

Publishing Director Katie Cowan
Art Director Maxine Pedliham
Senior Acquisitions Editor Stephanie Milner
Managing Art Editor Bess Daly
Editors Amber Dalton, Kiron Gill
Designer Sandra Zellmer
Illustrator Erika Lee Sears
Photographer Kim Lightbody
Prop Stylist Rachel Vere
Food Stylist Hanna Miller and Tamara Vos
Proofreader Katie Hardwicke
Indexer Vanessa Bird
Jackets Coordinator Jasmin Lennie
Senior Production Editor Tony Phipps
Production Controller Kariss Ainsworth

First American Edition, 2022
Published in the United States by DK Publishing
1450 Broadway, Suite 801, New York, NY 10018

Printed and bound in Latvia

For the curious
www.dk.com

MIX
Paper from
responsible sources
FSC™ C018179

This book was made with Forest Stewardship
Council™ certified paper – one small step in
DK's commitment to a sustainable future.
For more information go to
www.dk.com/our-green-pledge

CREDITS

DK and Anna Higham would like to thank James Lowe and Lyle's for the right to include the following recipes: Gooseberry sherbet with fool and oat biscuit, page 26; Baked cream, mulberry granita and thyme, page 38; Ricotta ice cream, blackcurrant leaf oil, page 46; Fig leaf ice cream with fig leaf oil and warm almond cake, page 83; Pear, oats and goat's cheese, page 104; Cocoa husk ice cream with warm Passe Crassane pear, page 107; Pumpkin ice cream with sage meringue and whey caramel, page 116, Meyer lemon sherbet with preserved lemon meringue, page 147; Buckwheat ice cream, chocolate mousse and caramel, page 191; and Cobnut ice cream with raw cobnuts, page 212.

All Photography by Kim Lightbody except pages 2, 3, 6, 9, 10, 13, 14, 18, 36, 218 by Miles Hardwick.

Fabrics used in photography throughout The Natural Dyeworks www.thenaturaldyeworks.com.

p6 Wendell Berry, excerpt from "The Farm" ["Go by the narrow road"] from *This Day: Collected and New Sabbath Poems* 1979-2012. Copyright © 1979 by Wendell Berry. Reprinted with the permission of The Permissions Company, LLC on behalf of Counterpoint Press, counterpointpress.com.

p235 Terry Pratchet, excerpt from "Notes from a Successful Fantasy Author: Keep It Real" from *A Slip of the Keyboard*, Doubleday, 2014.